THE ORGANIZATION OF JOURNALISM

THE ORGANIZATION OF JOURNALISM

Market Models and Practice
in a Fraying Profession

PATRICK FERRUCCI

UNIVERSITY OF
ILLINOIS PRESS
Urbana, Chicago, and Springfield

Library of Congress Cataloging-in-Publication Data

Names: Ferrucci, Patrick, author.
Title: The organization of journalism: market models
   and practice in a fraying profession/ Patrick
   Ferrucci.
Description: Urbana: University of Illinois Press,
   [2024] | Includes bibliographical references and
   index.
Identifiers: LCCN 2024017895 (print) | LCCN
   2024017896 (ebook) | ISBN 9780252046216
   (hardcover) | ISBN 9780252088292 (paperback) |
   ISBN 9780252047480 (ebook)
Subjects: LCSH: Journalism—United States—Finance—
   Case studies. | Newspaper publishing—United
   States—Finance—Case studies. | News Web sites—
   United States—Finance—Case studies.
Classification: LCC PN4888.F6 F47 2024 (print) |
   LCC PN4888.F6 (ebook) | DDC 070.4068—dc23/
   eng/20240716
LC record available at https://lccn.loc.gov/2024017895
LC ebook record available at https://lccn.loc.gov/
   2024017896

To Erin, for everything

CONTENTS

Acknowledgments   ix

Introduction: Recentering the Organization
in Journalism Studies   1

1   The St. Louis Beacon—The Digitally Native News Nonprofit   23

2   Defector Media—The Cooperative   45

3   The Colorado Sun—The Public Benefit Corporation   67

4   The *Boston Globe*—The Mogul-Owned Newsroom   89

5   The Athletic—The Venture-Capital-Funded Newsroom   112

6   The *Denver Post*—The Hedge-Fund-Owned Newspaper   136

Conclusion: The Organization and the Deprofessionalization
of American Journalism   157

Notes   181

Bibliography   201

Index   215

ACKNOWLEDGMENTS

You could say the idea for this book first began bouncing around in my mind when I was roughly six or seven years old. I mean, that would be a gross exaggeration, but it's kind of true. I grew up in a multigenerational household, living with my parents and my maternal grandparents. Every morning when I didn't have school, I would wait impatiently for my grandfather, Ernest Bertulli (1917–2000), to get home from whatever custodial job he had that morning with a copy of that day's *Boston Herald*. I wanted to read about the Red Sox, of course. But the real treat, though, was whenever we'd all head over to my other grandparents' house. You see, my other grandfather, Patrick Ferrucci (1921–2004), subscribed to the *Boston Globe*, and I just liked that sports section better. Even back then, I guess, I was starting to think about how different news organizations operated differently (or better yet, how one employed Bob Ryan and Peter Gammons and the other didn't).

But from then, almost four decades ago, to now, there's been a whole lot of people who helped make this book you're holding (or squinting at on some screen) a reality. So many of my colleagues in the College of Media, Communication and Information at the University of Colorado-Boulder were generous with their time and knowledge, even if they didn't know it. I'd like to thank the entire college. Specifically, I'd like to mention Karen Ashcraft and Nathan Schneider for pointing me in the right direction for some of the literature used here. Over the years I spent working on this book, numerous others also impacted this work. Most especially? Chad Painter, Greg Perreault, Kay Weaver, Pete Simonson, Scott Eldridge, Teri Finneman, Nick Matthews, David Wolfgang and, grudgingly, Jake Nelson. And, in a sentence by himself, Edson Castro Tandoc Jr. Jr. Jr. Nothing happens without great mentors, so I'd like to mention particularly Rick Sandella, Stephanie Craft, Earnest Perry, and Glenn Leshner.

My awesome colleague Mike McDevitt, through both his own brilliant work and dozens upon dozens of conversations over beer, really helped shape a lot of the ideas you're going to read in this book. An academic could not dream of having a department chair as great and brilliant as Liz Skewes. I could not ask for a better mentor and am so lucky to have wound up here and met Liz. The introduction of this book is, really, a reworking of a theoretical article I cowrote with Tim Kuhn of Colorado's Department of Communication.[1] As I've said, I've had these ideas for years, but Tim's assistance—and especially his own work—really helped me find the words to get them from my brain to the page. And you know someone is an absolutely great friend when they willingly read an entire draft of a book and give you really insightful feedback, the kind of notes that substantially improved this work. So thanks to Toby Hopp for giving up so much of his time to help on this here thing.

Tim Vos needs a new paragraph. Some of these ideas first hit a page more than a decade ago in my dissertation. Back then, Tim—and I'm paraphrasing here—said, "Pat, the way this is written sucks, but you're on to something." Seriously, nobody's been more integral to my academic career than Tim, and roughly fifteen years since he first became my advisor, he's still my advisor. Tim's awesome.

This book is a product of a whole lot of time spent with journalists. None of it was possible without the absolute generosity of those who allowed me to glean amazing insights from their experiences. I'd like to thank each and every journalist—at the organizations included here and the ones that ended up on the proverbial cutting-room floor—who gave me some of their time. I truly hope I presented their stories accurately and with respect and admiration for the increasingly difficult and important work they do.

I'd like to thank everyone at the University of Illinois Press for providing amazing support throughout this process. Mariah Mendes Schaefer is incredible to work with. The reviewers the press chose for this book improved the manuscript by several orders of magnitude. Thanks to them. Most important, thanks to Danny Nasset for being a great editor, believing in this book, making it so much better, and just being an all-around great guy.

And, you know, in these acknowledgements, we save some for last. Thank you so much to my parents—Paul and Diane Ferrucci—for decades of unwavering and unconditional love and support. I love you guys so much.

When the first words of this book were written—when I didn't know exactly what I was writing yet—back in early 2020, my son Owen was about seven months old. The amount of joy he brings daily truly inspires me to go to work happy and ready to write things like this book. I could not be a luckier guy getting to watch you grow up. I love you, bud.

And, of course, this book is dedicated to Erin Schauster, the best colleague anyone could ask for at home and at work. You're the absolute best. I've become so much better a scholar just listening to Erin talk about her own work all these years. Thanks for putting up with me, making me smarter, and listening (or at least pretending to) as I rattled off thoughts about this book (or some music I was listening to or sporting event I forced onto the ol' TV) for years and years. I'm a very lucky human.

THE ORGANIZATION OF JOURNALISM

INTRODUCTION

Recentering the Organization
in Journalism Studies

In early 2005, during a time when a technological revolution began to sig-nificantly disrupt newsrooms across the United States, the scholar David Ryfe conducted an ethnography of a "mid-sized American corporately owned newsroom."[1] When Ryfe started his field work, the newspaper just hired a new editor who deemed himself a change agent and believed that "reporters had to change the way that they gathered and reported the news."[2] Due to the newspaper's steep declines in circulation and its non-existent relationship with the community, this editor attempted to drasti-cally alter the historic routines that journalists at the newspaper had relied on throughout construction of news processes. The most salient of these changes came in the form a directive toward beat reporters: spend less time at the institutions you cover. On the surface and to an outsider, this may seem like a modest request, but to journalists, this change radically affects their job and self-understanding. As Ryfe noted, journalistic "pro-fessional identity is tightly bound to practice, reporters can quickly feel at sea when one of their key practices (like routine interactions with officials at public agencies) is disrupted."[3] To the surprise of virtually nobody with any newsroom experience, the journalists Ryfe observed rebelled directly against the new editor and, indirectly, the corporate owners of the newspa-per. In some cases, journalists complained, but more important, numerous employees quit the newspaper as they felt these changes impeded their autonomy, something absolutely crucial to a journalist.[4] In fact, journalists "are resistant and even resentful of what they see as encroachments onto their professional turf."[5] After spending eighteen months in the newsroom, Ryfe exited as the organization's journalists essentially proved victorious in their implicit rebellion against the new editor and the owners: basically, all historic routines returned to the newsroom, and the editor soon found himself transferred. Ryfe concluded that the "culture of professionalism in the newsroom is remarkably resilient and resistant to change."[6] Furthermore, most of the pressure imposed on the journalism industry to change is actually "exogenous to the culture of journalism. There is little pressure to change from within the culture of journalism."[7]

For decades, into the early twenty-first century, scholars have argued that the professional culture of journalism has remained stagnant and unchanged, that it is resilient against any effort to modify.[8] For journalists, culture is manifested through the concept of professionalism. The field began a process of professionalization in the late nineteenth century, a process that continued into the early twentieth century "with the proliferation of professional associations, schools, and codes of ethics."[9] Today, many journalists are still shaped by the socially constructed boundaries of their profession in journalism education programs before they even enter the field.[10] However, seismic disruptions to the journalism industry, mostly technological and economic, over roughly the last two decades began to impinge on the monolithic professional culture that Ryfe had observed in 2005.[11] In effect, if there ever was only one overriding professional culture or definition of professionalism in journalism, that is no longer the case. The scholars Herbert Gans and Gaye Tuchman—and, later, Ryfe—described an industry that acted remarkably consistently regardless of the organization.[12] But even as recently as 2005, the vast majority of the organizations populating the journalism ecosystem structured themselves in essentially the same manner: as advertising-funded news organizations producing general news. Fundamentally, the journalism industry recognized this structure, or market model, resulted in a profitable, replicable manner as early as the late 1800s.[13] But digital dissemination allowed for a multitude of new market models with various funding structures.

This book argues and will illustrate that the emergence of new market models into the field of journalism effectively splintered what was previously a monolithic professional culture. Organizations traditionally exerted minor influence over how construction of news processes occurred within newsrooms, but that is no longer the case. When studying influences or forces impacting journalistic practice, media sociologists often implicitly or explicitly separate the world into the five hierarchical levels of influence that Pamela Shoemaker and Stephen Reese conceptualized more than two decades ago.[14] These five levels are the individual; the routine; the organizational; the social institution, or influences beyond media;

and the social system, or ideological. As is the case with most hierarchical models, scholars have historically applied it by focusing on "boundedly rational actors at the micro level, influenced by inducements and punishments and internalizing" forces at the macro level, without accounting for the organization.[15] This argument contends that most research examining influences on news production often looks at individual-, routines-, social institution-, and social system-level forces because prior work found organization-level forces had little explanatory power.[16] That may have been accurate when Gans and Tuchman did their work, and even when Ryfe did his, but it is not anymore.

We can see how much influence the organization now exerts by examining certain forces that individual news organizations had no control over. At the individual level, all the way back to White's seminal "Mr. Gates" study, researchers have shown that certain personal demographics completely separated from the organization could impact news production.[17] In that specific study, White found that Mr. Gates had certain perceptions, both positive and negative, that influenced his decisions concerning which wire stories to run. At the time of the article, in the mid-twentieth century, journalistic organizations across the country primarily hired people from one demographic: liberal-arts-educated men.[18] In effect, a specific type of journalist was hired by almost all traditional news organizations at the time. Compare that with the situation today: for example, many local news organizations, tend to employ young journalists recently out of college as a way of keeping costs down.[19] On the other hand, when the digitally native sports news organization The Athletic was launched, it implied in its mission statement that it would value and employ journalists with significant amounts of experience, in the belief that this would lead to better stories.[20] Organizations that produce travel journalism often hire a very specific type of journalist, one complicit in flouting certain normative standards, but not all.[21] And, of course, as news organizations become increasingly ideologically driven, many outlets look to hire journalists with a very specific ideological belief system.[22] Whereas the swelling number of right-wing information organizations such as Breitbart.com can be seen as obvious examples of organizations that hire at least partly on the basis of political ideology, this also occurs, for example, at progressive alternative newsweeklies. Research also illustrates how different types of organizations also hire completely on the basis of skills, something that happened historically with platforms in the sense that broadcast organizations looked for certain skills whereas print organizations looked for others. But in a digital environment, organizations can hire for far more nuanced skills.[23]

Another example of a force situated at the individual level that historically the organization did not all affect is professional identity. In scholarship, researchers have called professional identity in journalism remarkably resilient in that it did not change as a journalist moved from job to job.[24] The key here is that, essentially, a robust economic ecosystem throughout the journalism industry catalyzed a very specific professional identity that permeated the whole industry, allowing journalists the ability to transition from one news organization to the next and keep their sense of professional self.[25] Daniel Hallin contended that this inflexible, fossilized professional identity in American journalism started to erode in the late 1980s, coinciding with the corporatization of legacy media across the country.[26] He argued this prior identity primarily considered a close connection to objective reporting and a strong autonomy concerning news selection vital to its makeup. To Hallin, the change was replicated in other parts of society at a time when faith in institutions and a confidence in professionals began to erode across cultural industries. But regardless of the correctness of Hallin's argument, his main contention centered on the idea that the professional identity American journalists held since, basically, World War II was changing. He did not argue that a uniform professional identity did not exist, only that it was becoming increasingly fluid. However, as digital technology became more and more ubiquitous across the industry, scholars began to notice that professional identity in journalism started to fray by transitioning to something a little less stable across the field.[27] In fact, recent work finds that professional identity in the field moved and can now be considered completely fluid.[28] This mutability can be traced back to the "decreasing autonomy of individual journalists, increasing job rotation and insecure careers" that now prevail in journalism.[29] One study concluded that although journalists still cling to traditional normative "ideals in particular in situations of crisis and uncertainty," their professional identities should be considered liquid in that they are definitively not stable.[30] Further research has concluded that professional identity could now be considered an organizational force, because "organizational attachment also functions as a clear line of demarcation" in terms of how journalists formulate their professional identities.[31] Also salient, this series of studies determined that organizational backing significantly influenced how specific journalists conceptualized professionalism in that individual organizations could impact a journalist's role perception, view of ethics, and other important elements of professionalism.[32] This work, for example, found that self-labeled "digital journalists" believed they were significantly different in terms of their jobs—or professional identities—than nondigital journalists, whatever that means. Therefore, "digital journalists seem to be defining their profession" and "distinguished themselves from traditional journalists" in a variety of ways, most notably in their perception of the role of the audience in their work.[33] With professional identity, then, it is possible to see how an organization can impact individual-level forces affecting news construction, something historically almost ignored in media sociology work.

Two examples of how an individual organization can have significant influence on communication routines can be seen through a contemporary examination of both ethics and sourcing. According to historical literature, communication routines are the patterned, routinized practices that cut across the journalism industry, the kind of customs present in almost all newsrooms. These are the practices that effectively, together make up professionalism in journalism.[34] As noted earlier, the emergence of standard codes of ethics in journalism was a harbinger of the professionalization of the industry. Through an almost universally standard set of ethical guidelines, the journalism industry developed its own media accountability system, a set of normative guidelines that governed the entire industry.[35] And when an incident occurred that no well-known ethical principle covered, the industry would step in to fix the problem. A popular example of this came in the early 1990s when *Time* magazine published the murder suspect O. J. Simpson's mug shot on its cover. The freelancer who designed the cover intentionally darkened the mug shot, which caused a sizable public outcry. Professionals from within and outside journalism effectively contended that "by darkening the photo of Mr. Simpson's face, *Time* gave him a more sinister appearance and was thus guilty of racism."[36] At that time, darkening an image through the use of then-new technologies such as PhotoShop had made toning ethics a popular topic within the industry, something the Simpson incident exacerbated. The National Press Photographers Association, the largest professional association in American photojournalism, took note of this increasingly visible issue and created a code of ethics for digital image altering.[37] Because the journalism industry boasted such a strong professional culture at the time, this new code of ethics became the criterion for dealing with this type of issue. Studies show that for at least the next two decades, a standard ethical guideline permeated the entire industry in terms of the editing and altering of photographs. However, recent work suggests this is no longer the case; research now posits that photojournalists are working "without industry-wide standards and not knowing how to adopt different standards from organization to organization, they are left to follow their own individualized ethical frameworks."[38] What this means is that organizations are now dictating ethical guidelines to their newsrooms. This could not have happened as recently as the early 1990s. Now, though, it can and does happen.

One more salient example of how individual organizations impact routine-level factors comes from historically normative practices. In the aforementioned Ryfe studies, an organization attempted to change industry-wide patterns and failed.[39] Now, though, a significant amount of recent research illustrates, both explicitly and implicitly, how an organization can change routines that, in prior times, cut across the industry. For example, Michael Schudson contended that quite possibly the most fundamental element of professionalism in journalism in the United States comes from the adoption of objectivity.[40] Now, though, using digitally native news nonprofits as foci, research illustrates that although longtime print journalists founded many of these establishments, the majority of them act more like alternative newsweeklies in terms of content production. Essentially, many of these organizations have taken a far different approach to sourcing, eschewing traditional expert sources and utilizing more community organizers, for example. This approach to sourcing results in content that would not be considered objective by, for example, traditional legacy media.[41] In another instance, researchers found that a small print nonprofit in the western United States relies on an open-system approach to content creation as a way to build a stronger sense of community among all relevant stakeholders such as citizens, journalists, local businesses, local organizations, and a board of directors. The result of this unusual framework can be seen in the sourcing of stories as the journalists in the newsroom often look to advertisers as sources, for example, something that is traditionally frowned on in journalism.[42] When utilizing web metrics as a focus, researchers have found that an individual organization can significantly influence how routines do or do not emerge. A series of studies that compared routines surrounding web analytics that looked at organizations with varying market orientations found that practices differed depending on how profit-orientated a newsroom was.[43] For example, newsrooms that skewed closer to a weak market orientation generated routines around using analytics as a way to make decisions that would strengthen journalistic content in a normative manner, whereas those with a stronger market orientation used information from analytics in a manner that strengthened business operations. Both ways, though, shaped journalistic routines. Through his work on web metrics, Edson C. Tandoc Jr. also found over the course of several studies that the adoption of this technology—an organizational-level factor—appreciably affected the routines that journalists performed in their daily work.[44] In short, as illustrated by recent scholarship, organizations absolutely play a much larger role in, for example, the manner in which ethics are determined and applied and how various routines emerge. This means that in numerous cases, communication routines no longer permeate the entire industry, but rather are becoming more and more organization specific.

Forces emanating from the social institutional level of influence also typically affected all journalism organizations in a similar manner, regardless of the organization. For example, all organizations in the United States are bound by government regulation. Historically, the journalism industry funded itself primarily through revenue from advertising, something that absolutely influences news production, regardless of the mythical wall that supposedly stands between editorial and business operations at an organization.[45] Other journalism organizations relied in some manner on public relations firms for what some scholars have called informational subsidies, in that journalists need help from outside actors such public relations practitioners to learn about news and broker conversations with powerful sources.[46] Although all of these examples remain true, in an age of numerous market models for journalism, organizations now have some power to determine what and how social institutions influence news practice.[47]

Advertising long stood as the primary funder of journalism in the United States, but the digital era and declining advertising revenues across the field catalyzed the need for a diversified funding structure. One type of social institution that began exerting more and more influence on the industry is the foundation. For example, the Knight Foundation is a philanthropic organization that is willing to help fund journalism. Newsrooms must apply for these funds, and that, of course, is an organizational decision. When a news medium decides to apply for foundation funding and receives it, the newsroom enters a relationship that will alter how it produces news. Recent work suggests that foundation funding leads to a focus on utilizing certain technologies, prioritizing certain types of sources, covering particular beats, and more.[48] In short, most types of funding inspire certain changes and prioritizations in a newsroom. Even the organizational decision to become a nonprofit newsroom will have legal ramifications for a news outlet, because governmental policies and laws will affect what the news organization can do in ways that do not happen at traditional legacy media.[49] Furthermore, the effect itself of advertising on newsrooms is now different depending on organization. In the past, advertising influenced news construction at all legacy media in the same way—albeit presumably to different degrees. That is no longer the case. Certain news organizations accept funding not just from traditional advertisers but also from potentially nefarious native advertisers, which absolutely affects how journalists do their jobs.[50]

In short, the precariousness of funding in the journalism industry leads to a diversification of operating revenue streams but also opens the door to more outside influence. Both Eldridge and Bélair-Gagnon and Holton have done extensive work in a general way about how the more prevalent need for revenue opens up the newsroom to numerous "interlopers" or "strangers," meaning employees of outside organizations that usurp some agency within news-production processes.[51] For example, this introduction previously discussed how the use of web analytics in a newsroom disrupts traditional routinized practices, but organizations that choose to employ metrics also sometimes allow web analytics companies into the newsroom.[52] When these nonjournalists encamp in the newsroom and apply different ethical frameworks when training journalists, outside institutions become more powerful in determining how news production occurs within an organization. Analytics are but one example of how journalism's recent focus on technological innovation provided entry into the newsroom for numerous types of technology companies, granting power to these ancillary organizations.[53] This is especially and potentially troubling because journalism is not simply a business but a public service, whereas most of these companies operate in manners commensurate with business.[54] In terms of technology companies, in a more macro sense, the journalism industry relies so much on Silicon Valley stalwarts such as Facebook, X (the artist formerly known as Twitter) and Google for dissemination, advertising, and even news-production tools that some researchers have argued that these companies are essential elements of gatekeeping, or news-production, processes within newsrooms, giving them significant power that would be unheard of in journalism even a decade ago.[55]

The co-occurrence of a diversification of revenue streams with an influx of market models in journalism did not only provide access to technology companies, though. Some larger for-profit and nonprofit organizations, for example, began to host expensive live events to fund journalistic operations.[56] These events, often sponsored by local corporations and organizations, often have a negative effect on journalistic authority, which then impacts journalistic practice in some salient ways. News organizations that choose to pursue more aggressive investigative journalism now also make themselves more vulnerable to outside institutions through the threat of lawsuits. Essentially, research asserts that many social institutions attempt to impact journalistic practice by suing news organizations that may or have published negative investigative journalism about those institutions.[57] This tactic is meant to take advantage of the economic instability affecting so many newsrooms; they will choose not to publish some negative information for fear of being sued by a wealthy company or person, even if the news organization knows the lawsuit is without merit. One more example of an organizational decision about a social institution or extra-media influence that affects practice can come through audience influence. For example, many newsrooms will alter their news practices in response to what audience members write in online comment sections, no matter how valid this content is (even from trolls).[58] In sum, although the obvious institutions of advertising, government, and public relations continue to influence journalism from the outside, the many disruptions, particularly economic, to journalism in recent years have compelled individual journalism organizations to decide whether other extra-media influences would enter their newsrooms.

Finally, because the point of this introduction is to illustrate how individual news organizations have amassed agency over influences from all levels of analysis commonly studied in media sociology research, the social system should be discussed. Influences from the social system, as previously noted, often involve culture or ideology and other, more nebulous, concepts. For example, the fact that all news organizations in the United States practice within capitalism significantly influences journalistic practice, regardless of whether a news organization is part of a conglomerate or a small nonprofit. Capitalism has effects on all news organizations. However, unlike in the past, individual news organizations can wield more power over how some social-system-level forces affect their journalistic practice. For example, many nonprofits around the country decided to limit the influence our economic system has on newsrooms. Many former journalists at legacy media organizations saw their newsrooms receive reduced funding and suffer massive layoffs, all in the hopes of increasing the stock prices of their parent corporations, so these journalists started nonprofit newsrooms to insulate themselves from these forces as much as possible.[59]

Typically, the country in which a journalistic organization operates significantly affects the role of journalism within its borders.[60] The most obvious example concerns the post-Vietnam and Watergate era in the United States; during this time, the watchdog role boasted increased currency in the journalism industry.[61] On the other hand, the watchdog role could never become popular in a country such as North Korea. More and more research across the world, though, illustrates how foreign countries have begun funding journalism organizations. When a news organization accepts this funding, though, a culture change typically is adjoined.[62] Whereas this is unusual currently in the United States, evidence from other countries provides insight into what could happen if government funding does become a more a viable stream for American journalism organizations. For example, much work illustrates how the Chinese government spends significant amounts of money each year funding journalism in various African countries. The results of this influence can be seen not only in pro-China content produced by African journalists but also in the way African journalists, in their daily work, act more like Chinese journalists compared with African journalists not working in organizations funded or partly funded by China.[63] Researchers have also found this phenomenon in Cuba, where a reliance on Russian funding significantly influenced journalism practice.[64] Here in the United States, it's possible to see how, more than ever, news organizations are able to push back against cultural norms in a way that would have never happened in prior decades. For example, one recent piece of research posits that in an attempt to engender a larger audience and garner increased attention, both for potentially economic reasons, Gawker published information that could be classified as the complete antithesis of then current cultural mores.[65]

This introductory chapter is an argument that, I hope, forcefully illustrates the growing power of the organization in the journalism field and successfully makes the case for more studies of individual organizations. This book features case studies of six different individual news organizations, all with differing market models: the mogul-owned, legacy city newspaper the *Boston Globe*; the venture-capital-funded, digitally native sports organization The Athletic; the public-benefit cooperative the Colorado Sun (owned by its journalist-founders); the journalist-owned cooperative sports and culture website Defector Media; the traditional, digitally native news nonprofit the St. Louis Beacon; and the hedge-fund-owned newspaper the *Denver Post*, which is part of a chain. The goal through examining these individual case studies is ultimately to demonstrate how organizational factors and, specifically, types of market model affect journalistic practice in a multitude of ways. This should provide a blueprint for conducting future case studies of journalistic organizations but also, ideally, should spur *more* case studies in the future. Considering the professional culture of journalism in the United States as still monolithic is a mistake that potentially hinders the insights emanating from journalism studies scholarship. Scholars can then look at these differing market models as archetypes for other similarly structured models and then test these conclusions, thereby further improving our understanding of organizational factors impacting practice. The field of media sociology needs to recenter organizational work in studies of forces affecting newswork, and I hope this book furthers this process.

Understanding Market Models and
Organizational Culture

In the late nineteenth century, the journalism industry found itself in a time of significant disruption. Before then, newspapers in the United States received funding primarily from political parties and, in turn, acted as organs for partisan views.[66] In the midst of this professional precarity, though, the industry evolved from one funded by political parties to a Wild West—like landscape featuring a seemingly endless array of alternative market models.[67] These models gave rise to a wide disparity in terms of journalism's culture and mission across the field. However, this situation changed relatively quickly. As printing became less expensive, literacy rates rose exponentially, and businessmen began to realize the economic potential of the news, the commercialization of journalism started in earnest.[68] This commercialization process meant selling news directly to the public and filling the pages of newspapers with advertisements.[69] Yet after a handful of controversies such as the birth of yellow journalism, the journalism industry was forced to reckon with how it governed itself.[70] At the heart of this self-governing watershed sat the idea of influence. With the commercialization of the press, the industry found itself straddling two domains: business and public service. The scholar C. Edwin Baker described journalism as a dual-product model, an industry that must sell itself to people—through quality, citizen-focused journalism—but then must sell those people's attention to advertisers.[71] The journalism industry observed by Baker mimicked the one Ryfe studied in the early 2000s; until very recently, advertising funded the bulk of journalism, and therefore organizations across the industry looked similar. For example, in seminal sociological ethnographies of newsrooms conducted by Gans, Tuchman, or Fishman, the researchers found very little difference in how news work happened across organizations.[72] At this time, and into the early twenty-first century, the journalism industry displayed a robust, strong, and rigid professional culture that would take precedence over any other type of culture an organization attempted to implement.[73] In fact, decades ago, in his ethnography of the *New York Times*, the management scholar Chris Argyris concluded that a strong organizational culture "requires continual self-examination and self-renewal. . . . [T]he communication media (and specifically journalism) has shown little interest in such activities."[74] The crux of Argyris's contention revolved around the *Times*'s existence within an ecosystem with such a strong professional culture in journalism that obvious changes to its organizational structure that he perceived would have produced positive results were met with little interest. In effect,

Argyris, a scholar of organizational culture, argued that journalism organizations did not really think about organizational culture due the industry's reliance on an omnipresent professional culture. Indeed, ethnographic studies of journalism organizations, very popular in the 1970s and early 1980s, virtually disappeared from media sociology scholarship in the 1980s and 1990s due to the fact that this type of research uncovered very few new findings, since journalism organizations essentially operated in the same manner across the industry.[75] But the disruptions catalyzed by the proliferation of digital technologies in the early twenty-first century and the increasing numbers of market models effectively created a schism in journalism's professional culture.[76] Now, new media organizations have created a disjointed field. Recent research illustrates how the culture generated by organizations is forming, for example, an ethical framework for news work that clearly supersedes professional norms and varies from organization to organization.[77]

Many in the field of communication argue that if scholars are studying any organizational variable, it should be within the framework of organizational culture; they contend, though, that "at the present moment, 'organizational culture' is once again declining in status in the field."[78] This is especially important in the field of journalism studies, a discipline that traditionally ignores organizational culture.[79] Even when this concept is studied, it is often in search of a viable organizational culture that will allow or celebrate the foisting of "innovation" on journalists.[80] But organizational culture affects far more than how technological innovation occurs within a newsroom. Therefore, for each of the case studies in this book, organizational culture is considered the primary object of inquiry. So, although numerous organizational-level forces are studied in each chapter—and these will be identified in the coming pages—these forces are considered within the context of each organization's culture.

Organizational Culture

According to the organization scholar Joanne Martin, organizational culture is typically studied via one of three approaches.[81] An examination of the literature on the subject illustrates that the majority of studies of organizational culture look for "consensus, consistency, and clarity" within an organization, effectively implying that there is one overriding culture in a single body, a culture often most notably dictated by leadership.[82] Other researchers believe that an organization is a system of subcultures that coexist in both harmony and conflict. The third paradigm for studying organizational culture sees an organization as not defined by a singular

culture or multiple subcultures but rather by a set of competing interests that together impose a sense of ambiguity across the site. In the first
paradigm, leadership plays a vital role.[83] To understand better how organizational culture works at a journalism organization, leadership needs
examination, not simply from the newsroom. Leaders from all areas of
the organization should be studied because they all, in some way, influence news production and the culture of the organization. This approach
would satisfy Martin's goal of incorporating elements of all paradigms of
organizational culture studies; studying all departments of a news organization implies examining subcultures to reveal the ambiguous overall
idea of the culture.

Organizational culture consists of the "elements of a group or organization that are most stable and least malleable" and the "result of a complex group learning process."[84] Slightly more than a decade ago, Thomas
Hanitzsch attempted to conceptualize a universal journalism culture.[85]
However, this approach no longer makes sense because, as this books contends, journalism culture no longer exists as a single, monolithic entity.[86]
Furthermore, if as prior research suggests, one monolithic market model
within journalism led to a very specific organizational culture across the
field, then new models would lead to the emergence of different organizational cultures. Now, then, we must begin to study how individual
organizations generate cultures and thereby make decisions about journalism practice. To do this, researchers should examine "the reasons for
firms' existence and persistence, their boundary locations, and the means
by which they operate both internally and externally."[87] An organization
is, effectively, impermanent and fluid, not an actual entity but rather an
action undertaken by a group of people who come together.[88] This type
of inquiry will inevitably uncover how power is dictated within an organization: "power does not reside exclusively in persons or offices, but is
encoded in discursive formations, linguistic distinctions, and material
resources."[89]

Essentially, although a universal journalism culture may not exist, a
universal journalism outcome persists: the publishing and dissemination of
information. All journalism organizations engage in this activity; therefore,
most organizational decisions affect this very activity. The case studies
in this book research how individual organizations make these decisions
and help readers understand how these organizations inhibit or facilitate
various forces that affect news work. Understanding the factors behind
these decisions is complicated because "what goes on at the surface of
an organization is not all there is, and that understanding organizations
often means comprehending matters that lie beneath the surface, matters

that some organizational participants may prefer not to know about."[90] Indeed, any study of an organization intended to determine how it creates a culture that allows or precludes certain influences must examine the totality of the organization—not only what members say occurs but also underlying assumptions and patterns of behavior. Specifically, case studies should not utilize only one method of inquiry but rather multiple techniques that can provide the researcher with more than surface-level behaviors, mission statements, or perceptions.

This book relies on the theoretical conceptualization of organizational culture explicated by the management scholar Edgar H. Schein.[91] This framework posits that to understand culture, a researcher must examine three levels of analysis. The first level is what Schein calls the artifactual level, which entails all the elements of an organization that are easily identifiable and analyzable by a researcher, components such as mission statements, the layout of an organization's workplace, its website, workday schedules, dress code, technology utilized, and so on. The second level revolves around espoused values, which are the elements of culture that one needs to investigate to uncover but are still surface-level factors. This level includes things such as communication patterns, what organizational members say about their work environment and their practices; this level concerns unearthing the shared assumptions of members toward their organizations. The third level of analysis in this framework reveals basic underlying assumptions. These are the elements of an organization that might not be published or spoken out loud but can be uncovered by a researcher through looking for patterns and behaviors that constantly appear in the data. In effect, this level is concerned with what the organization does, not necessarily what it says it does. For Schein, leadership is a foundational element of culture; thus leadership's effect needs to be interrogated on all levels of analysis as "culture begins with leaders who impose their own values and assumptions on a group."[92]

True understanding of the culture of an organization necessitates deep investigation: how communication occurs in the organization. To do this, the researcher must explore three specific concepts: structure, processes, and agency. Scholars define structure as the "arrangement of elements and their connections (like rules, responsibilities and communication patterns)"; processes, though, are the "activities or tasks that enact the organization and accomplish its varied aims"; and agency is, in historic terms, the "ability of social actors—usually individual persons, but also including groups and organizations—to make independent choices and engage in autonomous action."[93] Once again, to understand these complex concepts within an organization, the research must focus on their connections to leadership. Managers, or leaders, often exert a form of implicit control over these concepts; this control can be seen as "complicated, contradictory, and collaborative" in nature.[94] Inherent in how organizations operate and how the concepts discussed above manifest themselves is the discernable expression of power, which is a "quintessential aspect of social relations often ignored in contemporary debates" about how work is structured within organizations.[95] It is with power that leadership at all levels of an organization can exert influence on structure, processes, and agency, the very things making up organizational culture. Therefore, leadership is a significant focal point within the research for this book.

Organizational Influences

The case studies in this book also cover, within the context of organizational culture, how various organizational-level influences impact news work. For example, this book contends that how a newsroom adopts and utilizes technology is incredibly significant in terms of how news is produced and is therefore more than worthy of scholarly inquiry. But to consider this utilization separately from organizational culture would diminish understanding considerably. So all the following influences were examined, but all within a framework of organizational culture.

One clear influence on news work that an organizational culture will affect is *organization size*: the larger the staff the more it can itself affect organizational culture.[96] As noted in the previous section, actual study of organizational culture must examine it on three levels of analysis, necessitating the consideration, as much as possible, of *mission statements, staff policies*, and *leadership* and *leadership type*.[97]

Another influence considered for each case study is how journalists are socialized into the newsroom. During this process, "new employees observe how veteran journalists perform their roles, pay close attention to the behaviors rewarded by management and then model their behavior with this observance in mind. Through this process, an organization's rules, both official and unofficial, and culture are legitimized."[98] Socialization has always influenced how journalists do their jobs in a meaningful way. Some of the earliest work in media sociology focused on this very concept. Although Warren Breed's study of newsroom socialization is seventy years old, it still is just as influential as ever.[99] Finally, the use of *technology* will be analyzed in each of the case studies included in this book.

More than anything else, the case study selection process for this book was guided by *ownership*, because one of the goals here was to understand the impact of market models on practice. Another influence emanating from the organization, one intrinsically tied to ownership, is *market orientation*, or how closely an organization hews to traditional market philosophies. Randal Beam defined market orientation in journalism:

> The successful market-oriented firm identifies a potential market opportunity, selects a group of customers that it wants to serve and develops a strategy for efficiently meeting the wants and needs of those customers. The central business assumption is that long-run success depends on a strong, organization-wide focus on customer wants and needs.[100]

The key here is that individual organizations determine their market orientation, or how closely they plan to treat readers as customers versus citizens. According to recent work conceptualizing how market models align with market orientation, the definition of the term *market model* fundamentally sets how the news organization is funded. Each news organization has its own funding structure, which determines the market model. In the United States, of course, the presence of numerous market models provides a systematicity whereby, as David Ryfe argued in a relatively recent article, the economics of journalism, though historically ignored in scholarship surrounding journalism practice, cannot be separated from the work of journalism.[101] Moreover, the contention is that a specific market model brings with it a specific set of practices, because "given the importance of economics to news production, it is utterly predictable that when the economic logic of journalism changes, journalists will gravitate to new practices."[102] This is because, as noted in recent works on market models, an organization's funding structure will impact its market orientation, which will then definitively alter its practices; an organization's market orientation can, for example, influence how routines emerge surrounding audiences and technology, or how sourcing happens, or even how content is framed.[103] This book's case studies utilize the conceptualization of market orientation from a recent journal article that I wrote; this conceptualization updates and synthesizes the work of Randal Beam and John H. McManus.[104] In sum, it's important to understand that McManus argues that journalism organizations compete concurrently in four distinct markets: the market for audience, the market for sources, the market for advertising, and the stock market.[105] How strongly an individual organization competes in those markets dictates its market orientation. Of course, in 2024 the market for advertising is limiting; therefore, in my aforementioned paper I renamed this the market for *funding*. And since all organizations compete vigorously in the market for sources (not just for quotes but also for story ideas) and the market for audience (all organizations are at least weakly market oriented, since they need an audience to survive), the markets for funding and the stock market determine orientation. Both of those markets are primarily dictated by ownership. Therefore, for this book, market orientation is:

TABLE 1. MARKET ORIENTATION

Orientation	Ownership
Weak	Nonprofit
Somewhat weak	For profit, standalone organization, or ownership within organization
Somewhat strong	For profit, chain ownership, or ownership through outside entity that owns other things
Strong	For profit, chain ownership and on stock market, or owned by venture capital

These definitions are taken and adapted from Patrick Ferrucci, "It Is in the Numbers: How Market Orientation Impacts Journalists' Use of News Metrics," Journalism 21, no. 2 (2020): 244–61.

A Note About Method

To conduct the case studies featured in this book, I employed a combination of methods most conducive to understanding organizational culture.[106] For each organization studied, I combined three methods: participant observation, in-depth interviews, and textual analysis. The vast majority of the data collected come from in-depth interviews with both journalists and other, non-newsroom staff from each organization. Interviews typically ranged from thirty to ninety minutes. I conducted interviews within each organization until I felt I had reached a saturation point, a common ending for qualitative research.[107] The number of interviews for each case study fluctuated wildly from organization to organization, primarily because some, such as the *Boston Globe* or The Athletic have hundreds of staff members, whereas organizations such as the St. Louis Beacon or Defector Media have fewer than two dozen. In each case, I conducted some participant observation, nowhere near enough to consider these case studies ethnographic in nature. However, I spent time in newsrooms and/or with reporters as they worked remotely and made it a goal to observe enough to ascertain routines, employee communication patterns and social dynamics. Finally, because one must, as Edgar Schein contends, study both artifacts and espoused values of an organization to understand its culture, I conducted textual analyses of mission statements, employee handbooks, organizational memos, and so on.[108] Essentially, I obtained all publicly available material findable but also asked participants for materials such as handbooks, memos, ethics codes, and other company-only artifacts. To gain a true understanding of an organization, it is not enough simply to observe practice and conduct interviews, as many similar studies do, because "studying practice as a unit of analysis" means that one should consider "that practice never presents itself to researchers as an objective and unambiguous thing."[109] What this statement returns to is the notion that what can be seen or what is articulated, through both artifacts and interviews, is not necessarily all that makes up practice and, ultimately, what influences it. A researcher must analyze all of Schein's three levels of analysis.

When conducting case studies of organizations, the researcher must attempt to understand an establishment's organizational culture before they can make any significant analytic findings. "Culture" means "common patterns of behavior, beliefs and rituals," the kinds of things that require multiple modes of inquiry.[110] Once these inquiries are accomplished and if a case study is well chosen, although the results cannot be generalized in a typical empirical manner, one can extrapolate from them to make more comprehensive and sweeping findings.[111] When conducting a case study, the goal is to make the local universal, meaning that the researcher must choose cases that could represent other similar cases.[112] It is important to note that during the data-gathering portion of writing this book—which took years to complete—the models of some of these newsrooms changed considerably. For example, The Athletic is no longer funded by venture capital, but is a significant vertical owned by the *New York Times*. In each instance where a model changed, I did return to the case and conduct more interviews, which are included in the chapters. However, I would argue that these specific cases are less important for the impact of change than for what was happening while they adhered to a specific market model, such as the formerly venture-capital-funded The Athletic. That period in The Athletic's history can tell us a lot about current and future newsrooms funded by venture capital.

The Cases

The St. Louis Beacon—Founded in 2008 by the longtime St. Louis, Missouri, journalist Margaret Freivogel, a reporter and editor who spent more than three decades at the *St. Louis Post-Dispatch*, the city's major metropolitan newspaper, the Beacon was a digitally native news nonprofit that covered the city of St. Louis and its close suburbs, primarily focusing on education, politics, crime, and culture. The newsroom's mission was to provide engaging and important coverage to its community, the type of coverage that Freivogel and other leaders at the Beacon felt the *Post-Dispatch* did not generate anymore. The Beacon focused on it what it called "news that matters," which Freivogel conceptualized as reporting with "depth, context, and continuity."[113] The Beacon was part of the first wave of digitally native news nonprofits to emerge in the wake of the success of the Voice of San Diego. The site was funded primarily through a donor model. For example, in 2010, 59 percent of its revenue came from donations, 35 percent from grants, and 6 percent from fundraising events.[114] The newsroom employed roughly a dozen full-time journalists and several consistent freelancers. In 2013, the site was merged with St. Louis Public Radio. Data for this book comes from both an ethnography conducted in the early months of 2013 and follow-up interviews with journalists who worked through the merger. Due to its nonprofit status and lack of advertising, the Beacon would be considered a *weakly market-oriented* news organization.

Defector Media—First appearing online in September of 2020, Defector is a subscription-based, journalist-owned cooperative that covers sports and culture. This digitally native, blog-based organization began after a large group of employees from the sports website Deadspin quit to protest their new owner's orders to only publish sports news. Both the mainstream press and the business community consider Defector a major success. As noted by the *Washington Post* in Defector's early days, "at less than six months old, Defector.com is financially self-sustaining and entirely owned by its staff."[115] The site employs roughly twenty full-time journalists. All employees start with a minimum $50,000 salary, the result of a mission to provide staffers with a living wage. Defector publishes short, blog-style posts that primarily concern sports but also discuss many trending issues and stories in popular culture. Besides the short opinion or analysis posts, Defector also publishes some long-form investigative pieces, for example, stories about sexual harassment in the workplace that have garnered plaudits from across journalism. As at some other recent entries into the journalism ecosystem, the journalists at Defector created and published online its own ethical policy. According to the market-orientation continuum in Table 1, because of its for-profit status and employee-ownership model, Defector would be considered a *somewhat weakly market-oriented* news organization.

The Colorado Sun—Established in 2018 through a two-year grant from the blockchain organization Civil, a company that aimed to create a media platform for journalism that would be owned and operated by the public, the Colorado Sun is a for-profit public-benefit cooperative that now primarily funds itself through membership, donations, sponsorships, and grants.[116] It started in direct response to layoffs, funding cuts, and decision-making by the hedge-fund owners of the *Denver Post*, the large metropolitan daily where the founders of the *Sun* all had worked previously. The organization employs roughly twenty full-time journalists, numerous freelancers, and contributors, and is owned by its journalist founders. The enterprise primarily publishes stories concerning politics, culture, the environment, and education. The Sun focuses on "fact-based, in-depth and non-partisan journalism."[117] The organization covers the entire state of Colorado. According to the continuum in Table 1, the Sun would be classified as a *somewhat weak market-oriented* news organization.

The *Boston Globe*—Founded in 1872 as a place for news primarily aimed at Boston's Irish Catholic population, the *Boston Globe* is the largest newspaper in New England and the major metropolitan newspaper in the city.[118] Since 2013, it has been owned by John Henry, an investment manager who also owns the city's historic professional baseball team, the Red Sox. The *Globe* is a typical legacy media organization: a newspaper/online operation primarily funded through a combination of advertisements and circulation/subscriptions. Similar to most legacy daily newspapers, the *Globe* publishes a general mix of news concerning politics, education, arts and culture, sports, business and, fundamentally, all other types of news. This newspaper and online news disseminator employs almost three hundred journalists across multiple departments and platforms. Henry runs the *Globe* as a for-profit enterprise through a corporate venture called Boston Globe Media. The *Globe* is not part of a chain and is an independent, privately owned venture, meaning its parent company is not listed on the stock exchange. The newspaper would be classified as *somewhat strongly market oriented*.

The Athletic—Founded by two entrepreneurs in January 2016, this venture-capital-funded, digitally native sports news website claims more than 1 million subscribers, employs more than three hundred full-time reporters, and serves roughly forty geographical markets in the United States and Canada.[119] This news organization publishes all its content behind a paywall, meaning the only people who can read it are subscribers. Journalists have argued that The Athletic "has leveraged the resiliency of local sports writing and a willingness to pay for it to become one of the biggest sports publications in the country."[120] In its early days, The Athletic amassed both credibility and public attention by "pillaging" local sports sections through the hiring of prominent sports journalists known for covering specific beats in specific cities.[121] In theory, The Athletic eventually would fund itself and make profits through a robust subscription tally. But even at more than a million subscribers, The Athletic was not yet a profitable enterprise and still relied on seed funding from venture capitalists to operate until the *New York Times* purchased it in early 2022.[122] One of The Athletic's defining features concerns the type of stories The Athletic publishes: unlike the majority of sports news publishers today, the organization relies on historically normative notions of quality journalism to guide its agenda.[123] Therefore, The Athletic publishes a mix of long-form investigative and feature stories with a small amount of event-driven content. According to the market-orientation categorization outlined in Table 1, when most of this research was conducted, The Athletic was a privately owned, for-profit news organization. Therefore, this organization would be considered *somewhat strongly market oriented*.

The *Denver Post*—The *Denver Post* began its run in the late nineteenth century as a publication started by the followers of then former president Grover Cleveland, who would use the paper to publish propaganda that eventually won Cleveland a second term in office.[124] Once it delinked itself from Cleveland, the *Post* became a purveyor of sensationalism and a producer of yellow journalism well into the twentieth century. In the mid-twentieth century, new ownership moved the newspaper toward a traditional, objective, fact-based approach.[125] In 1980, the family that had owned the *Post* for decades sold the newspaper to the Times Mirror Company, which began the *Post*'s life as part of a corporation. The newspaper, the winner of nine Pulitzer Prizes between 1964 and 2013, serves the state of Colorado, primarily focusing on the state's Front Range and tourist areas. Like the majority of legacy news operations and major metropolitan newspapers, the *Post* focuses its coverage on an assortment of topics such as education, arts and culture, politics, business and sports. Since 2010, when an entity titled Digital Media sold the newspaper, a hedge fund named Alden Global Capital has owned the *Post*. The media columnist Margaret Sullivan, writing for the *Washington Post,* once called Alden "one of the most ruthless of the corporate strip-miners seemingly intent on destroying local journalism."[126] This sentiment is shared by many as Alden has earned significantly negative assessments from journalists, the public, and even the government. This hedge fund has been called a "vampire that bleeds newspapers dry" in search of maximizing profit with little concern for quality journalism.[127] The *Post* employees between forty and sixty journalists. It would be considered a *strongly market-oriented* news organization.

TABLE 2. CASES IN THIS BOOK

Organization	No. of Journalists	Platform	Market Orientation	No. of Interviews
St. Louis Beacon	approx. 12	online	Weak	Roughly 85% of all employed
Defector Media	approx. 20	online	Somewhat weak	Roughly 67% of all employed
Colorado Sun	approx. 20	online	Somewhat weak	Roughly 50% of all employed
Boston Globe	approx. 300	print, online	Somewhat strong	Roughly 25% of all employed
The Athletic	approx. 400	online	Somewhat strong	Roughly 25% of all employed
Denver Post	approx. 50	print, online	Strong	Roughly 40% of all employed

1

THE ST. LOUIS BEACON

The Digitally Native News Nonprofit

In early 2012, I began a four-month-long ethnography in the newsroom of what was then the St. Louis Beacon, a digitally native news nonprofit founded in 2008 by ex-employees of the city's longtime daily newspaper, the *St. Louis Post-Dispatch*. This fieldwork was the data-gathering portion of my dissertation. I chose the Beacon as my focus of scholarly inquiry primarily because of its status as a digitally native news nonprofit. My interest concerned how nonprofit status could affect the way a news organization operated; at that time, almost all American news nonprofits published digitally. As recounted elsewhere, early in my time at the Beacon, I witnessed the organization's education reporter, a longtime veteran of legacy news, struggling to adapt to a mandate from the site's editor in chief. Through his impressive Rolodex of sources accumulated over decades of experience, the education reporter learned that a large local university would soon fire a dean over a particularly noteworthy charge of sexual harassment. The reporter had the story cold. He had trusted sources. He verified the information. He knew the names of all those involved, even those that would not make the website for obvious reasons. He simply did not have on-the-record corroboration. However, he told me that at any other place he worked in the past, the story would run that day. At the Beacon, though, the editor in chief wielded more power over all aspects of the news organization than anyone in a similar position at any of his former newsrooms.[1] The editor would not run the story, even though the reporter and all the other people in positions of power in the newsroom believed in the piece's accuracy. The editor delayed the piece until the reporter had on-the-record corroboration of a few details, but by then, competitors had already broken the story, which the reporter remained convinced he had days before everyone else. About a month after the incident, the reporter told me:

> What really got me that day when I was making all the phone calls, and you were sitting right next to me and could see how frustrated it was getting me, was when I talked to the one professor who said to me, "OK, here are names and the email addresses of the two students who made these charges." And [the students] came back to me and said, "No, we didn't do it." But I knew that wasn't accurate.[2]

During an in-depth interview with the education reporter that took place near the end of my fieldwork at the Beacon, we talked about why he thought his current editor held the story, but that it would have run without issue at any of his prior journalistic gigs. His response meandered a bit as he searched for an answer, but two statements stand out: "We do things differently here," and "I guess being a nonprofit changes how we act in certain circumstances."

Although the Beacon became the digital news arm of St. Louis Public Radio in early 2014, the study of its organizational setup at the time still is useful in journalism studies research. Since the early 2000s, the digitally native news nonprofit began becoming a central element of the news ecosystem across significant geographic portions of the United States. These DNNNs are located in states such as Connecticut, Maryland, Texas, Colorado, Ohio, California, Florida, Michigan, Pennsylvania, Hawaii, and numerous other places.[3] In fact, although DNNNs make up only a portion of the number, more than four hundred nonprofit news organizations are operating across the country.[4] Like the Beacon, the vast majority of these sites are founded and run by former newspaper journalists, often veteran journalists who previously worked at legacy media outlets in the region.[5] This leadership setup, as described in the anecdote above, significantly influences how most of these nonprofits work.

Organizational Culture

The journalists at the St. Louis Beacon espoused a very clear mantra that functioned as a mission statement: "news that matters." Journalists consistently mentioned that slogan as their goal for journalism. The organization also printed the slogan on all promotional material. During the organization's founding, a lot of discussion centered on what the Beacon would cover. With a small staff, the founders knew it would be impossible to cover everything newsworthy, so they decided to cover only the "news that matters," a rhetorical device that allowed them to prioritize some subjects over others. One journalist described the genesis of this term:

> And I think coming up with the phrase, that was the first thing, peeling away and saying we're not going to do sports. And we're going to look at what the other media in town do really well, and we're not going try to duplicate that. So, we went in with the idea of burrowing in on hard news. That's the news that matters.

For Beaconites, as journalists at the organization called themselves, the news that matters revolves around context. The Beacon editors believed that all news reports should include contextual information. It was not enough for a reporter to write about what an issue means for the St. Louis area. The reporter must add contextual information, such as why that issue is important to St. Louis, how the issue is being debated by people on all sides of the argument, what experts believe about the issue, and how the issue affects other cities. In numerous cases, Beaconites discussed "surrounding an issue," a phrase that means answering as many of the questions noted above as possible. In a majority of organizational meetings concerning news production, employees would note the importance of context. The Beacon aimed not only to report what happened but also to explain why it mattered. An editor described putting stories into context as important because "you don't just say this is good or this is bad, but through reporting and context, you bring an understanding about it." One journalist particularly spotlighted the digitally native aspect of the organization as integral to achieving this mission, contending that the organization's digital format allows its reporters and editors to give readers this context. They said, "We have the opportunity to tell a story in-depth. And you know, we're not filling a daily news-hole the way a paper is, so we can come back to a story over and over in many different ways." Due to many of the Beaconites' long histories in legacy newspapers, they often compared whatever the Beaon would do with how a newspaper operates. One editor believed that newspapers try to produce quality news, but focusing on word counts does not allow for proper context, the "news that matters" within a story. Explained the editor,

> It's about context and that we're giving a fuller picture. I've long thought newspapers ought to sell themselves like, "OK, you've seen the headlines or you've seen the tweets, but here's where you come to get the backstory and find out how it relates." You know, here's this side and not just the two sides, but also the shades of gray. And that's what I hope we do.

The emphasis on context emboldened many Beaconites to call the organization a "daily magazine." Numerous reporters I interviewed used this term to describe the *Beacon*. They argued that magazines give journalists more room to provide context and depth to news consumers, and the Beacon's digital format and emphasis on "news that matters" gives them the same freedoms and responsibilities. One journalist said they describe the Beacon as a daily magazine whenever anyone asks:

> I tell people, when I talk about the Beacon, well, we do have some breaking stuff, which we do—we have that type of news—but I tell people I think of us as a daily news magazine. We don't cover everything, but what we do cover we try to do in depth. So there will be some duplications with the newspaper, but not too much.

Of the full-time, nonbusiness staff at the Beacon, only three had not spent time working at the daily newspaper in St. Louis. When they were founding of the Beacon, the journalists wanted to make clear to people both inside and outside the organization that they did not compete with the *Post-Dispatch*; rather, their goal is to "fill in the gaps in coverage" left by other local media. Beaconites embrace the relative smallness of the organization's staff by noting how little bureaucracy they must deal with. In interviews, reporters repeatedly mentioned the consistent availability of editors. The small staff allowed reporters to cover the stories of their choice. There is less competition for higher-profile pieces, noted a reporter. One editor described the Beacon this way: "We're small enough that we don't need rules. The bigger the organization, the more need for stringent rules. We don't have that problem. We're nimble." Many reporters and editors repeated the same sentiment. Because there are so few hard rules and so little bureaucracy, reporters say they can work on the stories that are most interesting to them. One reporter verbalized this:

> As a reporter, you know that if you're working on a story that you came up with, you're much more likely to enjoy it and invest in it than if someone gave it to you, even if it was an assignment that if you had been thinking about it, you would have come up with it by yourself. Everyone likes to work on their own ideas; that's just the nature of things.

So much of the organizational culture of the Beacon, a culture that espouses a belief in in-depth journalism meant to support civic democracy, came from the principal founder of the newsroom, Margaret Wolf Freivogel. In 2005, she and three other local journalists founded the Beacon after receiving buyouts from the *Post-Dispatch*. This occurred only after Freivogel and others attempted to purchase the *Post-Dispatch*. One of the journalists involved remembered the failed purchase as a good turn of events:

> We had some good legal advice on how to set something up called an employee stock ownership company, and that's how we were going to finance it. We got pretty far. We had a commitment of $850 million. We didn't have any of it in our pockets. We are very fortunate the [owners] told us to go away. We would have been in serious financial trouble. It would have been a disaster. First of all, we had no business experience at all. We had no idea. We knew how to do journalism, but we had no idea about business.

At this point, the four had not yet hatched a plan for the Beacon. In the summer of 2006, the quartet met after hearing about Voice of San Diego, an online, nonprofit news organization based in Southern California. One journalist went to San Diego to observe how Voice ran its news organization. "I saw that we could do it," they said. For the next eighteen months, the quartet planned the Beacon, focusing on generating a mission.

By the end of 2007, the four began assembling a staff. The Beacon first published content in February 2008. At the time, the organization called itself the St. Louis Platform, but soon after changed its name because the *Post-Dispatch* began a blog called The Platform. Rather than fight for the name, the founders simply rebranded as the Beacon. Before its merger with St. Louis Public Radio, a ten-person board of directors theoretically controlled the Beacon. Freivogel, who did not take a salary in her role as editor until 2010, was on the board. Richard Weil, one of the journalists who helped found the organization, was the chairman. The board made the major decisions. In the beginning, Weil was the person who pushed for a full-time staff reporter located in Washington, DC. One editor recalled that Weil thought a reporter at the capital would provide the Beacon with cachet.

> Richard was determined we would have a Washington reporter. So that was a top priority. I mean, frankly, if I made that decision, I don't know because I look at the local area and think we could do this or that. But I think Richard wanted something that would give us some prestige and even though, if you look at the [*Post-Dispatch*], they have one person, but he doesn't do a lot. This gives us something that others don't really have.

Despite a board of directors, Freivogel still controlled the Beacon, according to employees. Her opinions and decisions drove the culture of the newsroom. Because businesspeople who work for and run other organizations made up the board of directors, the board remained a hands-off entity. The board mostly consisted of prominent St. Louis dignitaries and major donors to the Beacon. Freivogel and the other founders insulated themselves from outside meddling and kept control of the organization they founded. The organization's funding model permitted her to stay in control.

The culture at the Beacon did not differ from those at many DNNNs across the country, many of which are controlled, at least operationally, by journalists themselves. Within a nonprofit, by having a journalist as the board chair and the editor as another engaged board member, the Beacon can act in a very specific manner, such as focusing on the "news that matters" mission at the center of its culture. That Beaconites' positioning of "news that matters" as different from legacy media is rather systematic across DNNNs. This occurs primarily because "nonprofit journalists may have taken on a narrower role of interpretative sense makers for their communities," meaning nonprofit journalists often believe their professional roles are different from those in mainstream news.[6] When removed from constant calls for measurable profits that are often omnipresent at mainstream media organizations, journalists can often practice a form of journalism that does focus on context, the concept at the heart of "news that matters."[7] This form of journalism, slightly different from traditional journalism according to some scholars, embraces many of the historical normative processes so entangled with journalism practice but also tends to push against the principal norm of legacy news: objectivity.[8] As previously noted, many DNNNs, including the Beacon, allow for a culture that both embraces historical journalism norms and pushes against what Michael Schudson considers the most fundamental norm of the field in objectivity.[9] DNNNs accomplish this through an organizational identity that aligns with the notion of filling "the gap as commercial news shrinks."[10] Therefore, by positioning themselves as an organization that covers the same type of news but in a different way, the Beacon and other nonprofits can practice many journalistic norms but not others by articulating this notion of being part of something while still being different. As one Beacon editor noted, "We probably couldn't be what we are if the Post-Dispatch didn't exist here." That statement affirms the idea that the Beacon and many other DNNNs consider themselves complementary to but different from legacy media. This difference can also be attributed partly to market model. In a traditional legacy news organization, the main marker of success could be considered advertising revenue, which is based on strict subscriber numbers or page views and the like. Because DNNNs such as the Beacon are often funded by a combination of donations, grants, endowments, and foundation money, their success metrics look different. In the case of DNNNs, "people who had given them money wanted to see results," results that often revolve around impact metrics such as policy change, something Beaconites often espoused as part of their own definitions of success.

The notion that the Beacon provided the city of St. Louis and its surrounding areas with "news that matters" also granted journalists the autonomy to decide what matters, a key part of the culture. At the Beacon, engagement practices allow the audience some input, but the organization strongly espouses the belief that journalists best understand what matters and that this understanding results in a better news ecosystem for the city. Beaconites strongly believe in letting their audience participate in the process of deciding what is news, but an underlying assumption of the Beacon is that citizens are not journalists, and that journalists need to make decisions concerning news. This means not only deciding what to cover but also deciding when to describe something in a story. For example, in one particular piece, a reporter wrote that something was "arguably" the most important facet to a story. One editor made another editor remove "arguably" from the story. "We need to know that this is the most important part," they said. At a meeting concerning an upcoming series about gun violence in the city, one editor said that the Beacon needed to talk to people in the community, do research, and then make decisions about what was important before it published anything. The implication is that in a sensitive series such as this one, many community members will have strong viewpoints they wish to express and concrete ideas about what is important to the city. But Beacon journalists need to know the community better and make these decisions themselves. One editor verbalized this belief very clearly at a meeting attended by two members of the community. During a discussion about how to frame a particular story, one of the community members provided their opinion on how that story is important to the community. This opinion contradicted what the original reporter believed. The editor replied:

> Look, our job is to tell the story. If you or someone else doesn't think this is the story, that's not our fault. What else can we say? [The reporter] knows this story. [They] reported it and wrote it. That is the story.

The journalists at the Beacon believe that the role of the organization is to contribute to the betterment of the city, to enhance St. Louis. This occurs not only through providing news and information but also through what they cover and who they cover. One reporter produced a series on transgender people. They did feature stories on people of all ages and races concerning their transition. The reporter described the series as a way to make the community stronger by providing a voice to people who otherwise might not have one. They said, "I like to bring invisible people into visibility. It's harder to hate or misunderstand people that you know." In the meeting discussing the gun violence series, a reporter and an editor stressed that the series needed to go beyond simple reporting about violence. They argued that a series like this could provide a lot of good to the community, if reported correctly. The editor said, "We need to treat this as a public health issue and not a political one. If 144 people in St. Louis died each year from skin lesions, everyone would be all over it, trying to fix the problem." The reporter concurred and added, "This is a big and important issue to the health of the community, but how do you intervene? We need to figure out how to reach the most people." When discussing what they believed is the role of the Beacon, the editor said,

> I believe in the improvability of the region. And I believe it's important. It's an old community. It's important in the history of the country. It has wonderful people living here. It's seriously divided by race and class, but who isn't? So there's a lot to be done. What we do, we believe as a consensus, we believe that what we're doing is material that has some roots and some meaning to people and can help the community.

Therefore, although a slogan or short mission statement such as "news that matters" might seem like a cliché or marketing device, it actually drove the focus of the Beacon newsroom and provided journalists a way to decide autonomously what news is important, based on what they desired to cover, while also positioning themselves as a news entity focused on bettering the community through news productions choices.

Leadership

In his ethnographic research about a technology company in Massachusetts, Gideon Kunda explored how organizational culture can be strongly shaped by a visionary leader.[11] Kunda found that although the company had hundreds of other employees, many in significant leadership positions, the role of a visionary founder can dictate an organizational culture, even when the founder is not present when a decision is made. Some organizational theorists liken some organizations as similar to political systems, with some "characterized by absolute and often dictatorial power."[12] This is not necessarily so nefarious as the word *dictatorial* implies; companies such as Apple under Steve Jobs would fit this description. Ideally, it could mean simply that a company takes on one person's vision and that vision affects essentially all-important aspects of the organizational culture. At the Beacon, Margaret Wolf Freivogel was the clear leader. Freivogel spent thirty-four years at the *St. Louis Post-Dispatch*, at various points running the newspaper's Washington bureau and editing the Sunday newspaper. When she took a buyout and left the newspaper in 2004, she immediately began wondering about her next step. Over the first five years of the Beacon, Freivogel's role at the organization shifted. At the start, employees said she played a much larger role in the organization's day-to-day operations. However, afterward she contributed to the overall focus of the Beacon but spent most of her time dealing with business issues. During the primary time period studied for this research, Freivogel focused a lot of time on the then potential merger with St. Louis Public Radio. She often attended meetings concerning the merger. She also frequently worked off site, editing stories while traveling to visit her children and grandchildren. Even when she was not physically in the newsroom, however, Freivogel's influence remained.

In the office, Freivogel clearly led the staff. At every meeting she attended, she controlled the conversation and facilitated discussion. Everything went through her. Other editors did not ask Freivogel specific questions about specific stories but rather questions about overall issues. For example, when talking about coverage of the State of the Union Address, Freivogel asked another editor how the Beacon planned to cover the event. When the editor responded that they would focus on "the facts," Freivogel agreed and made her vision known: "We don't need a narrative. If there is one, great, but if not, just the facts." She said her primary focus with the *Beacon* is quality. "I'm worried about good journalism." When a reporter discussed how they dealt with editors, they inadvertently illustrated Freivogel's role at the Beacon:

> I talk with my [direct] editor all the time. We have many conversations about stories, and [they know] what [they're] looking for. I talk with [another editor] occasionally, when [my editor] is on vacation or if I'm doing an arty story or a more feature-y story. Occasionally I talk to [a different editor] if it's health related, but not very often. [Freivogel] sometimes gets in the mix as a person who pushes you in the right direction or something.

That quote explains how Freivogel sets the direction of the news organization without becoming involved in the day-to-day decisions about coverage. Other editors also said that Freivogel occasionally became very interested in a particular topic, and that meant that coverage needed to focus on that issue. Freivogel would not explicitly assign the coverage or inform an editor to do that task; she simply would say that she found something interesting. An editor said that Freivogel was very clear on direction.

> One thing is that [Freivogel] does set direction. She makes it clear. You know, she gives us a lot of leeway and I think [another editor] and I, well, we pretty much manage the daily. I was going to say paper, but you know what shows up every day. But I think [Freivogel] is very clear about giving direction about the kinds of things she thinks are important.

One manner in which she often dictated culture and decisions without doing so explicitly was through setting the ethical direction at the Beacon. Employees looked to her for the "right" decision. In multiple interviews, Beaconites noted that whenever they found themselves unsure about how to deal with an issue, they contacted Freivogel. This illustrated her role because not one reporter discussed Freivogel as playing a large part in how they produced stories. When a Beacon reporter said "my editor," they meant their direct editor, not Freivogel. But ethical decisions came from Freivogel. For example, an organization in a partnership with the Beacon became outspoken concerning a certain ballot item. Nobody in the newsroom knew exactly how to deal with the issue and immediately turned to Freivogel for answers. "I don't want to overreact to this," she said, "but we cannot be involved in a partnership where they're strategizing with one side." Another time, the Beacon accepted a grant from an arts organization. The grant called for the Beacon to hold community meetings to discuss issues in the arts. Freivogel found herself a little indecisive about the experience at first, but after the meetings, she thought the partnership worked well. During a morning budget meeting, she cited this experience as a blueprint for how the Beacon should approach grants in the future:

> If you were going to articulate a guideline for us, this seems like a start. This felt a little uncomfortable for me at first because we were partnering with an organization that was giving us money and we report on them. But they were also genuinely wanting to know what was going on. So that's a sort of guideline for the future. There are probably organizations we don't want to partner with, like a liquor store that wants to know where liquor is sold.

An employee on the business side of the Beacon noted the tension between the business side of the *Beacon* and the editorial side:

> There's never really a bad monetary opportunity for grants or whatever, I think. The editorial side might disagree. The bottom line is it comes down to [Freivogel]. I mean, she has such a great background with journalistic ethics that, like, the line does end with her. So basically, we have

to feel out what feels right and then think about it. In the end, we ask [Freivogel] because she'll have the right answer.

At one point, the Beacon worked on a series of stories concerning obesity in the inner city. The Missouri Foundation for Health essentially funded the series. One editor noted how the editorial side of the Beacon worked with the business side of the organization on this type of story:

> It's very touchy and it was hard for [Freivogel] to say, "OK, we've got to go out to these foundations and get money." This is new territory for journalists of course, but it's also our future. So we went. We've been very, very careful. [An editor] looks carefully at our stories. They take a political test on all of them so [they feel] they are unbiased. [Freivogel] looks again, as she reads every story. But it's something we're all really careful about.

Some of the journalists at the Beacon consider Freivogel a mentor or an idol. In interviews, numerous Beaconites lauded Freivogel's experience and remarked how much they had or hoped to learn from her. One editor communicated that Freivogel was the primary reason they came to the Beacon and that they considered Freivogel a person to look up to professionally.

> When [Freivogel] called me and invited me to come, I've always had respect for [Freivogel]. I came to the *Post-Dispatch* right out of J-school. I got a scholarship from [University of Missouri]. So I've known [Freivogel] since I was eighteen years old. And I've always had a lot of respect for her. She's always kind of been a role model to me. You know, she's not that much older than me, just four or five years, but she was kind of setting the pace for things I wanted to do.

Freivogel influenced the culture of the Beacon at both micro and macro levels. When she was in the newsroom, the Beacon's work environment became more formal. The staff held budget meetings and engaged in fewer personal conversations; the workday seemed more structured. On days when Freivogel worked in the Beacon newsroom, all major decisions concerning editorial went through her. This did not appear the case on days when she worked off site. On the macro level, Freivogel built the foundation of the Beacon, and the staff enacted her mission for the organization daily. She still retains a firm hold on communicating that mission.

Freivogel embodied the "news that matters" approach taken daily by the Beacon. When in the office, she sometimes verbalized this approach concerning a story. When discussing a particular piece with a reporter, Freivogel said, "Start with people directly affected and then you build around them, not the other way around. You need a place to start. We need a vehicle." This advice clearly articulated her vision of an online newspaper utilizing context to tell stories. When Freivogel was out of the office, other editors ran the day-to-day operations, but Freivogel's mission remained omnipresent. On a day when Freivogel worked away from the office during a trip to Vermont, another editor told a reporter over the phone that a story needed more people affected by the incident, thus continuing the mission. For the series on gun violence, Freivogel called a meeting to brainstorm ideas. Before the meeting, she told two other editors that with all her obligations concerning the merger, she could not oversee the series as closely as she would have liked. She implied that this meeting would allow her the ability to communicate what she wanted out of the series, even though she would be only tangentially involved. Freivogel originated the idea for the series and called the meeting to make sure Beaconites understood her vision. In the newsroom, she said to the other editors,

> I think the key would be doing it in a way that would let people see the patterns of gun violence. Maybe we pick a block that's in the middle of this and see who's here, what's happening and how this intersects with these bigger trends. I will send this note around and say, "Let's make a big deal out of this." But I'm doing that without knowing if it is a big deal.

When the Beacon faced the quandary of whether to publish a racist cartoon about the city's mayoral race, the staff looked to Freivogel for the decision. Freivogel verbalized what she saw as the predicament. The Beacon could run the cartoon, letting the community see the depiction but also spread a racist image. Or the organization could describe it and not give it any more prominence. Eventually, Freivogel decided on the latter. "I'm inclined to describe it and not print it. People can find it if they want," she said.

Overall, like many other digitally native news nonprofits started by former journalists, the *Beacon* took on the personality of its chief founder, Margaret Freivogel. Even when she was not present, her direction led the newsroom. The notion of the Beacon as a form of autocracy potentially sounds dictatorial, but that was not the case. Beaconites clearly saw Freivogel as a visionary leader whose internal credibility allowed her to control essentially every aspect of the organization, from making decisions about funding, to leading the vision on individual stories, to deciding the mission statement that really defined how the Beacon operated in terms of story selection and topics covered.

Routines

The Beacon held a budget meeting each morning at 9:30 a.m. On Thursdays, however, the meeting began around 11:00 a.m., after the weekly staff meeting. In general, these budget meetings were low key. The three principal editors, Freivogel and two others, would turn their office chairs around to face each other and discuss what the reporters were working on. Most of the discussions centered around stories that the editors planned to publish the next day or in the coming days. Freivogel drove the vast majority of the conversations during budget meetings. On the days when she was not working at the office, the other two editors typically did not hold the budget meeting. On occasion, roughly two or three times a week, a display/technical editor would participate in these meetings. In the Beacon's final year, before it was absorbed into St. Louis Public Radio, Freivogel began inviting the organization's general manager, a nonjournalist, to these meetings. Freivogel explained the decision:

> The point of [this person coming each day] is because we make decisions with what we're covering during these meetings and decisions about how we're covering them. We're trying to increase [each story's] impact, and we can do that better if [the general manager] is part of the process.

The Beacon traditionally published around ten to fifteen stories per day, so editors often discussed the "count." They did not want certain days to have only a few new stories and other days to have more than fifteen. These morning news meetings sometimes went off topic, involving conversations about current pop culture, personal lives, or content produced by the *Post-Dispatch*. These meetings typically lasted roughly thirty minutes. At the conclusion of each morning budget meeting, the three editors would go over a rundown of stories each reporter expected to finish in the future, not that day or the next day. They would come up with an expected publication date for each of these stories after examining when they expected other stories. For example, if one editor expected a story on a Tuesday, but that day featured a lot of other expected stories, the three would collectively decide which piece to hold. At the end of each meeting, Freivogel would send out an email with the daily budget to all Beacon employees.

Each afternoon, at around 3:30 p.m., the Beacon held an afternoon budget meeting. Again, only the three main editors attended this meeting, which occurred in the newsroom. These afternoon assemblies lasted for roughly fifteen minutes, about half as long as the morning budget meetings. Unlike earlier, there was very little small talk. Each editor updated Freivogel on stories and that evening's plan for who is going to do what from outside the office. Editors discussed most of the information shared at this meeting earlier in the day. At 9:30 a.m. on Thursdays, the Beacon held a staff meeting for all full-time newsroom employees. On some occasions, the business staff would attend these, but predominantly only editors and reporters would attend. A discussion of content already produced by reporters took up most of the time at these meetings. Journalists would share anecdotes; they and other Beaconites would also talk about upcoming work. Freivogel ran these meetings. When she did not attend for some reason, another editor took over. At 2:30 p.m. every Friday, editors held what they called a "news storming" meeting. At one such meeting, Freivogel asked the general manager, who ran the news storming meetings, "Remind me what we're trying to do in these meetings." The GM described news storming by saying, "We're looking for ways to further engage people with what we're already trying to do." The general goal of news storming was to discuss with the GM, a social media expert, and the organization's strategic development manager what the journalists were working on currently. The conversation was a brainstorming session on how the news organization could present or publish stories in ways that would reach more people. The GM generated the idea for news storming meetings after attending the South by Southwest media conference.

> I started thinking, What does the *Saturday Night Live* version of the newsroom look like? I mean, do people from the community come in and say, "I am really mad about this issue, and I want to tell you why"? And then do people in the newsroom say, "Here's why you can't do that"? And they have a fight about it and in the end come out with a story—or not. . . . So in the world of the Beacon, I pulled that way, way back and I said, "You know, let's see if we can take some stuff we're already doing"—and I tried to make people realize this isn't more work and we're not going to start reporting on something based on what we know might be popular—"and let's look at how we might package our content to see if we can make them land in a different way." Then we could reach a new audience.

In general, when reporters worked from home, they communicated with editors via phone, email and GoogleChat. Reporters maintained that working from home rather than at the office did not negatively affect how they did their jobs. Each had worked in a newsroom before and predominantly noticed only positive differences. One journalist said they found that the routine of going to the office each day stunted productivity and that the Beacon's structure helped them avoid that.

> It alleviates the pointless things like having to get all dressed up and get downtown to sit at an office and do what? I was already, when I was at the *Post-Dispatch* the last few years, occasionally I would work from home especially if I was in the writing stage on a big story. . . . And, also, the way we have our email system, we're all on GoogleChat so they know when you're on, when your little green light is on. I mean, [my editor]

usually sends me a note every day around 10 or 10:30 if [they haven't]
seen my light on and says, "What's up?" or whatever. We usually talk on
the phone. I would say we average about once a day on the phone—more
than that if there is something breaking.

Another reporter noted that editors were "constantly online and instant
messaging." A different reporter, who worked from the newsroom more
than any other reporter, noted, "Frankly, there is nothing I can do at the
office that I can't do from home, but sometimes I just don't want to sit
home all day."

Because the Beacon was an online news organization, it did not have any
hard deadlines for content. However, over time, the daily routines of the
editors contributed to informal deadlines. Unless a reporter was working
on breaking news, if an editor was going to publish a story the next morning, the story needed to be edited before the editor left the evening before.
For example, if a nonbreaking story needed to run Wednesday morning, it
would have to be edited by 5:30 p.m. Tuesday night. This, however, did not
always happen. Reporters would upload stories into the Beacon's content
management system after 5:30, and editors would edit the story from home.
Typically, the Beacon published the majority of its daily stories before 8:00
a.m. This, editors believed, maximized the chance people would read the
stories with their morning coffee or when doing other activities before
work. The Beacon also published some stories throughout the day, but
hardly ever anything after about 4:00 p.m. "If we publish after four, the
story will just get lost," said an editor. Over the weekend, the organization
would sometimes publish stories but would limit them only to breaking
news, because editors do not believe people follow the news so closely on
weekends.

At the Beacon, very few of the reporters had a beat. Most were general-
assignment reporters. Each reporter produced about three to four stories
a week. All the reporters interviewed noted that they typically worked on
about two or three stories at once, and possibly one long-form piece.

Engagement

The Beacon identified engagement with its audience as an integral part
of its mission. The organization's general manager defined engagement:

It is an exchange of information. Somebody at a conference last year was
talking about cross-cultural engagement, and she said it's not enough to
say, "I invited you." Or "I invited you, and you didn't come." Or "I reached
out, I invited you, I engaged you." You have to be able to say, "I invited

you; you said no. I asked you why you said no. And then I changed my
invitation, and you came." And that's the idea of it being an ongoing
conversation that isn't even two ways, but sort of like a partnership
toward a shared goal of understanding.

One editor, possibly recalling their experience at the *Post-Dispatch*,
remarked that for engagement to work, there needs to be "a deep, huge
and clear disconnect between efforts to monetize and making connections and having these ongoing connections." The Beacon engaged with
its audience in three main areas.

Open dialogue. As part of engagement, the Beacon undertook many
different initiatives, ensuring an open line of communication between the
organization and the community. One editor introduced a "community
program" that eventually became a weekly radio show titled *Beacon &
Eggs*. The goal of the program revolved around organizing meetings at
libraries, schools, social clubs, neighborhood stores, and other high-traffic
spots to ask, according to the editor, "regular people about their problems
and enthusiasms." Beaconites believed that you could not just wait for the
community to speak, you had to bring the news organization to the community. "The idea," said a different editor, "is to make us regularly available.
We go into a neighborhood saying, 'We want to hear from you.'" Editors
said reporting on these events was not the purpose, although some ideas
did arise from them. The Beacon held its news storming meetings partly
as a form of communication with readers and citizens. The Beacon invited
members of the community to many of the meetings to discuss future
stories and what the news organization could be do better. People who
were invited tended to know about the subjects that would be discussed.
"People you invite to the table," explained one editor, "are people who have
a sort of knowledge or are a stakeholder with something to offer. They
are people we want to reach and inform, so we ask how we can do that
better." The Beacon also utilized the Public Insight Network (PIN, part
of American Public Radio), which helped create conversations between
the Beacon and the community. PIN allowed citizens to contact editors
and reporters directly and also to see what the Beacon staff plannned on
covering in the future. "PIN really opens the door. It finds people and gets
them thinking and we tap their insight," said one editor.

The news agenda. One editor referred to PIN as another way for "regular people and community folks to set our news agenda." One reporter
explained that through talking to people all around the city, they found
that gender transitioning was one of the bigger talking points in the arts
community. They then began *Beacon & Eggs*, which focused on gender
transitioning. One reporter noted that they spoke to political and civic

groups as a "way to find out what they're thinking about." The reporter then used those findings as news subjects. Finally, the Beacon collaborated with a local arts organization to hold a series of open-mic events. On four consecutive days, the organizations visited four different St. Louis neighborhoods and invited residents, artists, and organizations from that community to discuss the issues important to them. "And the whole purpose," said one Beaconite, "was to really listen to the community and pull out some key topics or initiatives." The Beacon then used these topics and initiatives as the basis for its news agenda concerning the arts.

Accessibility. One of the Beacon's stated engagement goals was to take complicated issues that usually appeared in the news and making them more accessible to readers. Too often, one editor said, a news organization would print stories about an issue without fully explaining it or making it clear how and why it affected the community. One reporter added, "Almost anything we do, well, it's to make stories more accessible and relatable to the audience we're trying to reach." One of the stated ways Beaconites attempted to attain better accessibility was through applying more narrative to stories. They consistently discussed how narrative allowed readers to connect with other people and understand the issues better. One reporter explained.

> We need to get personal stories. It's one thing to do a story on, for example, obesity rates in America and use statistics and a relatively superficial interview with an individual, but it's a whole other thing to have an in-depth with an individual, with their family, maybe spending a day with the family, watching how they interact, listening to the individual challenges. You know, we're going to be with a group of individuals for a long time.

Beaconites also pointed to interactive graphics that made statistics relevant as a way to make information digestible and easier to understand. Staffers noted that statistics meant something to people and helped tell fuller stories, but without putting the numbers in context, many times the statistics left readers wondering what it all meant.

Galvanization. When the founders established the Beacon, one editor explained that they knew that "if we don't use what's good, we're not going to, well, we will cease to have any influence or impact at all. It'll just be more, sort of noise." The Beacon identified, in other media, an overreliance on bad, negative news that did not provide readers with any potential fixes. One editor said they thought communities reacted to this by simply stopping listening and reading, adding that news organizations must discuss the issues in a way that can make the community better, not frustrate it.

Technology

The Beacon staffers primarily used technology to connect with its audience. At the time, technology did not play a large role in most other news production processes. Using social media allowed the news organization to connect with readers. For example, the Beacon's Facebook page was open; anybody who "liked" the page could comment. Beacon staffers would often comment back through the Beacon's account or comment directly using their personal Facebook accounts. The same could be said of Twitter. The general manager said that creating these lines of communication through social media allowed the conversation to happen openly rather than in private. One editor said that technology was "absolutely essential to us communicating with our readers and them communicating with us." Another editor noted that consistently communicating with people over social media allowed the community to begin trusting the news organization. Some younger reporters mentioned using social media to communicate directly with the audience, but that practice did not occur across the newsroom. One reporter on the younger side said that "technology is all about starting conversations" and that they believe the Beacon's own commenting system illustrated this idea. They said readers could comment on the organization's website; those comments would be conversation starters between readers and journalists. When Freivogel decided the Beacon should host a "conversation about race," she looked to the website as the place to hold this conversation. The staff then posted numerous stories about the topic and directly asked readers to comment to start the discussion.

One example illustrates how the news organization harnessed technology to provide citizens some influence is the Public Insight Network. Once signed up, these members could communicate directly with Beacon editors about what news they wanted to see. The PIN editor periodically sent out messages to all PIN sources asking what was on their minds. For example, the Beacon received a grant directly from the national Public Insight Network for its series on obesity in the city. This allowed the editor to communicate directly with the targeted audience about what they wanted to see in this series. It also allowed the Beacon to invite all members of the PIN to the meetings and discussions held on the topic. Because the Beacon was a digitally native news organization and thus unburdened by printing costs, its relatively small operating budget was enough for the organization not to institute a paywall. In fact, part of the Beacon's stated mission was to be free and open to all, with internet access. One reporter said technology allowed the Beacon to break down information and inform its readers more easily:

> Technology, it just allows us to do stuff you can't do in a regular newspaper. That engagement element is about more than just giving people something, but also holding yourself accountable. And the fact that the Beacon is an online newspaper, I think there is a lot of necessity to harness content, to harness technology to make our content more attractive and accessible to people, to make it so they can understand it. That's so important.

Beacon staffers noted that video, which was used sparingly, could sometimes help the audience to a story. The reporter working on the story about gender transitioning explained,

> With the gender series, I'm interviewing people and it's hard to talk about someone without them. You've got a teenager who was born a girl but feels like a boy and is a boy for all purposes. How does he look when he talks? What does his voice sound like? How does he present? You can take a still picture and write about this stuff and you still don't get that flavor, but when you hear him talking it's like, "Huh, he's just a guy."

Advances in technology made it easier for Beaconites to accomplish their chief goal of "news that matters."

The Merger

Not every DNNN merges with another organization. The vast majority of DNNNs are run by their founders. As an organization matures, those founders will move on at some point. When a founder—particularly one with as much agency over the entire organization as Freivogel—exits a nonprofit, that departure is "often disruptive for the organization and emotionally charged for the people involved."[13] In a sense, because so much of the organization's DNA is connected to the vision of the founder(s), a period of destabilization often results when the founder exits voluntarily, such as through a merger, sale, or retirement, or even involuntarily. In fact, because founders such as Freivogel command such large amounts of power within an organization, they provide a significant amount of stability to others within the firm, but their exit can be particularly traumatic because others rely on that stability for everyday decisions.[14]

After months of meetings, in late November 2012, the Beacon and St. Louis Public Radio agreed to merge operations.[15] Sixteen full-time members of the Beacon staff officially became state employees, because St. Louis

Public Radio is owned by the University of Missouri system. The merger
was "watched by other public broadcast stations and online startups"
because it could be seen "as a model for the future."[16] Originally, Freivogel
stayed on and supervised the Beacon staff through the merger. The new
organization's website used the names St. Louis Public Radio and the St.
Louis Beacon, but by March 2014, the new organization went by only St.
Louis Public Radio while retaining the "news that matters" mission.[17] "We
moved buildings, but at first, it still kind of felt like the Beacon," said one
reporter of time right after the merger. "Soon, though, it really was
tough. We didn't exactly have a direction, you know. We were trying to find
our place in this new thing, but we were supposed to be part of the new
thing." Interviewed years after the merger, numerous Beaconites who had
made the transition described how odd it was not having Freivogel in the
middle of everything, making the important decisions. Said one journalist,

> You know, I could sort of turn my chair around and talk to the person
> who was in charge of everything, [and they] could just decide whatever
> and then do it. And now, in most in cases, that's very much not the case.

Over and over, what journalists missed most was having leadership easily accessible and right in the newsroom. Having a university, an entity
not present in the newsroom, in charge, took getting used to. "We have a
general manager, but it's not the same," said one journalist. "They're not
the one making important decisions. You could say the buck does not stop
with [them]. So that's a huge change we had to get used to."

Although the mission or slogan "news that matters" remained after the
merger, journalists overwhelmingly believe that the manifestation of that
mission changed. "That was kind of our lighthouse, the thing that guided
us," said one journalist.

> Or we thought so. But really, I think, looking back, it was just [Freivogel].
> How she basically defined what news meant is what we did. We kept
> news that matters, but it didn't mean the same thing really. It started to
> mean what [St. Louis Public Radio] meant for news. We still did amaz-
> ing work and many things that I'm really, really proud of, but it was
> different. It was different because [Freivogel] was not, you know, in
> charge anymore.

So although some DNNNs do not go through mergers such as that at the
Beacon, numerous others experience the loss of a founder for other reasons and must deal with that disruption. Large DNNNs in Minneapolis,
Austin, San Diego, and other places found themselves in this situation,
which illustrates the foundational influence of leadership at DNNNs.

Conclusion

The St. Louis Beacon, like many small digitally native news organizations, particularly nonprofits, founded in the twenty-first century, featured an organizational structure effectively revolving around one person, its founder Margaret Wolf Freivogel. This form of organization, common in startups, typically results in a culture dictated by one person's vision. At the Beacon, Freivogel felt that she understood, after decades at the *Post-Dispatch*, where and how that major metropolitan newspaper was failing the community. She believed that the city and its residents needed more news with context and, therefore, imbued the Beacon with its mission of providing "news that matters" to its readers. This mission statement effectively defined newsworthiness for Beaconites. Due to the small staff and a hands-off board of directors, Freivogel could, in consultation with other top editors, effectually take ownership of all important decisions in the organization. As one journalist described it, all anyone at the Beacon needed to do was turn their chair or hop on GoogleChat or make a phone call and they could easily reach Freivogel, and she could quickly provide guidance or answers. As longtime veterans of newspapers, Freivogel and the other top editors at the Beacon all had had experience with what one top editor called "the bosses telling us to play with shiny new toys." This perception of technology as more often than not aimed at generating higher revenues and not better journalism, impacted all decisions around technology in news production. Therefore, the organizational culture of the Beacon was framed, in a significant manner, by one person's belief in what news should be and what, they believed, was wrong at their former place of employment.

This organizational culture worked well for the Beacon. Observing the newsroom and interviewing all employees underscored the staff's unwavering support of Freivogel, their faith in her decision making, and her ability to make complicated ethical decisions such as how to create boundaries between, for example, funding from foundations and the news-work it underwrote. As noted earlier, the Beaconites simply trusted Freivogel; they believed her stellar background as a journalist meant she would always prioritize quality journalism over all else. The issue faced by the Beacon and by other newsrooms in similar situations was that eventually, visionary founders leave. At the Beacon, a merger with the local public radio station effectively ended Freivogel's status as the lead organizational decision maker. This created a significant disruption that forced the Beacon to become an essentially new organization. In his theory of organizational culture and how it is affected by leadership, Edgar Schein extensively discusses how the original founder's values are often the compass for the company, how companies started by visionary founders face significant problems under new leadership, and how a new leader will inevitably make decisions differently.[18] That happened after the merger, and the former Beaconites who made the transition initially struggled to adapt. One reporter said,

> By that point [of the merger], I could, I bet, know what [Freivogel] would do 95 percent of the time. So I knew what I was supposed to do. You get so used to doing something one way and then it changes. It was tough.

All digitally native news nonprofits, especially smaller ones, will face this issue at some point. The story of the Beacon illustrates the need for a predetermined plan to work through an eventual change in leadership. As more and more news startups enter the journalism ecosystem, those founded by visionary leaders need to strategize early on about what a leadership transition would involve. The Beacon case study involves a DNNN, but this lesson can be extrapolated to any new news organization where one or two people's vision casts a long shadow across the organization. This is particularly the case at DNNNs, where these leaders wield more power over the entire operation than would happen at a more traditional news-organizational alignment with distinct editorial and business operations, with the business side often having more decision-making agency.

2

DEFECTOR MEDIA

The Cooperative

In late October 2019, the relatively new owners of the sports and culture website Deadspin were momentarily stunned. In April of that year, a company named G/O Media took over Deadspin and began making some very unpopular changes, unpopular at least with the journalists on staff. Whereas staffers prided themselves on covering both sports and culture, the G/O-installed CEO instituted a mandate for the journalists: "Stick to sports." Deadspin's interim editor in chief, Barry Petchesky, who had been at the site for years, said no—and promptly received his walking papers. But G/O did not expect what happened soon after as a "sign of protest and solidarity": more than a dozen staffers quit in protest.[1] At a particularly precarious time for media workers, staff members decided they'd had enough. Despite daily headlines "announcing another round of media layoffs," the Deadspin journalists "decided they would choose when to leave and how to go."[2] Without new jobs to fall back on and with many of them having spent years working together, the former Deadspin journalists began collectively thinking about what they would do next. "That was the hardest part," said one staffer, primarily because it "took the longest time." Very quickly, most of the former staffers knew they wanted to start something together, but what that something entailed took a significant amount of time to determine. Explained one journalist who quit Deadspin, "We all left Deadspin right at the end of October. And, you know, we all stayed in touch with each other," they explained.

> Pretty quickly we realized we wanted to try to do something to, like, start a [new] thing. And I would say for like most of the months after that, all of those conversations were around securing funding from somebody or some source.

The journalists coalesced in a nineteen-person group. They agreed that they all wanted to start a new journalistic organization together, but they were all journalists, not businesspeople. Together, they studied the media ecosystem, looking at various potential market models, but realized they did not know the nuts and bolts of starting a new business. "We, at first, we were, like, you just can't start something with nineteen people because we can't pay for someone to create a website. We, like, we wouldn't have salaries," said one journalist.

> We always knew we wanted to do a subscription model, but we, for a long time, were just operating under the assumption that unless some rich guy gives us, you know, three million dollars to start with on day one, like it's just not going to happen. So we spent a lot of time feeling that out, seeing, you know, if we could find a rich guy to do that. And there were a lot of different pitch meetings and conversations that went to various lengths. We got pretty close with some fund that was going to give us money, but then the coronavirus happened. So that was in March [2020], and at that point like our person just immediately pulled out.

The notion of having affluent backers help them fund a news startup seemed, at the time, the only option to most of the former Deadspin journalists. "We really had no idea there was another way," said one journalist. "It, like, literally didn't even cross our minds we could do it ourselves, but then [the] pandemic happened, and we needed to think, I hate this cliché, but outside of the box." That different thinking led to the idea that maybe this group of nineteen could do it themselves by utilizing a less-seen market model in American journalism: the cooperative. "We realized," said one staffer, "we could build a website, we could have the paywall and we didn't need millions of dollars up front to accomplish something." Another noted:

> We're like, OK, well we can do this. And at that point we went into it thinking, we'll have the website, none of us will make a salary possibly for a year. It's going to be really tough. I mean since then everything's gone great. Like, you know, the subscriber number is really good. We're not rich or anything yet, but we are on a great trajectory and things have worked out, I think, better than we could have even thought. So, in some ways we sort of dodged a bullet not actually taking funding.

On September 10, 2020, the group launched a sports and culture website called Defector, an employee-owned cooperative that is a subscription-based, paywall-enforced site devoid of advertising.[3] By the time of the launch, the nineteen founders wrote that they "want[ed] to be a website that [readers] will actually want to read," and "hope to give [readers] a publication that exists not just as a name that occasionally pops up in your various social media feeds, but as a daily destination."[4] For the first two years of its existence, Defector earned slightly more than 95 percent of its total revenue from subscriptions alone, and the other roughly 5 percent from advertising on podcasts, merchandise, donations, events, and other small revenue streams such as the monetization of social media platforms.[5] In an almost unprecedented manner, the site became profitable almost immediately, spurring the *Washington Post* to contend that "in a world of endlessly distressing media news, the Defector story is a bright spot and maybe a small miracle."[6]

One key difference in Defector's business model lies in its tiered subscription costs. Many news organizations charge different prices for subscriptions. For example, the *New York Times* monetizes certain elements of its content, such as games, or cooking stories through higher subscription costs. In contrast, Defector charges $79 per year for standard access to all content on the site, but $119—roughly a 50 percent price hike—for the ability to comment on stories, participate in question-and-answer sessions with journalists, and receive email newsletters. The founders believed that, through engagement, they could monetize their readers and take advantage of "answering only to that loyal audience."[7]

Organizational Culture

To most organizational theorists, the strongest, most adaptable, best-functioning organizations think explicitly about culture and spend time "talking about a process of reality construction that allows people to see and understand particular events, actions, objects, utterances, or situations in distinctive ways."[8] Although these conversations around culture might not mention it explicitly, the act of unambiguously defining what an organization should be creates shared values among employees within the ecosystem; these values allow members to see their experiences within the organization in a similar manner. For the founders of Defector, the time they spent working toward finding a market model left them much time to think about what they wanted this news organization to be, exactly. Before the purchase by G/O Media, many of the former Deadspin staffers now forming Defector lived through multiple ownership changes. Originally part of the Gawker group of websites, Univision Communications purchased Deadspin (and all of Gawker) in 2016. Univision then sold to G/O about three years later. After years living through various ownership groups, the first thing the founders of Defector wanted to avoid was a feeling of powerlessness. "You know when you're working somewhere and just super bad decisions keep coming down all around you, and you can't do anything about them?" asked one Defector founder. "That's really what we said was not going to happen here." To that end, the founders very intentionally set out to establish an open organizational culture, one where everyone felt equally powerful in decision making. "From the beginning, everyone is part of these decisions around the company. It kind of just helps get people used to the idea right off the bat of like, 'No, this belongs to all of us,'" explained one founder.

> Every single one of us gets to have a say [in] what happens at this company. And that doesn't always mean that, you know, everyone's in total agreement. Certainly not. . . . But it feels like everyone is kind of being called to be a part of it in a way that definitely did not exist at any other place I've ever worked.

Another founder noted, "I guess the culture, for lack of a better word, is open because there's no real turf to protect." This concept of an open, complete democracy within the company manifests itself in myriad manners. To Defector employees, the decision to found the organization as a cooperative is what makes fostering this culture possible.

Although media cooperatives are much more prevalent in Europe and South America, particularly Greece and Argentina, they are beginning to become more common across the United States. Scholars define a media cooperative as a "self-managed and collective work organization" that remains outside the structures and logic of the media conglomerates."[9] The ability simply to start a website and begin publishing journalism, as Defector did, allows for media startups to exist in a way essentially impossible two decades ago.[10] And although numerous different types of journalism startups have become more common across this country in the last two decades, many of them adopted the same standard normative ideas of legacy journalism, primarily because their founders came from legacy journalism.[11] But regardless of where the founders gained experience, cooperatives are drastically different due to their governance structures, which are built around notions of full democracy. Even in the most democratic of newsroom, "canonical notions of corporate structure and governance, even when they encompass a wide variety of stakeholders, tend to affirm the practice of granting ownership and control to investors, since they bear direct financial risk."[12] In short, funders often have the ultimate power in corporations because they fund the operation. In a cooperative, everyone collectively funds the operation. Despite a long history of media cooperatives in the United States, many are historical and fall outside what would be considered mainstream journalism.[13] At

Defector, the notion of open ownership is fundamental to its organizational culture, a culture that is focused on openness across all dimensions of organization. "When we all quit Deadspin, there was this idea that came up pretty immediately that was like, 'You know, we could do something here,'" explained one founder.

> We could maybe do something. And I was of the opinion that if we were going to do anything, being worker-owned, being a coop of some sort should be, you know, like the main goal. Like if we were going to build something that was relying on [venture capital] money or was going to require a wealthy benefactor to support us, then it's not to say it wouldn't have worked. But to me personally it didn't seem like it would have been worth doing.

The concept of ownership is not simply an economic one, but rather the Defector founders wanted to hold each other accountable, wanted to have the power to succeed or fail on their own terms. "It is very comforting to know that if things blow up and things collapse, if things fail quietly, it'll be because of something we did," explained one founder. "It will be, you know, there's a justice to it. If we fail or if we succeed, it'll be on our terms."

Although there are numerous types of cooperative structures, the founders of Defector very clearly manifested their notions of organizational culture through their choice to implement a cooperative plan that prioritized equal power, not only for the founders but also for any new people who joined the company. The founders also made sure that all the power lay with people in the organization, not with anyone who might leave the team. This was very important to members of the newsroom. "The structure we have is extremely focused on just current employees as the ones making the decision and getting the money," explained one founder.

> What we have is like after a year, anyone who leaves, they keep their equity but they're not going to be getting revenue disbursements or anything with that equity. It's only of value to them at that point is if we sell, they'll get a percentage. So, if you leave, you keep your equity, but you don't get to vote on things anymore, you don't get to get a check at the end of the year for however much revenue was made, which we all thought was fine. You know, I mean there's probably part of us, some people, in the back of their heads were like, "Well we're the founders. If I leave in five years, I'd kind of like to still have payments or something." And we were like, that would also sort of be against the spirit of this. It's like if it's a media [cooperative] and if the people who work there at any given day are the ones who matter, they should be the ones making all the decisions and stuff like that.

The founders still maintain a larger share of the equity in Defector, but they implemented a plan—often called a phantom equity plan—that makes sure that newer members of the newsroom get an equal say in all decisions and, perhaps more important, feel like an equal part of the organization. "That was really important to us," said one founder. "What we didn't want was someone to come here and feel like it's us and them. I don't mean us versus them; that would never happen. But even us and them would go against what we're trying to do." When someone new gets hired into the organization, they receive a quarter of a percent of the company, but also get full voting rights as members of the cooperative. "Their vote and everything carry the same amount of weight as everybody else's. They have a much smaller chunk of equity, but we figured that was OK since the founders, it made sense [for them] to have a bigger chunk," explained one founder. "All that really matters is that they get to vote and have the same influence over everything as everybody else." When a new member gets hired, everyone in the cooperative's equity gets diluted a small amount to reflect the equity now given to the new member. Therefore, hiring affects everyone, "which makes us, I think, so much more intent on hiring great people from now on," explained one founder. A nonfounder discussed how this setup immediately made them feel comfortable at Defector, and let them know that the newsroom's espoused values concerning an open democracy within the company truly existed in practice. "It's hard to underscore how much this feels like a team, in really every way," said one nonfounder.

> There are people here who didn't get jobs and kind of put their lives, you know, sort of in some ways on the line gambling whether this would work. And I get to come in and have the same say as them. That's crazy. I'm an owner of this place. It really makes me focus on doing the absolute best I can. Not that I wouldn't otherwise, of course, but, you know, it just feels different when you and all your friends are really the only ones responsible for the success—and that means, like, real-life financial security for all of us.

The founders believe that making these decisions about "what kind of place do we want to work at" before even delving into the journalism part of the company potentially had a big impact on what they consider the installation of a successful organizational culture. "I think we always knew we wanted to be a better version of Deadspin, so we didn't have to talk about it that much. And we really didn't," recalled one founder. "What we did was try to describe a place we would all want to work at, regardless of whether we did awesome blogs or just, I don't know, manufactured something." They started this by making policies around what they wanted the company to be. Very early in the process, Defector founders, hired a human relations consultant—since none of them had any experience in the area—and through some workshops with the consultants, began to understand that policy work in the early stages could really set the tone for the future of the organization. "Like, as cheesy as it sounds, we wrote an employee handbook, right, and like did our best to put our values in the handbook. And we wrote an ethics policy, and we wrote a diversity policy," recalled a founder. "You know it's normally the type of thing that gets handed down to you from a corporate overlord and you roll your eyes at it. But now it's like well, OK, actually now we can't roll our eyes." Another founder discussed how everything changed in the ideation of the company once they realized a rich funder wouldn't bankroll the organization. "It was a, like, an a-ha moment," explained a founder, contending that when they realized they were going to start the site themselves, it became a reality that they would really need to come up with the mission and culture of the news organization themselves. "You know this, of course, but we talked to some experts about our options, but then we just made decisions," they recalled. And again, the founders consistently noted that these conversations revolved not around journalism but rather around a corporate structure that manifested their values and goals for a company, not necessarily a newsroom. "It was all on us," said one founder, adding,

> That opens up the possibilities to where, you know, we can do this thing however we want. So what we did was we had a smaller group of us sort of work as a committee, draw up, like, a basic, you know, vision for the structure and everything for the company. A lot of the basics [revolved around the idea that] we all want the same ownership over it, you know, it's a collective whereas if there are big company-defining decisions that need to be made, that's like a full staff where everyone's vote counts equally. Stuff like that. And that was where we just sort of got into the nitty-gritty and the specifics of the structure. I think what we were trying to do was thread the needle. You know operationally there was a fairly standard hierarchy. You don't want, like, a full staff vote on should this [story get published] or not or should we hire this guy. So with that in place we then sort of overlaid on top of that much more of the flat cooperative model for all the big decisions. It's all about building checks and balances. And, like, that's where we decided that we can vote out the [editor in chief] at any time. That's kind of crazy. But, like, that really is a necessity if you're actually going to be committed to having the cooperative thing. Because if we didn't have that, [the editor] could be an asshole and start running the site crazy, and then a cooperative does you no good at that point.

Beyond the organizational structure of Defector, staffers enacted these values of open democracy and prioritizing quality work over economic gain while also making business decisions. "It's actually a really good testing point for people," explained one journalist. "You know, do we make this decision that could absolutely make us all more money, or do we make the right decision?" Many journalists recalled a relatively early hiring meeting. Defector members interviewed multiple people for a business position within the company, consistently asking the various job candidates what they thought the newsroom could do better in terms of generating more revenue. These interviews, according to one founder, proved that Defector clearly believes in the mission and culture of the organization more than anything else, including maximizing profits.

> Everyone kept saying, "You should buy Facebook ads." And [we said], "Our whole staff is morally opposed to Facebook ads. But thank you for the suggestion, but we're not doing that, you know." Also, Facebook is killing our industry, um, no, we're not doing that. Like, no, we're not buying Facebook ads. Although they were right in terms of pure profit margin; they are not wrong. But also, we're not going to do that. Thank you. But here there actually is a direct line between what goes on the page and our company culture. And so, I think [it was] really important for us to have that pretty explicitly laid out from the beginning, just because it plays into a lot more of your actual day-to-day work experience and what you're producing.

Numerous journalists spoke about the mission of the organization but noted that some decisions around economic issues also potentially could be affected by previous work experience. For example, a handful of staffers believed the organization made conservative decisions surrounding the use of company funds. "I think one of the things is that it's our money that we're spending. We have budgets and all that stuff and it's all very well managed," explained one founder. "Yet I think we have not necessarily exploited all of the potential resources we have because we're so used to working for belt-tightening owners."

Beyond the founding of the company and major decisions undertaken by all cooperative members, Defector manifests its culture in the day-to-day workings of the newsroom by setting up, empowering, and staffing a variety of committees charged with making decisions, suggestions and conducting research in their particular areas of emphasis. Virtually all Defector staffers sit on a committee, mostly of their choice, and work on important issues. The newsroom formed a Growth Committee, a Culture Committee, a Podcast Committee, an Events Committee, a Merchandise

Committee, a Public Relations Committee, and more. The point of these committees was to empower cooperative members in areas of their choice. "Think about it," explained one staffer, "almost of all our committees make decisions about things that would normally not be made by us journalists. Someone outside of, you know, a newsroom would dictate this." One of the founders explicitly discussed the committee structure as an intentional choice to make sure their company's original goals around democratic governance are made real beyond large company decisions.

> We could have made this place, Defector, and said we're a cooperative and all that entails. And then we could come together and make the big decisions together, but we could have hired a couple businesspeople or whatever to do the work of the committees. You could say that would really make sense since we'd get some extra time to do the posts or stories. But that would really defeat the purpose of this whole thing. This is ours. We're responsible. We kind of envisioned, you know, everything. It's our job to make sure what we said we wanted and what we said we valued is what we actually do. Well, making all the decisions is how you make sure we're a true cooperative.

Leadership

The structure of leadership at Defector is instrumental in the manifestation of the desired organizational culture within the company. The founders did choose Tom Ley as editor in chief, and he has the same duties and responsibilities as a chief editor in any newsroom—and more when considering how much the staff oversees the business end of the cooperative. However, the notion of power, particularly hierarchical power, is essentially missing from Defector. "I think the main way I would describe this," explained one journalist, "is we have an editor in chief, but we don't have a boss." To many of the staffers, the editor in chief essentially works in the same way as the rest of the newsroom, but with some extra duties. One founder described the editor position as someone who "does the stuff that everyone else also does, and then also just some of the annoying things like keeping track of calendars and shit like that. And, yeah, then mostly just kind of stays out of the way."

As previously noted, the founders intentionally crafted the cooperative structure with an eye toward limiting the power of the position, making it possible to vote out the current editor in chief with a two-thirds majority vote. "It's really to ensure we're doing what we say we're doing," explained one staffer, adding, "We all make collective decisions, but out of necessity, whether it's Ley or someone else, that person makes decisions, and we need to hold him or whoever accountable." Even if the nominal leader makes decisions alone, staffers contend that the two-thirds majority vote to remove anyone from the position forces that person to make decisions in the best interest of the group. "Not that they wouldn't, since we all want the same things," said one staffer, "but I think it's impossible for that not to matter." A founder recalled how this setup embodies the democratic governance structure that is so important to the mission of Defector, and how even when they disagree with a collective decision or one made by the editor in chief, knowing that it's a democracy changes the way the disagreement feels. They explained,

> A decision we all made as a group when we were setting up Defector is we want to be a subscription model. And then that trickles down to how we run the day-to-day. So I think I always say the biggest surprise for me working at Defector was, like, genuinely realizing how much time and heartache and grief I spent at all my other jobs. Even in various positions, whether I was, like, a starting-out reporter or an editor, what I got [was tons of pressure from decisions made]. All these decisions made by higher powers, they trickle down to you and they affect you in all these ways. And I don't have that at Defector. I always say I realize I get to like the people I work with a lot more because we spent so much time dealing with the aftereffects of decisions made by others. And then understandably that causes stress, and you get in fights because I think it should've been handled this way and this other person thinks it should have been handled that way, you know. And now it's, like, well, "What if we didn't have to deal with that problem at all?" And it's definitely a lot easier to get along with people and to strike compromises, you know. Obviously, I still don't always get what I want. But that's just an easier thing to live with when you're just dealing with a person on the same level as you.

Implicit in that statement is the collectively held notion that, at Defector, whether someone is a new blogger, a founder, an editor, or even the editor in chief, everyone has the same status, with the same decision-making power. This is fundamental to the mission of the organization. It creates a level of transparency that makes disagreements much easier to understand and recover from for the organization. This would not be possible if the leadership structure of the organization did not align with the mission of the organization. "We could have said all the right things at the beginning, but then if certain people because of their title or maybe their prestige had more weight, what's the point?" asked one staffer. "We would have basically had all the same problems as I've seen everywhere else. Transparency would have sucked. People would hate each other. That doesn't happen like this."

Ethics as an Espoused Value of Culture

The vast majority of traditional journalistic codes of ethics focus on the nuts and bolts of reporting, on the value organizations place on matters directly connected to reporting, such as the audience, sources, truth, and the like.[14] To make sure staffers' values are reflected in their work, Defector created an ethics and values document that explicitly tells subscribers what the company prioritizes and how it will operate. This document highlights transparency first and foremost, making it clear that Defector will act in a transparent manner not only internally but also externally, so that subscribers and the audience will always know "where to direct their questions about the health or direction of Defector and can expect those questions to be answered thoroughly and promptly." The policy makes it clear to the audience that although Defector is loyal to them through its transparency, there is a strong focus on making sure those within the organization feel supported and empowered. The policy notes that if an employee believes that "they or their colleagues do not have the support or resources they need to be successful at Defector, they can expect those concerns will be sincerely heard by the rest of the staff and by Defector's managers."

The policy lists six values:

1. We maintain transparency among ourselves and with our audience.
2. We act with intention.
3. We practice mutual care and solidarity.
4. We uphold high standards of integrity, both internally and externally.
5. We respect the hard work that lies ahead.
6. Eat shit.

Of the six organizational values clearly stated in the policy, one also makes it clear that Defector will always prize an open workplace where staffers should enjoy the work they do. This value, "eat shit," explains that Defector will "take this seriously, but not too seriously. We support each other and show affection while still being goofy rather than sentimental, nostalgic, or stuck in our ways." The point of the policy, explained staffers, is not just transparency but also to make clear to each other what they want out of Defector. The policy affirms that Defector journalists are humans first and journalists second. This implicitly means that historical norms of journalism matter at Defector only if they align with the values of the organization, which, again, supersede journalistic values. In the policy, said one staffer,

We were clearly articulating this idea that our experiences and opinions and thoughts are not a liability to us and to our work as journalists. These are benefitting our understanding and our readers' understanding of what's going on, and we are being transparent about our positions and where we come from. We're reporting fairly. The reporting process is not changing, just the way we are presenting it to our readers. We're really putting a whole different framework on the site, on the idea of what journalism is or should be. And so that's really been the biggest difference, really feeling empowered to operate from this position of not having to kind of like tiptoe around these ideas of journalistic norms and objectivity. But really being, like, "Well this is how it's done, and this is how we're doing it."

To Defector journalists, this is why transparency across the entire organization, in both the journalism and the cooperative structure, is so fundamental to the company. The journalists desired the ability to do things in an ethical manner; but that manner could, in some instances, not necessarily align with historical journalism ethics. To staffers, as long as complete transparency remains a focus within newswork, the audience will allow positions, as the quote above calls them, to infiltrate content. One staffer pointed directly to the *New York Times* to illustrate why they believe it's so important to be true to yourself and the audience within stories. They believe that is why Defector prioritizes transparency over objectivity. "Look at what [objectivity] prevents," explained one journalist.

I think it prevents people who are most knowledgeable and informed about a subject from covering it to the fullest extent of how it can be covered. I mean, you see that. For example, Michael Powell at the *Times* is the culture war reporter, and he himself, you know, he's operating under this guise of objectivity and is really pushing one set of values at the *Times*. If they had hired someone who had more facility with things like trans issues or had been a student on campuses more recently, for example, I think a lot of his coverage would look very different. Or if Michael Powell was more up front about his own biases, which from a reader's perspective, at least if you follow his work, are pretty clear, then I think it would just [be different]. But the *Times* is the *Times*. I don't think it's an accident that the *Times* hired Michael Powell to be their culture-war reporter. That's kind of where [and how journalism] reinforces the status quo. I guess that's the best way to describe it. If we as journalists are interested in challenging power and the status quo and systems, which I think we all are, then we have to break out. That also means challenging the status quo and systems of our actual work and the norms that dictate how we do our jobs. So I guess that would be the most important part [of what we do at Defector].

Technology

The Defector newsroom is a room in name only; the operation does not currently have a centralized office that everyone works from. Staff members primarily work out of their homes. At first they feared this could make it difficult to create a cohesive workplace culture. "I think anyone who's ever worked in a newsroom knows the impact of a newsroom," said one founder. "I mean, without ever anybody saying much, the newsroom kind of dictates" the organizational culture to those within it. Due to a lack of a newsroom and staff members located around the country, the founders of Defector thought quite a bit about how to create an overall culture. Although many newsrooms in the 2020s utilize the messaging platform Slack as a communication hub, Defector chose to incorporate this technology in a foundational way, as a platform that undergirds the entire organizational culture. As one founder explained,

> We have a very active Slack, I would say. That could certainly probably be a little overwhelming at first for people who may not be used to a very busy Slack. But, you know, 95 percent of the stuff that happens on Slack is not work related. It's people shooting the shit, it's people making jokes, people sharing pictures of their pets or a cool photo of a bug they saw online or just whatever we want to talk about. And since probably half to three-quarters of the staff isn't in New York, everything is done remotely. So everything happens in Slack anyway. No one's really missing out by not coming into the office every day.

For staffers, Slack is a platform on which they can put their professional mission in place, but it's also a foundational driver of two goals: keeping the staff connected and helping make collaborations happen across the organization. Most of the time, these collaborations are not multibylined stories, but rather a way to talk about ideas, brainstorm stories, or get suggestions. Therefore, although Slack serves a vital work purpose, it also brings people working around the country together in a meaningful way. "I mean, the real thing is that it's a clubhouse, it's where we hang out," explained one founder.

> And, you know, we talk about things that have happened and we drop links in, and we talk about them. And usually from that conversation comes the idea for a post. You know, we actually had a thing called Slack Law that happened at Deadspin where Tommy Craggs, who was the editor at the time, said, "Hey, if you keep talking about this shit without blogging it, if you keep talking about this shit in Slack, you are going to have to eventually blog it because it's clearly interesting you enough,

you have enough to say that you ought to make a post out of it." And that has carried over and that has remained. And there are times when I like going to Slack just because it's my place to hang with my friends, you know what I mean? Like, I go in on weekends and stuff like that just because I want to. And, in fact, we've had to put policies in place or suggestions in place to make sure people aren't in Slack all that often, because we want everyone to have outside lives and also, we want to influence each other to have outside lives. I'm one of the main offenders who doesn't do that. So because I don't really see [these] people all that often in real life, that's sort of my socializing time. But from that socializing comes the work.

That quote illustrates Slack's importance in Defector in multiple ways. First, it connects employees and provides a place for them to share experiences, deepening their personal connections. Those bonds, contended many journalists, make it easier to move forward after disagreements over any decision. Second, it provides a platform to catalyze shared ownership over content, because journalists can comment, make suggestions, and brainstorm around other journalists' stories and ideas. Third, suggestions around the usage of the platform allow Defector to manifest its values—in this case, the concept that work is not everything and that a healthy organizational culture requires a healthy work-life balance, something implicit in the "eat shit" principle of the values and ethics policy previously discussed.

For many, Slack is a driver of content. "It is most useful as a way to bounce ideas off my coworkers and sharpen my ideas, sometimes come up with ideas," explained one journalist, adding, "It's useful to state my argument and then have people be like, 'Well, but actually,' or 'What about this?'" But even beyond news production, Slack provides a platform for effective, democratic, shared governance, the bedrock principle of Defector. "We have this one channel [on Slack] called Big Discussions," said one journalist. "[It's] where we talk about stuff that could either result in structural changes or changes to compensation or hiring. Anything that may or potentially could lead to a staff vote, we talk about it in this Big Discussions Slack." Without Slack, so many of the facets of organizational culture desired by the staff could not be so effectively implemented. When starting the company, the founders understood this. "We set up our Slack situation, you know, the ideas of how we'll use it, early. We had to," recalled one founder. Because of this, it became an essential driver of culture, something vital to implementing the espoused elements of culture deemed so important by founders.

Socialization

Even before they officially started Defector, the founders began to think about the day when they would welcome their first new hire. At the beginning of the organization, all the staffers had a shared history together, having spent time, in some cases considerable time, working together at Deadspin. "I would say that everyone working there and then, you know, everyone quitting together, that bonded us. And we understand that," explained one founder. The founders worried that the main effect would be that a new person without that shared history would start and immediately feel left out, regardless of the ownership equity or the equal voting rights that come with membership in the cooperative. Therefore, the socialization process became extremely important; founders spent considerable time hypothesizing about a process that would make new hires feel completely part of the organization. "So many of us worked together for so long and we are a very talkative group and lively [on Slack], and, you know, if you just threw a new person in that, it could be overwhelming," explained one founder. Another explained how they decided to combat this potentially detrimental issue:

> We have a couple of things that we do. One, some of them are silly but valuable and some of them are more normal. One of the silly ones is that [one founder] started just, like, keeping a glossary of all of our bits and inside jokes that happen in Slack all the time because those are extremely alienating if you don't know what's going on when you're a new person. So anytime we hire a new person, they receive that glossary and get to sort of mainline all the worst and dumbest parts of working here just to see what that's like. Then we have on the more serious side, we have a values document that we wrote at the beginning that we give to new people. We usually, anytime a new person comes on, assign someone on staff to sort of be their buddy through the first couple weeks or months. They take them out to lunch, like, just catch up with them and be available for them to ask questions.

To the Defector journalists, these multiple socialization tools are immensely important. Even some founders, for example, explicitly noted the glossary of terms and inside jokes as invaluable. "I didn't even know some of them. And I honestly didn't want to ask, so it's great. I know what people mean now." That glossary and the buddy system are essential entrees into Defector culture. "It's a whole glossary of terms referenced in Slack, or inside jokes or things like that, and we send them to people when they start because there will be these little words and phrases and

memes and jokes" in Slack or conversations, one journalist explained about
the glossary. "And this glossary says where they came from, and it helps
people feel like they're in on the joke."

One new addition to the staff found that the way the buddy system
was described by the journalists made a "world of a difference" in their
socialization. They said that when the buddy system got explained, "it
was clear I could ask [my buddy] anything and not worry about judgment
or anything. I just found it so refreshing—and necessary, really—that I
could rely on [my buddy] for a real understanding of the place." The staff
of Defector, particularly the founders, take the socialization process very
seriously, primarily because they believe two things: (1) If everyone truly
understands the mission and values of the organization, it will run more
smoothly, and the entire staff will make decisions that align with their
shared beliefs, or at least better understand decisions that they disagree
with; (2) Because Defector is a cooperative, every staffer is an owner, and
the current journalists want to make sure they are onboarding like-minded
people. "We're a small staff, you know, compared to a lot of places," said
one journalist, "and if we bring in an asshole or someone who just wants
to make a ton money, it's going to affect the mood. The way we [socialize]
helps everyone to know what we do and aspire to do."

Engagement

The staff at Defector takes engagement very seriously, so much so that
engagement practices are tied into the business model. As previously
noted, subscribers who would like to participate in a robust commenting community must pay a roughly 50 percent premium for an annual
subscription. However, commenting is just one engagement activity that
the Defector team prizes. The journalists participate in numerous other
engagement practices, such as question-and-answer sessions; activities,
events, and "hangouts" on platforms such as Twitch; and direct contact
through email or social media. Defector semiregularly hosts various Q&A
events, sometimes via a platform such as Twitch or Amp, other times in
special comment sections. Often, Defector calls these sessions "office
hours." Staffers almost universally regarded these types of events as a way
to truly know their audience and community. "We have a pretty good idea
of the demographics of our subscribers," said one journalist, "but actually,
kind of getting to know about them, not personally, but understand them,
it's really helpful and I think makes us closer." Another journalist described
how these more personal exchanges with the audience helps them better
appreciate what the community expects from them. "A lot of times it's just

kind of jokes and shit like that in these [sessions], so maybe we don't always think of them as super valuable," the journalist said, "but when I sit back and think about them, I really start to get to know the community better, which then, even if I don't realize it, helps me do my job for them better."

Another form of engagement the journalists discussed involved various kinds of events. For example, journalists often will play new video game releases on Twitch while chatting with subscribers. Defector very rarely covers video games, but these events "are of interest to subscribers and, um, really fun, so we do them," as one journalist said. The site also regularly hosts Thursday Trivia Night, an event where Defector journalists compete against each other in a trivia contest that subscribers can watch live and comment on throughout. Sometimes these events are simply what the site calls "hangouts," which are essentially less focused, but still centered on discussion between staff and audience. "These are all really fun things that don't feel like work," said one journalist, "but they also make the subscribers feel a part of this. And they are. We don't exist without them. We need them to feel part of this."

Like the majority of journalism organizations, Defector makes the email addresses of its staff public and provides links to social media accounts. This gives subscribers a way to connect with staff directly, "which is different than comments," as one staffer noted. One journalist discussed how direct contact affects the way they go about their job:

> Like, there are definitely subscribers who have emailed me to be, like, "I read that thing and it sucked and that's why I unsubscribed." And like, does that feel bad? Yes, it definitely does. But I also have to remember, like, maybe that reached, you know, two other people and caused them to subscribe.

Journalists believe that direct contact can implicitly affect how they do their job, but more important, Defector staffers value this type of engagement, even when it is negative.

The principal engagement practice at Defector is hosting, modcrating, and facilitating a vital comments section. The staffers all noted they believe this is the most important thing that drives subscribers to pay for the more expensive premium tier of subscription. The participants stress they need to moderate the comment section relatively little, because subscribers feel like it is "theirs." As one journalist described,

> You know that it's almost its own culture, and I guess when you pay for the privilege of commenting, you tend to value it more. So the reasons to be uncivil are greatly diminished. . . . So in a lot of ways, that's the part

of the site that belongs to them. So I think they're relatively proprietary
about it in a good way.

This self-moderation of the comments helps free journalists up to participate in commenting if they desire, but also spend more time creating
the content subscribers want. One journalist, echoing many others, noted
that moderating comment sections can take a significant amount of time.
They said,

> I think you know one of the things we were worried about is, like, there's
> not a ton of us on staff. And, you know, moderating comments is kind of
> a bear of a job, and not everyone wanted to be doing that all the time. So,
> we thought, like, "OK, if we attach this to not just a subscription, but like
> an even higher tier, that will sort of initially weed out a lot of the people
> who will tend to be there just to be trolls or whatever."

Beyond moderation, though, journalist spoke consistently about using the
comments section to find or shape story ideas or just to communicate with
subscribers. For example, one participant noted they were "happy to go
in there and talk" stories over, hoping to learn more about what they did
right and what they did wrong. Another journalist talked extensively about
the quality of the comment section, which makes engagement that much
more valuable. They said, "It's just people wanting to sort of continue the
conversation in ways that entertain them, but not at a reductive level, but at
a really interesting and entertaining level. It's a little bit elevated." Numerous staffers also spoke about how because the commenters are made to
feel like they are part of the Defector community, there is a mutual respect,
which makes engagement within the comments more valuable. They said,

> You can go through responses and get feedback, which is always good
> for any writer. If it's feedback from someone you respect, and we respect
> the commenters, then that is going to inform your work in a way that's
> very positive and good in the long run.

News Production

It is within the processes and practices of news production that Defector
most resembles any traditional news organization. The newsroom boasts
a relatively conventional hierarchical structure, with editors and writers
and the same traditional roles that go along with those titles. The site aims
to publish roughly eight to ten stories, or what they call blog posts, per day.
Some of these posts are on the shorter side, roughly four hundred to six
hundred words; others can be much lengthier. As one reporter commented,

editors "have basically a story schedule. Like, you know, OK, who's working on this? They want to make sure that the story budget is full and running [because] we usually aim to get ten posts up a day." That story budget, or list of ideas, typically gets filled in a variety of ways. When describing the entire process, one editor basically recounted a process that has occurred in newsrooms for decades.

> Either an editor will pitch a reporter, or a writer will pitch an editor, or pretty frequently the editors in their own separate Slack will be like, "We should do something on this. Who would be good for this?" And so, an editor quite often will do that. I guess that's called assigning, but ideally, this doesn't always happen. But ideally an editor talks it out a bit with the writer before the writer sits down to write. You know, they toss some ideas around, see what the angle is, see if you're in agreement on what the angle is, that stuff. Then they'll go do their thing. They'll write their blog. Usually, it'll get written in our CMS, the content management system, [in] which we use a WordPress thing. Then the writer will Slack me, "Hey, you know, take a look. Here's my draft." And I will do my edits in the CMS and leave notes in the CMS. Slack is just used if I have any immediate questions about something that they don't need to specifically address when they go back for a second draft. Just like, "What did you mean by this?" So I leave my notes, kick it back to them, they address them usually; sometimes they'll push back, which is fine. We can have that out in Slack. I'll look at it again, usually that's good for most posts, a second draft. Then once I've signed off, then it's on me to coordinate with the other editors and our editorial budget to see when this is going to go up, and it's up to the editor to actually click "Publish" and put it on the site.

The site implements a system that allows people working on more complicated, investigative pieces to have the time to report on them without the burden of producing other posts. On Tuesdays and Thursdays, one editor and two reporters will enter what the staff calls a Blog Cave, which is essentially a conversation on how the two reporters can produce some content to alleviate the production burden on reporters working on longer stories.

Within news production, particularly around story-idea generation, Slack once again plays a large role within the Defector ecosystem. One reporter described the role of Slack when the site brainstorms content:

> We're all on Slack a lot, talking a lot, so a lot of the stories will just come out of somebody dropping a link in the Slack and they're, like, "Oh look at this." And then a couple other people are, like, "Oh yeah, I think this and this about that." And then at some point if that conversation is leading somewhere interesting, you know an editor might say, "Does anybody

want to write about this?" Or they might think to themselves that I think the person leading this conversation should write about this, and they'll just DM them and be like, "You should write it." Other times it's just a writer will come to an editor and be, like, "I have an idea. I want to write about this." And they're, like, "Sure."

Even when conversations on Slack are not about specific story ideas, they can be the basis for a story idea. "We are probably a little more collaborative than most places because we are smaller and we all like talking to each other," explained one editor about how so many conversations take place on the platform. "A lot of ideas and things that end up on the site sort of naturally come out of whatever the hell we're just talking about that day." Those collaborations are, again, essential to the mission of Defector. The myriad ways that collaboration happens within the news-production process is a tangible example to staffers that the values of the organization play a role in the day-to-day work routines lived by the journalists. One editor noted that "any dumb conversation can be turned into a blog that goes on the site, and that happens. It's one of the things that I really enjoy when it happens, and it's for serious things too, not just for silly things." They went on to argue that this is an example of a "cooperative site in action" and that it gives everyone ownership over all content. "Everyone can kind of play a role in everything we publish this way," they contended. Because of this process, there is a shared sense of ownership over content, regardless of byline:

> When we're discussing [story ideas] in Slack and someone will say something really smart or funny about something and then when a different person eventually is, like, assigned to write about it, they'll say, "Hey, I'm going to steal that sentence that you put in Slack, like, word for word and put it in the blog." And they're like, "Great." I love when that happens."

Conclusion

Perhaps due to its relatively short lifespan, Defector appears to be unilaterally succeeding. Among founders and new hires alike, there is a resonant belief that through its strict adherence to a set of democratically established values, the site has become a professional and economic success. The staff at the site believe the reason for that success lies primarily in alignment across the organization. "We could be making more money doing things a little differently," contended one staffer, "but I'd bet you'd be hearing a lot more complaints if we did that." In general, between quitting Deadspin and launching Defector, the founders took the necessary time to brainstorm exactly what they wanted out of their next venture. They realized that "it didn't make sense to start by thinking about what we wanted to write about," recalled one founder, but rather to start by coming up with a shared set of values. Once those were in place, they then attempted to find a market model that would best operationalize those values. From there, they crafted a values and ethics policy so that the staff and their audience would understand how those values would be incorporated into the journalism. That alignment—along with focused decision making geared toward living out those values—allows Defector to feel like a success.

The other very key decision the founders made concerned equity. Defector easily could have been a cooperative that granted ownership equity and equal decision-making power only to the founders. "That might have worked at the beginning," guessed one founder, "but once we started to grow, it could have taken down the whole culture for everyone." Both through decisions surrounding ownership but also within their implemented socialization practices, these founders understood the importance of maintaining a thorough democracy within all facets of the organization if they wanted to fulfill the mission of a newsroom based around true, open democracy. As one founder noted,

> I know we're just a little website, but we are an example of another way to do it. This is an alternative. Maybe it won't work for everyone or maybe you're not even in media or whatever, but, you know, here is, like, a little glimmer of something that's different. So, yeah, I hope we're working toward more of, like, being an example of, you know, it's almost like we're kind of redefining what success can look like, I guess.

When starting the site, the founders knew they could rely on publicity from their much-covered resignations from Deadspin, and they could rely on the built-in audience staffers would have from publishing to a large audience on Deadspin for years, but they knew this wouldn't last. This perception informed decision making throughout the early days of the site, particularly around hiring. The founders wanted to emulate what they loved about working at Deadspin, particularly in the years under Gawker Media's ownership, but also do far more in terms of its journalism. "I think when we started, the whole idea was we were only going to be able to play the "Hey, you remember us from Deadspin" card for so long, particularly after Deadspin relaunched," explained one founder.

> And [Deadspin's] a piece of shit now, but, like, it exists, right? So we were only going to be able to bank off of that goodwill for so long, and I think

we exploited it for all it was worth. But in order to continue being, you know, a media company, we had to be our own thing. And that's why we made a conscious effort when we were hiring.

In discussing organizational culture, Edgar Schein strongly argues that companies must truly think about mission alignment on all levels of organization or face consequences that often include a damaged organizational culture.[15] The staffers at Defector had an advantage in this process not afforded to non-startups: It did not have to change its organizational culture and mission, rather determine it and then apply it to all subsequent decisions. This likely made starting and maintaining an open, democratic newsroom somewhat easier, but perhaps the most essential decision occurred when the founders chose a cooperative structure. The impossibility of creating this democracy and shared governance within the organization would more than likely have become very salient for staffers once imbalanced power dynamics became visible. By adopting a cooperative ownership structure and then implementing the phantom equity plan, the founders chose a model that manifested their values, allowing them to maintain their desired culture even through growth and transformation.

It's relatively clear, then, that if a new media organization ponders adopting a cooperative structure, its founders should consider the experience of Defector. Simply creating a journalistic coop is not enough to instill a democratic organizational culture; all decision making at the beginning of the organization and throughout its evolution—especially at the early stages—should align with democratic ideals. Organizational alignment is key; a new organization cannot simply say it wants to be a democracy. All decisions—long before actual journalism is considered—need to align with the overall goal for actual success and positive organizational culture.

3

THE COLORADO SUN

The Public Benefit Corporation

In early April 2018, following the announcement of another round of lay-offs from its hedge fund owners, Alden Global Capital, the *Denver Post*'s editorial department engaged in an "open revolt against its owner."[1] In what became known as the Denver Rebellion, the *Post*, led by the editorial page editor, Chuck Plunkett—who did not inform ownership or even the paper's chief editor—published a series of opinion columns under the headline "News matters" that called Alden "vulture capitalists."[2] The editorials asked Alden to sell the *Post* if it did not care to provide the paper with the resources needed to support the community with quality news. In the years since, people have described that editorial section as "both tribute and alarm bell."[3] Although he was not technically fired, in the days after the Denver Rebellion, Plunkett resigned from the *Post*, foreshadowing a wave of resignations in the following weeks. Ultimately ten journalists—not including Plunkett—founded the digitally native, for-profit public-benefit corporation the Colorado.[4]

A little over two months following the Denver Rebellion, several Sun founders sit around a conference table at the University of Colorado-Denver. The journalists are speaking with an interdisciplinary group of professors from the University of Colorado-Boulder about potential ways to make the not-yet-launched Sun a sustainable news organization.[5] While still at the *Post*, a couple of senior members of the Sun began conversations with Civil, a startup that wanted "to test a unique blockchain system for sustaining journalism."[6] Civil promised two years of funding to the Sun, providing the new organization enough time to develop a plan for sustainability—hence the meeting in Denver.[7] Even before the

Sun's launch—while the whole idea of the organization remained in a flux funded by blockchain technology, which the founders did not even truly understand. The founders, after years of living through economic precarity at the *Post*, understood what they wanted their imminent news organization to embody. A little less than five years after its inception, one founder recalled how concrete the goals of the Sun were, even before its launch. "From the very beginning, we've all been extremely aligned on our mission. By that I mean nobody, we're a bunch of journalists, right, so none of us really got into this business to strike it rich," they said. They added, "We've never had any internal battles or anything like that over, you know, turning a profit or something like that. I mean, we understand all too well that we do have to make money." This sentiment—the idea of creating a sustainable journalism organization focused on quality explanatory coverage—has always guided the formation and future decisions at the Sun. The founders realized early on that initially focusing coverage on only what they could do well was key. "We knew from our days at the *Post* that when you try to do everything and lack the resources to do anything really well, that's when you fail," explained a founder. "We wanted to start by focusing on things that matter and things we could do well. And then we can expand in terms of staff and coverage as we can."

Although in those early days, not counting the two-year grant from Civil, the Sun did not follow a true business model, the staff understood that its success, both in terms of its civic goals and its economic goals, needed to involve its audience. "We knew," said one founder, "that the key was to develop a base of premium subscribers that really help supplement the creation of all of this news that we're giving away for free, essentially." In a sense, from those early days, the Sun focused on providing free, quality journalism to everyone interested, while building a foundation of audience members willing to pay a membership fee that would undergird nearly the entire economic operation. This foundation became necessary earlier than expected: Civil's pledge of two years of funding was meant for payments through May 2020, but the payments ended in October 2019, leaving the Sun to figure it all out a little earlier than expected. "We were forced to move out on our own before we wanted to," said a founder, "but we did that, and I think built something everyone can be real proud of." Another founder noted, "I've joked with [a lot of people] that we've just had to learn things the hard way, and that's worked for us." That hard way resulted in the ten founders of the Sun taking on equal ownership of the newsroom and setting forth as a company.

Organizational Culture

From the beginnings of the Colorado Sun in mid-2018, the founders espoused a culture of collaboration, a culture that still permeates much of the organization. After coming from what they described as a very hierarchical top-down power structure at the *Denver Post*, where, as one Sun journalist described it, "You just stay in your lane," the founders envisioned the Sun as a newsroom that would harness each journalist's strengths into one cohesive, collaborate team. One Sun journalist explained,

> We created the most collaborative workplace that I have ever been in. I mean, I've been in a lot of newsrooms, had a lot of other jobs, you know, before that, and by far this is the most collaborative place I've ever worked.

Over and over, this sentiment came up in interviews with the newsroom's members. One younger and therefore less experienced journalist talked about how pleasantly surprised they were by the collaborative nature of the newsroom, something they did not expect but have come truly to appreciate. "I'm working with a lot of [people] with more experience, who I really admire," they explained, adding, "If I have a question or need to talk through a story, I pick up the phone and call them and we talk it out. ... And that's always been encouraged. That's what I'm looking for really in a newsroom." The perception of "the most collaborative newsroom" that reporters have ever experienced, real or perceived, clearly seems to be an articulated and espoused value that has more currency among the Sun staff than any other. This collaboration often takes the form of what the younger journalist quoted above described: an open forum of sorts around stories. Journalists at the organization are told, both explicitly and implicitly, that they should harness the full institutional intelligence of the Sun staff whenever they want or need to do so. Therefore, this primarily comes through story discussion. The Sun's founders, and some other more recent staff additions, bring with them decades of experience in covering the state of Colorado, so the credo is that anyone can help anyone else improve a story through some targeted guidance, a source referral, or just some knowledge gained through experience. "Discussion is really the priority," said one journalist. "I know, because I'm told, but I've also seen it with other colleagues, how a discussion can make my pieces better." Numerous journalists discussed how the founders, especially the editor, often explicitly discuss the power of collaboration and celebrate it as a key attribute of the organization's culture. In meetings, stories or projects that feature collaboration are also celebrated—"a bit more than others, and it's noticeable," said one reporter—and that makes for a more explicit espousing of the attribute.

Although interpersonal communication is the dominant practice that enables collaboration to occur, numerous staffers noted the creation of a newsletter as the optimal example of this collaborative nature. The news-letter The Sunriser reaches Sun subscribers each weekday and highlights some of what the staff deems the best journalism across the state of Colo-rado. From the beginning, founders saw this newsletter as a manifestation of the culture they wanted to create. One explained,

> For instance, the Sunriser, a newsletter you read hopefully every day. We have a big old editing party around between 8:30 and 9 [a.m.], the whole staff. Everybody who's available jumps into a Google Doc and reads it, offers suggestions, offers items, edits, writes, whatever. That just doesn't happen elsewhere. It does not happen. The people at the *Denver Post*—or, you know, pick a legacy news organization—their newsletter writer is sitting there at a desk somewhere at home and they're knocking it out, and they're lucky if they've got one other person who will read it over for them, a copy editor or whatever. A lot of them have gotten rid of copy editors as you know. This [whole process] was an organizing principle for us.

According to the journalists interviewed, the choice of collaboration as an organizing principle seems to have had an almost uniformly positive effect. Almost of all Sun staffers discussed the potential of collaboration as one of, if not the best, attribute of working at this news organization. Even journalists who admitted to not actually participating in much of this collaborative work spoke hopefully and positively about both participat-ing in the future and the potential improvement of the work that comes through this process. "I'm really proud of that for us," said one journalist:

> I think we wanted to create a news organization that was collaborative and to create a news organization that was really open to people wanting to, kind of like, raise their hand and say, like, "Hey, I want to do this," and just sort of giving them the chance to do that. So [it's] empowering, I guess, in that way.

However, a small number of reporters, particularly new members of the staff who perhaps did not have a strong foundational relationship with the journalists who came from the *Post*, felt this talk of collaboration did not mirror their experience or, potentially, was an attribute not available to them. "It all sounds good, you know, but I'm not sure I've felt collaboration is an option for me," said one journalist. "I'm invited to things like the Sunriser, and maybe I'm not a very open-to-collaboration person, you know, but I've never felt like I can just call up [a founder] and have [them] collaborate on a story with me." Others said similar things and implicitly hinted that although the Sun is a great place to work and a successful newsroom, maybe it is, as one person described it, "two different places in one." In other words, it might be a newsroom featuring one overriding, espoused culture that is available primarily to the founders, but underlying assumptions of the Sun actually differ. Even certain founders noted this possibility, but it became a more lived experience for nonfounders. "I love working here and think, honestly, we do, bar none, the best journalism in the state of Colorado," said one journalist, "but it is different if you're an owner [of the Sun] versus someone like me that's, you know, an employee." Regardless of position at the Sun, it is fact that the team understands that the business model significantly affects the entire organizational culture. There is a distinct difference in terms of where people feel they fit into the culture at the Sun depending on if they are a founder/owner or not.

Even the founders reluctantly admit that the Sun's distinct business model is a large part of the culture. In the early days of the organization, members knew they had roughly two years of funding from Civil, but they did not know exactly what their business model should be. In fact, in those early days, they were a limited liability corporation; they debated numerous different options from a nonprofit to a cooperative. Even today, according to one of the founders, the model could be changed. "You know, we might end up being a nonprofit someday," they said. "Or a lot of us like the idea of having an [employee-owned stock option]." But the ten founders landed on the idea of a for-profit public benefit corporation, a company equally owned by each of the ten founders. A public benefit corporation, a legal designation allowed in more than half of the states in the United States, describes a company that by law must pursue both a "public benefit in addition to its responsibility to return profits to the shareholders. It is legally a for-profit, socially obligated, corporate form of business, with all of the traditional corporate characteristics but with required societal responsibilities."[8] Essentially, this legal distinction allows the Sun to operate as a traditional business but with the goal of advancing the public good. In many ways, this frees the founders from an obligation "to consider stakeholder interests" first and foremost—even though they themselves are the stakeholders.[9] For this type of business, the designation "public benefit corporation" is important because "this system—built on internal and external mechanisms—enables a company to hold itself

accountable to its stated public good."[10] At first, the Sun's founders seemed
particularly afraid that outside funders potentially might somehow accrue
an ownership stake in the news organization and attempt to move it away
from its social mission. Being a public benefit corporation provides some
legal cover against this possibility, because this status forces companies to
be accountable to the designation. In Colorado, this means that any public
benefit corporation must publish an annual benefit report with

> a description of how the company promoted the public benefits listed
> in the company's articles of incorporation and any obstacles the com-
> pany faced in promoting those public benefits and an assessment of the
> overall social and environmental performance of the company against
> a third-party standard.[11]

The founders interviewed noted that their time working for the *Post*
clearly had scarred them in some ways, saying that with every ownership change at this legacy newspaper came a more and more precarious
labor situation that also included far fewer resources to accomplish the
civic mission of the paper. This meant, at the beginning, really thinking
intentionally about how a business model could protect the mission of the
organization. One journalist recalled, "You know, when we were able to
start fresh here, every single person who worked in the newsroom was part
of the design of the business goals." By setting this standard, they said, they
were able to "make sure everybody knew what the goal of our news was,
which was tying our mission to our revenue, which is, just like, 'Let's get
this in front of as many Coloradans as we can.'" Another founder noted that

> Civil got us off to a strong start by saying, you know, "Here's a pile of
> magic money. You never have to pay us back and you crazy kids go do
> good journalism and we'll figure out the rest." This was fine for starters,
> but we knew from the very beginning that because of our experience
> with Alden and others that we couldn't trust that. And we're journalists
> anyway: We don't trust anybody. So we had to act with fear from the
> very beginning, fear that it could all go away and be taken away from us.

To the founders, then, tying the market model of the organization to the
public mission of the organization was vital.

For the founders, this alignment of revenue and civic mindedness really
forms a large part of the culture. After they spent years of working for
owners that they felt did not care at all about the need for journalism in a
community, the Sun's model makes that explicit. As one founder explained,

> For me personally, there's a big difference in that this is my business. It
> makes a difference that it's owned [by us]. For many years at the *Denver*

Post, I was able to sort of separate the ownership group and what I was doing. Until literally, Pat, I woke up one day and I'm like, you know what? I can't work this hard for assholes. Like, I just had a personal whatever. Call it a come to Jesus, whatever you want to call it. I just couldn't work that hard and give that much effort to people who were just terrible human beings. And I didn't want anything to do with them. I didn't want to work for them. I didn't want to serve them in any capacity. And I just had to leave. . . . It makes a big difference for me to be working for something that I own. You know, it's not necessarily a financial motivation. It's something that we just want to help other outlets and shine a light on a way to do this without being terrible, if that makes any sense. Like, it's possible to recognize the value of journalism is not monetary, right? It's not a monetary perspective. Yes, we need to be able to find a way to make money and make this thing work, of course.

This feeling of pride in ownership clearly affects the culture of the organization. Numerous founders talked extensively about how much more they care—and as one said, "Believe me, I always cared too much and now I care even more"—about how well they serve the community, how intentional their decisions about sustainability questions are, how much more they think about whom they plan to hire and add to the team. "Seriously, every decision seems huge now because it's our place," said one founder.

However, the Sun first realized the potential problems tied to their model when one of the founders left. There was no mechanism in place to assess a fair-market value for that founder's shares in the company. Essentially, the Sun had a procedure that said, if any founder leaves, the rest of the founders have the right to buy those shares, but there was no process for valuing the shares. The organization figured it out, and now nine journalists own the Sun. But this ordeal illustrated to everyone in the organization and its board of directors the fraught potential linked to having a company of twenty-five employees where roughly 40 percent of those employees are owners and 60 percent are not. "Whether I like it or not," said one founder, "I own this place and others don't. And it can definitely get weird." Another founder said that they hope a plan emerges in the near future that would allow for some "equitable distribution of some ownership," but they don't know what that could look like. This schism between owners and nonowners rarely matters in the day-to-day work of the journalists at the Sun, but it does impact how connected nonowners feel to the company. Without prompting, many nonowners said that they really admired the mission of the Sun but felt decidedly less "part of everything," as one journalist said, than the owners. "Look, it's not just the ownership thing although [I don't know] how can I be just as much a part of this thing as people who own it," explained one journalist, adding, "It's also that the owners have all this shared history with the *Denver Post* and started the Sun here. And they own it. That's a bond that definitely separates us from them."

Yet despite this apparent division between owners and nonowners at the Sun, the focus and goals of the organization clearly bring all the journalists together. Regardless of which journalists were interviewed, there is overwhelming agreement that every decision made by the founders seems to be in the interest of quality journalism. "Can you imagine that?" asked a nonowner. "Such transparency in a newsroom and an indisputable thirst for good journalism over profits." This piece of the culture also dates back to decisions made by the founders, decisions that focused on specifying exactly what the Sun would be and what it did not plan on doing. One founder explained that, before launch, "We decided we were not going to try to be a mini *Denver Post*, right? We were not going to be the full-service [grocery store] where you go in and get everything you need for tonight's meal." They went on to explain that the Sun is not meant to be the only stop for journalism in Colorado, but rather a specific piece of it. They added,

> Certain types of journalism [at the *Post*] were falling by the wayside. It's a lot cheaper to chain somebody to their desk and have them rewrite press releases. And it's cheaper to do that and you can generate more page views. . . . But we decided we're not going to be in the page-view business anymore.

The goal of producing the best possible "explanatory and investigative" journalism in the state is something that aligns with all journalists' professional goals as well, creating a symbiotic newsroom.

Leadership

In his influential book *Images of Organization*, Gareth Morgan discusses several types of organizations, often utilizing metaphors in his descriptions.[12] One chapter discusses the concept of organizations as systems of government, delineating different structures of government according to their power dynamics. Much like the Sun's overall culture, the perception of the leadership structure does differ depending on one's position within the organization. Although the news organization does have an editor in chief in Larry Ryckman, the founders talk about a freedom within the organization, a freedom that gives everyone the power to lead. As one founder described it, "At the Sun, it's a relatively flat leadership structure. It's a manageable size where everybody knows everybody else." About the lack of leadership outside the newsroom, they added, "There's no mysterious layers of bureaucracy or anything happening above the editor level. It's all the same people." These founders will often talk about Ryckman's position as a mere formality, as if resigned to the idea. As one founder described it, "Someone needed to step up and run the business. Larry fits the role perfectly. I don't think we think of him as a boss or anything, but just the person best equipped to step up." Over and over, the founders provided some variation on the notion that there is no hierarchical structure at the Sun but rather, as Morgan would call it, an organizational system of democracy.[13] In a sense, they believe the leadership structure at the organization is just something that had to happen. One founder described it this way:

> I never set out to be a business owner or entrepreneur or any of that. I had no desire to, you know, God forbid, own a news organization. You know, we did it because we felt like we had to, and so we started off from a good place and, you know, that it was about public service from the very beginning and not about building vacation homes in West Palm Beach, Florida, or something. For us, I would say, [we just decided to run the business side of the organization also] because, in general, journalists are terrible about asking for help.

Inherent in that statement is the resignation mentioned above, the realization that if the founders wanted to accomplish the civic mission of the Sun—something they felt very much needed in Colorado—then someone would need to step up and handle the business side of running a public benefit corporation.

Quite clearly, this decision to have one of the journalist-founders become the business side of the organization, despite having virtually no training, arose from the same fear that led the Sun to becoming a public benefit corporation. After years of working in legacy media, especially under the ownership of Alden Global Capital, the founders took every precaution they knew about to make sure they maintained control over all aspects of the organization, a control they believed essential to the overall accomplishment of their mission. One founder noted that under Alden, "I never felt that my news coverage was guided in any way by the owners. But I will say that some of the stuff that was printed in that newspaper became challenging for me as a journalist." They added, "Just because there was so much confusion among a lot of readers how to distinguish between [what the journalists chose and what the owners chose]." They went on to note, "I don't feel that that's the case at the Sun, so that's a stark contrast." Again, implicit in that comment is the fear of influence from actors outside the newsroom, particularly any ownership entity that is not a journalist. This clearly influenced the leadership model at the Sun, which the founders describe as including the freedom for any journalist to act as the leader, do what they believe to be in the best interest of the journalism, and have a leader in name only.

However, the nonfounders perceive two different realities. Some of these journalists agree with the founders' assessment of a nonhierarchal newsroom but wish that was not the case. "Many of the founders have decades of experience and just know what to do," explained one journalist, "and that shows in their work. I sometimes wish I was given more guidance, which I understand goes against the spirit of what they want, though. I want that guidance, though." This particular feeling is not lost on the founders. One recalled that after a conversation with a nonfounder, they started to realize some people wanted overt, consistent leadership. They said,

> It's been really interesting, because [there's] an interest in having a more hierarchical structure than I think we envisioned, which was going to be reporters doing their reporting thing and seeking out what they're interested in. And then, knowing when you have a responsibility that you have to go cover something, but also just pursuing what really intrigues you. And, you know, now [we're wondering if] editors should be assigning stories. Should we have goals that are articulated? Or should there be consequences if people aren't reaching those goals? You know, it's been interesting for the company to evolve in that way.

Another subset of nonfounders also understand that the founders have articulated this notion of freedom from leadership mandates, but they believe that unspoken power dynamics make this espoused leadership structure something of a mirage. One noted that the founders often call everyone colleagues, but "we're not colleagues since you're a shareholder and you have more security and standing. That's common sense." One founder noted this, articulating this conundrum as, "Having the idea of, 'Hey everybody just raise your hand, say what you want to do, don't worry, as long as you're happy, we're happy' didn't really work." They added, "Maybe it's because [the nonfounders are] younger, but probably also because of this power dynamic, they want more 'Tell me what you want me to do. Tell me when I'm achieving what you want me to achieve and when I'm not.'" Since leadership often drives culture, this disconnect between what the founders intended and what they experience, compared with newer additions to the staff, obviously affects the overall manifestation of the organizational culture at the Sun.

Socialization

Due to the overall differences between the founders (who spent years or decades working together at the *Denver Post*) and many of the newer additions to the staff (some of whom also worked at the *Post*), the Sun journalists, both founders and newcomers, recognize the need for a more structured socialization process. One issue felt acutely at the organization concerned COVID, as most of the growth experienced in the newsroom occurred during the height of the pandemic, which made an already rarely used newsroom even more desolate. In fact, although the Sun does have a newsroom space in downtown Denver, virtually nobody interviewed admitted to using it often. This is fine for the founders, who share an institutional and social knowledge base that relies less on in-house newsroom experience. "The more experienced members of the staff, you know, a nod of the head, you understand what the other person means," explained one journalist. They added, "We can't assume those things with some of the newer folks. And we've had people who very much felt isolated because they were new and had limited exposure to the rest of the staff." Some members of the staff very much agree with this sentiment, with the idea that founders and others with a shared history all feel connected, whereas newer organizational members do not. "There was some late onboarding, but I wouldn't say that had much to do with becoming part of the Sun," said one journalist. "The honest answer, man, is I don't feel part of the Sun. I feel like an individual hired to a job that I think I'm capable of doing very well and I think the people who hired me appreciate." That sentiment sums up the differences between the two groups: The founders very much feel like they are part of a larger, vibrant organizational culture, whereas some newer journalists like their jobs but don't feel they're part of something bigger. The founders acknowledge that solving this problem is difficult for the Sun, which has employees spread out over a large state without a much-used newsroom, something that the vast majority of journalism literature accepts as a key mechanism for socialization.[14] After acknowledging that the pandemic made socialization everywhere more difficult, one founder explained,

> We started as a newsroom with ten people who had worked with each other for a long time and kind of had established social relationships. And now we have a lot of new folks who are coming in, including some from out of state, so they don't necessarily have long-standing social connections here. And how do you re-create the sort of the social integration of a newsroom without really being in person? And one part of our flexibility and wanting to give people the chance to kind of live their lives as they want has been to not be super insistent on where people are based.

As noted above, the Sun's founders recognized this socialization problem and have made efforts to solve it. They have instituted a mentorship
program that remains in its infancy. But the more tangible changes come
in the form of written policy, something the founders recognize the Sun
lacked. In the early days, even something as basic as an employee handbook
did not exist. "Why do journalists need one of those?" one founder joked
about the lack of clear organizational policy, adding, "To me, that's one
thing we missed on that could communicate, 'Hey, this is the Colorado
Sun' to new hires." Another founder explained,

> Early on we had no need for an employee handbook. We were doing
> journalism. We've over the past two, three years created an employee
> handbook and we've, you know, had to professionalize things. Like, OK,
> what is our family leave policy? Early on it was like, 'Hey if you need
> time off, go take time off. You know, just make sure you do your work
> and be considerate of everybody else.' Well, again, that was fine with the
> founders, but maybe not as fine for somebody who's coming in, they're
> twenty-five years old and they need more guidance than that.

The company also now regularly thinks of its ethics policy as a clear acculturation tool. The Sun considers its policy a living, breathing document
that truly, implicitly, illustrates its main mission as a news organization:
to do important, ethical journalism. The organization created the policy
in an open manner, gathering input from both the Sun staff and outsid-
ers. "If you go look at it, it's this massive thing," said one journalist. They
added, "We just put a call out to people and said like, 'Hey if you have
something you want to see from an ethical news organization, let us know.'
To me that was really important." The ethics policy became well known
within the journalism community; multiple Sun staffers reported that
other journalism organizations contacted them to emulate it. This document, as one founder put it, "tells our audience and our journalists what
it means to work here"—or, in other words, what being a Sun journalist
entails. Yet, despite a more professionalized operation with policies and
tangible, espoused values, the founders still understand the difficulty they
face, now and into the future, as a geographically disparate startup with
fewer acculturation tools than might have existed in prior decades. "We
know it every day. It is so difficult to train a young, vibrant, smart new
journalist without a newsroom," said one founder.

> Like, it is really hard to do. It's incredibly hard to do. In fact, we aren't
> sure that it's possible, you know. It's just, it's terrible to probably admit.
> That culture is really important, and back then [for me], we didn't really
> have the internet stuff. We had one terminal in the *Denver Post* news-
> room that had the internet, and you signed up for it. And, you know, I

could walk over and talk to these just brilliant journalists at any time and say, 'Hey, do you know this person? Hey, what's a way to approach this story? Hey, how can we do this new?' It's massively influential in how we became journalists, every single one of us that founded [the Sun]. And then now we've got these super bright, incredibly intelligent and eager, creative, wonderful journalists, and we're like doing this Zoom stuff to try to socialize with them. Like it's truly, truly a challenge and it's a great problem for us to solve.

Routines

For reporters at the organization, most of the routinized processes involving story production are based on their own individual preferences. Moreover, because most of the journalists work from home, they make their own routines. There are, however, a few clearly defined organization-wide routines that affect news production. At the beginning of each work week, typically Monday morning, the entire organization will have a meeting via Zoom "where we all talk about stories and whatever else is going on," as one journalist described it. Beyond that meeting, the Sun holds office hours with editors on Wednesdays. These office-hour Zoom meetings are optional. The newsroom also holds irregular meetups in person but attended primarily by the people living closest to Denver. Especially in terms of editor-reporter communication, the regular routines vary, depending on the editors and reporters in question. For one reporter, when they come up with a story idea, they will often talk to their editor almost immediately. "I try to go straight to the editor, and we'll have a conversation about where I think this is going," they said, adding, "I'll then start immediately making calls and start writing." Other reporters described talking to editors about stories only when they're perceived to be done or if a problem comes up. These varying processes belie, in a sense, the espoused collaborative nature of the newsroom. "In that way, the Sun, I would say, is less collaborative in that sense," one journalist said. "It's much more like lots of individual people trying to at least, from my point of view, trying to make choices about how to best cover things for our readers in [their] specific defined area."

Whereas the early stages of news production routines vary by journalist, the process of a story once the reporter deems it complete is relatively standard at the Sun. One journalist described the whole process as:

I do have basically two editors. Kind of like one direct editor, and then another sort of editor above that. But basically, the Sun would like me to do in the ballpark of two stories a week. And they don't really care what they are as long as they're good and in the world in which I'm

supposed to be covering. Then, when I'm done with them, I try to communicate with my direct editor or really with both of those people when
I'm going to be done with any given piece. And when it's done, I drop
it in a channel, a Slack channel, that's basically like a "Please edit this
channel" channel.

In a sense, reporters mostly work on stories individually. When they deem
a story complete, they will start a communication process with an editor
or two—via Slack, Zoom, phone call, or email—about the nature of the
piece. Then the piece will be uploaded onto either a Slack channel or
Google Docs, allowing for the editing process to begin. Unless a journalist decides to share ideas via a Zoom meeting, Slack conversation, or the
like very early in news production, the collaboration process perceived to
be an essential element of the organization cannot occur. One journalist
explained, "Collaboration definitely happens here, yet it's kind of a minimal amount really. I think the thing is when it does happen, it's glorious
or whatever, you know. But it's rare and not all spontaneous, at least in
my experience." For this collaboration to happen, journalists will need to
implement very intentional practices, such as posting a story idea on Slack
and asking for some assistance in brainstorming, or reaching out directly
to other journalists in the organization who might help with sourcing
or idea generation. In most cases, though, journalists do not implement
these practices, so the routines of news production have become highly
individualized at the Sun. "We could absolutely be more collaborative than
we are, and that's what we always hope for," said one journalist. "But the
thing is, there is always the ability or freedom to be as collaborative as we
want, and that is highly attractive, at least to me."

Technology

Colorado is the eighth-largest state in the United States by geographic size,
with a land area that is technically more than double the size of eighteen
other states and more than 25 percent larger than thirty-five states. In its
early days, the founders of the Sun determined that although they would
not cover the same breadth of news as the *Denver Post*, they did aspire to
be a statewide source of news, something the *Post* essentially had aban-
doned in prior decades. Therefore, while Sun has an office in downtown
Denver, in the same building that houses the offices of Rocky Mountain
PBS, not only do very few Denver-based staffers use it but it is absolutely
not an option for, say, reporters in other metropolitan areas such as Colorado Springs or in a mountainous area such as the Western Slope region

of the state. "It's kind of a waste of time, to me, to deal with the traffic and time it takes to get downtown," said one reporter, "when I can just work from home. It's more productive that way." Add to that the fact that most Sun journalists do not use the newsroom with the Sun's espoused value of freedom or autonomy over stories, and you're left with a newsroom, as at many other digitally native outlets, that relies on computer-mediated communication between staffers. Or, as one person put it, "Oh, man, communication here is all Zoom or Slack." Therefore, for many, technology has become a facsimile of the newsroom.

To the founders, this lack of an occupied newsroom is less important. One founder noted, "For the older staffers, the founders, you could drop us in the middle of a desert, and we would find water and find a way to find a story and file it. We would find a way." But this person acknowledges that this setup occasionally makes communication far more difficult. "I think, ninety-five percent of the time, everything works the way it's supposed to. But, really, our lack of easy, regular communication definitely hurts us when it's needed." The organization holds regular news meetings over Zoom, and although it utilizes Slack, it does so less than other similar newsrooms. In other places, Slack can be newsroom-like, a place to distill culture and truly find vibrancy in non-face-to-face interaction. At the Sun, Slack use is far more perfunctory. There is some editor-to-reporter conversation on the platform, and some reporters do use it as a way to brainstorm ideas or, really, manifest the type of collaboration the *Sun* espouses. However, it is not used regularly by all staff. "I've been at places where Slack is, you know, the lifeblood of everything happening in the whole place. That's not the case here. Only a few of us use it all the time."

Engagement

The Sun's relationship to its audience could be classified as traditional in nature; it is not at all a place that espouses notions of engagement as loudly as many other recent journalism startups. Furthermore, this relationship is decidedly a one-way street: the journalists maintain agency over the news agenda. Therefore, although the Sun absolutely aims to engage its audience and understand its audience, both of those goals are accomplished through ways designed to provide the journalists complete authority over news production. This is not a form of engaged journalism where some power is shared with audiences.[15] The Sun imagines its audience as using far more anecdotal information than data. The journalists believe that their experience and expertise as professional news workers gives them unmatched insight into what's important for their audiences. For those at the Sun, the very structure of its organization is a connection to the audience. They believe that a journalist-started enterprise resonates with Colorado residents looking for quality news. One founder compared the Sun with the *Denver Post* as a way to explain how market-model differences can catalyze different relationships with the audience.

> I think there's a deeper connection with readers. When readers realize what it is we're doing, they connect. I think at the *Denver Post*, when I quit, there were people striking and going out and marching with signs. You know, the journalists in the newsroom were. So, readers were always, like, "Wow, you know, your owners suck." And I'm like, "Yes they do." And there was this filter through which [they asked], "Should I not subscribe [to the *Post* because of that]? Is my money going to this guy that has all these homes in Palm Springs?" I have to be, like, "Yeah." And it was just a pain in the ass to have to be like, "Please do subscribe." You know even after I quit, I was, like, "Please do subscribe to the *Denver Post*." I can't imagine Colorado without the *Denver Post*. Like, we already lost the *Rocky* [*Mountain News*]. You know, it would be a tragedy. So I think it's just a more intimate connection maybe or just a closer connection with readers who are really proud of what we do at the Colorado Sun. We work hard to make our readers proud, and [they know they're paying for quality and not houses].

By the very nature of their market model, Sun journalists also believe they publish higher-quality news, on average, than any other Colorado news organization. And this quality, they believe, is a principal reason for their perceived closeness to the audience. One journalist noted that this sentiment is expressed regularly when they are in the field doing journalism. "On many occasions when I've called someone for an interview, they tell me how much they love reading the Sun and how much it is a value to the community, which is the nicest compliment I could hear." Some journalists believe that the process by which they practice news is the reason for the quality, which then translates into a stronger connection to the audience. One journalist explained, "My role is to do my best to talk to as many people as I can in the world that I'm [assigned] to cover." They said once they do that, they "work as hard as I can to select the most interesting stories that I think are most valuable to our readers [and] write them as well and as clearly as possible." This process, believed this journalist, produces high-quality work, which engenders more trust and loyalty from readers who will then engage more passionately.

One common tool that is utilized as a means of audience engagement across the field of journalism is social media, which is ubiquitous in journalism practice.[16] At the Sun, though, social media is used primarily for dissemination. Although at times journalists discussed specific news stories—such as the 2021 wildfires in Boulder—that warranted a robust and audience-friendly use of social media, the vast majority of this usage did not involve directly engaging the audience. "Social media is not my thing," said one reporter. "I try to do that type of engagement in person, when I'm covering my area." This response seems to equivocate between in-person and social-media engagement, but the reality is that relying on in-person engagement alone significantly limits the amount of engagement and how well a journalist can know their entire audience.[17]

The way the Sun engages with its audience in the most granular fashion comes through its use of web metrics. Although this news organization does not use metrics as vigorously as many newsrooms—nor does it involve the data across multiple decision points—web metrics do help it understand its audience better.[18] For example, one editor described how the Sun completely changed the way in which it organizes stories on its website due to a better understanding of how its audience wanted to consume content. They said,

> We actually encourage our readers to go to our home page and scan it every day. And we actually get a lot of traffic. When we first started, I assumed that OK, we don't have to think too hard about the home page because I know from my experience at the *Post*, people are going to be coming in sideways through an article, and so we need to really focus on the article page. I was blown away. People come and browse our home page, and that is a primary driver of [story traffic]. And since we figured that out, we've gone to great lengths to try to, like, really help sort and really provide opportunities for serendipity among our readers.

Like many organizations not strongly market oriented, the Sun does not apply the knowledge gained through metrics to generate story clicks and make economic decisions, but it does help journalists understand what its readers want.[19] This is a very intentional decision rooted in a desire always to prioritize quality over economics. One journalist explained,

> You know we're not doing clickbait headlines. We're not doing things just to trick enough people to show up to move the needle on a [corporate performance management] count to get us over a certain hump and get us to a certain milestone. And by removing that, we've been able to, I think, produce a lot more long-form and nuanced and much closer to what I think everybody can agree is like the truth about something than necessarily the shorter things that are sort of tailored for [search engine optimization] or to go viral.

Although these numbers exist and the Sun's editors make them available to the entire staff, unlike in other newsrooms, journalists do not have to view them. One reporter said, "I don't ever go look at the numbers. I don't really feel like I need to. I get enough feedback from different places, whether it's readers writing in [or] whether it's sources who I talk to later." For those journalists who do use the information gleaned from web metrics, it is only a means to think about raising the quality and engagement of the journalism. "We have a dashboard, but I don't know that it's shared proactively. I think you can choose to look at it," explained one reporter, echoing the prior quote.

> I do [look at it]. And, you know, there's sort of the sweet spot for I feel like what you're looking for in terms of web traffic. You know, if the story didn't get a lot of clicks, you're like, 'OK, I did something there. The headline wasn't right, the approach to the storytelling wasn't right.' If the time on site was lower than it normally would be, you say, 'OK, I did something, right? I didn't make the story engaging enough. So, I do find that useful. [I feel like] it's not we're click agnostic or click atheists or however you would put it. We just wanted to get away from the tyranny of click counts. But they are still useful for looking at. On the other hand, if you have a story that gets like a lot of clicks, that starts to become less useful because it got into some distribution channel.

News Production

The practice of producing news at the Sun is very intentionally traditional. Considering many of the founders have decades of experience in legacy news, it should not be surprising that they still use those same general practices. The chief difference, as noted previously, is that almost all the time, the Sun journalists have complete autonomy over their beats, choosing stories and sources as they see fit. Unlike at other newsrooms, there are very few editor-assigned pieces. Once a reporter chooses a story, they go through a very conventional process of writing it up, sending it to an editor and then, if necessary, going through a communication process meant to alleviate any concerns or take care of any perceived issues. This orthodox process, though, is guided by some of the boundaries in coverage implemented in the early days of the Sun, boundaries that have evolved over recent years. When they were defining their news production processes, the first step for the Sun founders was to delineate exactly what reporters should cover. As one founder noted,

> We want to cover rural Colorado because the *Denver Post* and the *Rocky [Mountain News]* once upon a time had bureaus all over the state, but

the *Rocky* is long gone, and the *Denver Post* has had to pull back, and they don't really cover rural issues so much anymore. So we decided early on that we were going to do what others aren't doing, to fill the gaps, to do the stories, to do the long-form, investigative, explanatory narrative stories that we all are passionate about, and the readers can't find as much of elsewhere.

This mandate allows Sun journalists to understand exactly what their role is, which then dictates story generation. It also forces many of the staff to live and work far away from the main office, which means less room for any experimenting in terms of news production processes. Early conversations focused on not only where the organization would cover news but also what they did not want to cover. "We also don't just match stories. If the *Denver Post* or [Colorado Public Radio] has a story, it's like, 'Hey good on you. Hey readers, go check out the *Denver Post*,'" said one founder. "We don't waste our time trying to reinvent the wheel. . . . Yes, compete when it comes to politics, but everything else, let's fill the gaps. Let's do the stories that others aren't doing, or let's do things better." These guiding principles tell journalists to avoid issues that legacy news might cover, or, if covering something that overlaps with legacy media, try to make coverage different by focusing on different angles or sources or narrative devices. For journalists at the Sun, defining what is a "Sun story" proved tantamount to defining news production practices. Some of this process included grappling with the idea of breaking news.

In the early months of the Sun, the organization adopted a no-breaking-news policy, instead focusing on developing long-form, explanatory journalism. But this policy needed adjustments as journalists began to understand better how the community needed them. "The pandemic came along, George Floyd and the social justice protests came along, and it became pretty clear that as we got bigger, that people looked to us as a leader," said one founder. "And it was going to be a statement on our part one way or the other if we turned around and didn't report on them." That forced the Sun to decide what to prioritize. "So, we didn't go out and cover every single night of the [Black Lives Matter] protests in downtown Denver, for instance. But we did report on them, and when the pandemic came along, we've never stopped," said one journalist. Another journalist added,

When the King Soopers shooting happened [in Boulder], we rolled on that. When the STEM school shooting happened, we rolled on that under the theory that, God forbid, there's another Columbine or whatever, we would go in and own that story because we can. You know, the

Denver Post once upon a time won a Pulitzer Prize for its coverage of Columbine. We have more people on staff who covered Columbine than the *Post* does today. We have the institutional knowledge. We know how to do breaking news. We have these conversations still a lot. Like, early on it was, "OK, this is a story, but is it a Sun story?" So, for instance, the King Soopers shooting, yeah, we rolled on it, and we wrote the breaking news along with everybody else. But we quickly then pulled back and did the deeper stories and tried to zag when everybody else was zigging. And the same with the Boulder wildfires. We rolled on that, full-court press. I will put our coverage up against anybody on spot coverage of those fires.

With the parameters in place around what type of coverage the Sun provides its readers, journalists then decide on coverage primarily through what so many interviewees called "gut feeling." The Sun's journalists all say that they completely understand their responsibilities and what's best for their readers, and they use that information to determine coverage. "It's basically just real standard reporting. Like developing sources, talking to people, being curious about the world that I'm asked to be curious about, talking to more people," explained one journalist. "You know, when you finish a conversation going, 'Huh that's interesting. I didn't realize that.' Or, 'Geez that seems like that'd be a good story.' It's just the very organic process of me trying to be a good reporter." Another journalist likened their ability to know a good story to something that translates to readers, noting, "It's, like, something that sparks my interest is likely to spark someone else's interest. So, it's hard to quantify. It's just sort of a gut reaction." Another said something similar. They explained, "It's just things that are interesting are interesting. I don't apply metrics to it. And I'm not always right. It's sort of just like a gut-reaction thing." Overall, the Sun's news production processes are defined primarily through its definition of what the organization should cover. Once reporters understand those parameters, they produce coverage in a very traditional manner, guided by their own freedom to explore their work as they see fit.

Conclusion

Designating the Colorado Sun a public benefit corporation plainly establishes a clear mission within the news organization. Overwhelmingly and without any disagreement at all, the journalists interviewed for this chapter—even those less connected with the Sun's founding—believed that every decision the company made was aimed at improving quality of coverage. Journalists kept noting that the entire team is aligned with a similar goal: producing the best news in Colorado. "You may disagree with a decision here or there from someone," explained one reporter, "but I, like, literally never believe something is happening with bad intentions. We all want the same thing, and we're always trying to deliver it." A legal designation that forces the Sun to be accountable to a civic mission means that the organization looks at all decisions through this prism. It is, without much doubt, the driver of a culture focused on quality above all else. Freed from the historical legacy of the *Denver Post*, the founders also successfully parsed out the Sun's coverage goals, implementing a newsroom culture that perceives consistent success. In a sense, by deciding to cover only what it had the resources to effectively cover, the newsroom does not feel inadequate, a feeling many of the founders articulated when discussing their time at the *Post*. "We used to cover the whole state [at the *Post*]," said one founder, "and then that stopped, and we just weren't doing our jobs anymore." Inherent in that statement is a belief that cutting back coverage, in an effort to align with current resources, made the newsroom feel like a failure. That does not happen at the Sun because the founders intently focused on making coverage decisions according to where they believe success is possible.

The most important struggle within the culture of the Sun arises from the gulf between the nine founders and the sixteen other employees who have no ownership in the company. All the founders acknowledge this problem and understand the need for a solution but remain at a loss as to an implementable plan that could alleviate the issue. Although the newsroom successfully created a healthy and positive culture around the work, it still falls short around a perception of equality. As one journalist explained, in many legacy newsrooms, the journalists can band together and unite over a typically absentee ownership group; at the Sun, the owners are colleagues. Often they do not explicitly articulate the obvious difference in power dynamics and sometimes ignore the ramifications of this disparity. Nonfounders understand there is no easy solution. They mostly do not even particularly want an opportunity to obtain a share of ownership but rather some mechanism to alleviate the problems caused by the power dynamic. "It's a problem that I wish they would deal with," said one nonfounder, "and it does stink when I hear the word *collaboration* over and over again, and I'm not really comfortable sometimes. But I will say that negative piece is easily overshadowed by all the good here." And although the founders expressly attempt to espouse this notion of collaboration—and it definitely does exist throughout the newsroom—another underlying assumption that is so clearly dispersed across the entire organization involves notions of autonomy and journalistic agency. The Sun's culture is very traditional in that it implicitly prioritizes individual reporters' autonomy over coverage. Although staff members discuss the audience and their connection to it often, they do not even consider giving up any agency over the news agenda. This is a clear effect of having a journalist-owned public benefit corporation where journalists, and only journalists, have the ultimate say over norms and practices.

In considering the clear fissures within the organizational culture of the Sun—the fractures caused by the owner-non-owner dynamic—it's possible to hypothesize they exist because some decisions were not made during the beginning of the organization. Essentially, instead of making all decisions about organizational structure with the notions of collaboration in mind, the Sun's founders clearly focused on embedding autonomy into the culture. They succeeded by ignoring the overt power dynamics embedded in an organization equally owned by ten founders who make up roughly 40 percent of an organization but created different cultural issues in the process. However, the espoused value of making all decisions with journalistic quality at the forefront minimizes, to some extent, the issues caused by the power alignment.

4

THE *BOSTON GLOBE*

The Mogul-Owned Newsroom

Late last decade, an award-winning reporter with more than twenty years of experience began working as a journalist at the *Boston Globe*, the major metropolitan newspaper of Boston, Massachusetts. They arrived at the *Globe* after working full time at four other newspapers and after interning at two others earlier in their career. "I'm from the area, so getting to the *Globe* was always my dream. I don't think I ever made a career decision without that goal in my mind." After the first few weeks on the job, learning the ropes and beginning to understand how the news organization operated, the reporter got assigned what they considered their first big story for the paper. "It was so exciting," they recalled. "I'd done some small things in my first couple months, but I was itching to prove my worth, you know, make everyone see that I belonged." Right after the story was assigned by an editor, the reporter knew this particular story had a chance to be big, but they didn't anticipate a lot of things they would uncover during the reporting process. "You've worked in journalism, so you understand," they explained. "It was one of those pieces where I get thinking I was done and ready to write, but something new would come up and I'd need to chase down another thread." As the story grew in both scope and importance, the journalist decided it was time to speak to their editor. "I was probably a week into reporting the piece and maybe four days in, I could see an end game, but [now] I couldn't anymore. I was kind of getting nervous I'd be looked at as a deadbeat in the office." After a weekend filled with more researching and finding sources, a Monday meeting with their editor is when the reporter began to realize that the *Globe* differed significantly from any paper they'd worked at in the past:

I'd worked at a bunch of different places before I got here. I'd been at places owned by a local family, but mostly, you know, places owned by all the chains we all know and don't love. I mean, my entire adult life has been spent in newspaper newsrooms. When [this story] started getting bigger, I knew I was supposed to get nervous. Here I was, the new [person], a new person with a pretty good reputation, I think, and I am at a little more than a week without filing a story. [My editor] was, like, "Don't worry about it. Go get the story. Write your story." There was literally no push back in the whole meeting. Only support. [They] didn't say anything about having column inches to fill or expecting this thing a few days ago. It was just, go write the best story possible. There was even, and maybe I'm just remembering this too fondly, a question of, like, "What can I do to help?" I knew then this place was different.

This reporter's implicit assessment of the *Globe*'s newsroom echoes what so many other employees across the organization believe: under the ownership of the billionaire John Henry, the *Globe* had transformed itself into a serious, journalism-first, multimedia enterprise that values quality content.

In October 2013, only one month after Amazon's founder, Jeff Bezos, far more publicly purchased the historic *Washington Post*, Henry agreed to send $70 million in cash to the New York Times Company for the *Globe* and most of its online properties.[1] At the time, most people in and around the Boston area knew Henry as the successful owner of the city's famed professional baseball team, the Red Sox. In his time as owner of the Red Sox, the team broke an eighty-six-year championship drought by winning four World Series titles between 2004 and 2018. For most of its history, the twenty-seven-time Pulitzer-winning *Globe* was managed by a local family, the Taylors. After its founding in 1872, the Taylors ran the paper from 1873 until 1993, when the New York Times Company purchased the *Globe* and its subsidiaries for $1.1 billion.[2] Although a family controlled the Times Company, it was also publicly traded on the stock market, making the *Globe* more overtly susceptible to market forces. As the Northeastern University journalism professor Dan Kennedy explained when writing about the *Washington Post*, "private ownership moves away from the will of the market, which [included] the fiduciary responsibility of trying to maximize profits or at least minimize losses."[3] Henry's arrival at the *Globe* brought with it a new culture described by the journalist above as different, but that another *Globe* reporter called it "incredibly rare and maybe unique for a newspaper, at least in my experience."

Over and over, when describing what it is like to work at the *Boston Globe* under John Henry's ownership, journalists kept repeating the same phrase: a "writer's paper." It effectively sums up the organizational culture of the entire enterprise. As one journalist said, "We're basically Shangri-La for writers. I think if you fancy yourself a writer's journalist, you want to be here." This overall notion may have been prevalent before Henry took over as owner, but it exponentially increased in the years after his arrival. One editor with multiple decades of experience at the *Globe* explained it thusly:

> We've always thought of ourselves as a real national local newspaper, if that makes sense. We did work with the quality of the [New York] *Times*, but we did it in this little provincial city. When [Henry] came in, we restructured a lot of things, lots of people lost their jobs, and a lot of other people were hired. The consistent message throughout was really about doing the best work possible, telling the best stories. And that meant focusing on storytelling and great writing.

For many *Globe* journalists, this change to an organization that celebrated great writing meant a significant shift in normative notions of work. As one journalist explained,

> I'm taking more time to do fewer stories, and so we have fuller conversations about, like, how do I effectively spend my time? How do I prioritize? Whereas before, I kind of did those decisions on the fly because the production expectations were so much higher.

The culture of the *Globe* as a writer's paper manifests itself in an environment that celebrates quality storytelling, one that puts resources in place that allow reporters to do their best work. "A lot of newspapers are much more top down and sort of traditional, like, you know, most papers are editor papers," said one journalist. "They're not writer papers, they're not reporter papers." When asked to elaborate, this journalist talked about giving reporters the autonomy to choose stories and then make decisions on how best to tell them. This journalism-first mentality provides reporters with a perceived freedom to succeed or fail on their own terms. "Every journalist wants to feel supported," explained one reporter. "Here, I may disagree with something now and again, but I never don't feel like they want me to do my best." Most of this feeling comes from the reporter-first, editor-second mission that permeates the entire newsroom. One reporter noted,

> It's the best-resourced newsroom that I've worked for. It has the largest staff, the most ambition, and it gives you latitude to work on stories that you might be interested in yourself. So, there's some reception to ideas that are generated by the journalists instead of a mostly top-down structure.

In many ways, this reporter-first, writer's paper mentality also gives the *Globe* a collegial feel, partly because most employees feel in control of their own work. "A lot of papers have real competitive, nasty sides in the newsroom," said one editor. "A lot of kind of passive-aggressive fighting over who gets what story is everywhere in news. It's not so much here because everyone kind of controls their own destiny."

Beyond the writer-first approach that pervades the newsroom, the collegiality that comes from less internal competition also stems from the perception of far less precarity within the newsroom. "The *Globe* is a pretty collegial place. I would say that it's one of the more collegial places that I have ever worked," said one journalist, noting that it is far more difficult for this kind of collegiality to occur at other newspapers. "Most places are owned by corporations who could[n't] give a shit about journalism, right? Those places have layoffs all the time." Another journalist directly connected the threat of layoffs to collegiality. "In my past, when I've worked at places with frequent staff reductions, we were friends, but weary friends, if that makes sense. In a way, it was always about one of us might survive, so there was competition." At the *Globe*, due to an ownership structure that many believe does not prioritize profits over everything else, the precarity that comes from constant layoffs doesn't exist, and this lack of dread in the newsroom leads to more overall collegiality. One journalist noted,

> I think there's definitely a much greater sense of job security, a much greater sense of commitment on the part of the ownership to the product, and that's evident. You know we've been hiring people; we've been putting money into projects. You know we sent a dozen reporters and photographers across the country doing this big project. . . . And it was, you know, that was pretty expensive.

The job security that comes from working in a newsroom that continuously adds resources, both financial and human, as opposed to subtracting them, gives journalists a strong assurance that the people they work with could be around for a long time. Countless journalists discussed how, before Henry took over, they felt like so many of their other colleagues throughout the journalism industry; they felt as if they could never get comfortable at a job because the field of journalism offered virtually no stability. "No matter where you work," explained one journalist, "you'll hear countless legendary—and I mean that jokingly—stories about these guys who worked there for decades and casted a huge shadow. They were lifers." The reporter went on to describe how everyone in a newsroom heard about these "lifers" and their escapades. "Again, it's like they're legends. And, you know, newsrooms have that kind of deep mythology, no matter how big or small they are. That comes from institutional memories of sorts. And I fear that's leaving journalism now." The journalist went on to say that the *Globe* has many of these "characters," people who worked in the newsroom for three or four decades and left large legacies. "Frankly, now I think any of us here [in this newsroom] could be like that because you get the feeling the opportunity to make a career out of this job is here. It's awesome."

Although the overall culture of the *Globe* feels revelatory to many of the journalists in the newsroom with, say, two decades of experience or less, many long-time journalism veterans do believe that Henry's ownership actually has brought back a more traditional journalism culture to the organization. "You're asking about the organizational culture," said one veteran journalist, "and it is different now than it's been in my time, but some of the parts of it that I think about really remind me of the [1980s]." That journalist and others with numerous decades in the field believed that before the significant economic disruptions brought on by plummeting advertising revenue attacked the journalism industry in the late 1990s and, more salient, in the early 2000s, there was a clear feeling of autonomy in the newsroom. "A lot of it has to do with why you think someone is giving you orders," said a veteran editor.

> In the past, nobody bothered us—most of the time, let me stress that— because we made money and that's all that mattered. It just got to a point where a lot of us felt like we lost a sense of control because every other day some other scheme to make quick cash was floated. Under the Henrys, that happens infrequently.

Another seasoned reporter echoed those thoughts but made a clear distinction between, for example, the 1980s and the 2020s, or, even more, the New York Times Company ownership and the John Henry ownership. "It's different," they said. "Yes, there's less interference—at least we think so—compared to the last years the *Times* owned us. But reporters didn't have the power we do now back then. Unless you were a star, editors really ran this place." The journalist went on to explain that the organizational shift to placing reporters—and therefore stories—at the center of the newsroom's ecosystem as the most identifiable and distinct piece of the newsroom's organizational culture most definitely coincided with the early years of the Henry ownership. "It always surprises me," explained one veteran of several newsrooms, "that these owners never get that people buy news and important stories, and if you cut those down, fewer people buy the news." They went on to say that although it should be common

sense to invest in the stories produced by the newsroom, the Henry ownership made noticeable decisions to provide resources to journalists and
"pivot towards making the actual newspaper or the website or whatever
better. It was refreshing, if not obvious, you know."

This culture shift at the *Globe* did not start the moment John Henry
purchased the paper, and that's important, said numerous journalists. Due
to the gradual nature of the shift, the results seemed more permanent and
notable. One editor said,

> We went through sort of a reinvention process. We rethought what our
> beats are, we rethought how we, you know, [how we think about] what
> our newsroom culture is like, and what's important to us. And so, you
> know, so when [we] did that [the idea was] we don't, we no longer want
> to be the paper of record. We want to be the paper of interest. And so
> that was a clear signal to the department heads about the direction [we
> were going in].

This shift toward a paper of interest rather than a paper of record might
seem like a rhetorical device or a public relations cliché, but many journalists interviewed noted this exact phrase as the key to a change in organizational culture. This alteration significantly affects news production,
shifting focus from event-driven breaking news or spot news stories and
instead places a premium on more narrative feature work. Journalists
overwhelmingly believed this change in direction empowered them not
just to do the same old things that journalists have been doing for decades
but rather make decisions based on quality. "It means we don't have to
write stories the same way people did fifty years ago," explained one journalist. "And that means we can now do the real journalism, the writing
that's going to matter to people and make them care about the news."

Organizational Culture

Altough its overriding organizational culture focuses on writing and
storytelling, the *Globe* certainly features numerous subcultures within
its newsroom. It's imperative to understand that a homogeneous organizational culture such as the one described above might permeate an
entire newsroom, but the organization could still include several het-
erogenous subcultures that all combine to form that overall culture.[4]
When attempting to understand how various subcultures exist within
a homogenous overall organizational culture, it is vital to comprehend
how each subculture's "power and position" within the larger ecosystem
exists.[5] In the totality of an organization, each subculture subtly shapes or

alters the overall culture until something relatively stable appears.[6] At the *Globe,* subcultures can be made visible by studying the various departments, each with its own leaders and norms. For example, some department leaders—or section editors—have five or more assistants, creatings a distinct micro organization within the newsroom. For example, one sports reporter made it clear that the sports department, though clearly part of the rest of the newsroom, does things very differently. "So many of us don't come to the newsroom often or at all, even before COVID, so we've always had a different thing going on," said the journalist. "It's like, really, we have completely different rules—for lack of a better word—and policies. We bring people on board differently. We talk to each other differently. It's different." When discussing how stories are ideated or how reporter-editor relationships work, journalists said that although there are similarities across the organization, each department head is empowered enough to create their own processes. The result is several subcultures within the main one. In discussing a new department that arose during COVID, when almost the entire newsroom worked remotely, one reporter described the building of a new subculture. Referring to the entire newsroom, they said,

> The *Globe,* innately, they take the work really seriously, they take themselves very seriously. [But] I came to this particular team after they were remote for two years, and while we were still remote, I don't know if there really was a sense of [overall] culture, initially.

The reporter went on to describe the process by which the members of the team began to build their own culture, a part of the entire newsroom, but still distinct. A different reporter on the same team explained, "We're much closer, all of us together. We celebrate birthdays together and we go out. Maybe it's because we're smaller, but that closeness is different than what my friends [at the *Globe*] describe of their teams."

The overall culture of the newsroom is decidedly reporter focused, but editors clearly play a prominent role in the building of subcultures. One journalist, a veteran of numerous teams within the newsroom, said, "a lot of it depends on the editor" in terms of those micro cultures. A different journalist with similar experience across multiple teams said, "Yeah, working at the *Globe* is [just] working at the *Globe* in a lot of respects. But your main editor, well, they can really impact the experience of that team in a bunch of ways." The reporter went on to describe how an editor can create a family-like dynamic and influence how conversations happen between team members and editors, as well as how much communication platforms such as Slack play a role in the subculture, and how basic processes play out. Numerous reporters noted that this was by design, and more larger news organizations should pay attention. One explained, "More and more—and I think this is residue from the corporatizing of, really, the whole country—companies want to make everything look the same." They went on to clarify that news organizations should have an overarching mission "in terms of what we're trying to do," but there are differences between departments that need to be celebrated, not diminished. "Sports isn't the metro desk, and the metro desk isn't arts," they said. "Those teams need to have the ability to kind of be what they should be and not conform to what some manager thinks is good for all." One reporter described the overall culture of the news organization as allowing for a real sense of belonging, but each team's subculture shapes the "uniqueness" of the *Globe*. They said,

> I think that most people get along really well because of the shared experience of being journalists. You know, I think that like a lot of professions, you know there's that sort of band of brothers kind of feel to it, and I think that that really helps. You know, and then, of course, within [my team], we kind of do our own thing. We know [what we are]. We understand that.

The underlying message in that quote illustrates how because the overall organizational culture provides a clear goal for all journalists, it allows for camaraderie to develop. But to get optimal results in terms of reaching the overall goal, each team or department needs to understand exactly what they are, and then move forward with the processes that allow them to achieve as much success—as defined by the overall goal—as possible. When asked to describe the organizational culture of the news outlet, one editor summed it up by explicitly using the term *subculture*. They said, "We're a writer's paper, that's what we all like to say. And that does kind of, you know, explain the feel of the place." After discussing how the term "writer's paper" affected the "feel of the place," the reporter added, "But we're also a bunch of different teams, subcultures, I guess, that each kind of have our ideas of what a writer's paper means."

Leadership

Although John Henry bought the *Boston Globe*, and although he's officially the publisher of the newspaper, numerous *Globe* journalists point to his wife, Linda Henry, as the person who leads the company. Linda Henry is the chief executive officer of Boston Globe Media, the company that owns the *Globe*. In combination, the Henrys have overwhelmingly led the cultural changes at the organization. In a book about billionaires purchasing news properties, Dan Kennedy labels these owners "moguls," contending that Henry's style of building culture at the *Globe* involved attempting numerous innovations that do not affect newspaper culture.[7] In a sense, the Henrys understood that innovations to the news organization, particularly those aimed at increasing profitability, needed to work sensitively alongside traditional journalism culture: changes in journalism culture often create overt anger in newsrooms and fail.[8] Some research suggests that because "owner influence is greater where voting power within the company is concentrated in the hands of individuals and families rather than companies," it is bad for a news organization's editorial independence when one rich person owns the operation.[9] This sentiment is echoed in the notion that there is a "democratic deficit caused by private ownership and unaccountable state coordination of the media."[10] This camp of media scholars believes that all private ownership of media is inimical, but perhaps the most negative consequences are felt most acutely when one powerful individual owns the organization. However, *Globe* journalists affirm that after the Henrys took over, their editorial independence became far stronger. "And that's the main reason why he and his wife are looked at favorably, really," said one reporter. Over and over again, journalists noted the vastly superior, journalism-focused culture encouraged by the Henrys compared to the culture promoted by the New York Times Company. One prominent article published after the sale of the organization to Henry noted that although the *Globe* clearly needed help getting its financial situation in order, the best way to strengthen its commitment to public service and the quality of the journalism would be simply through "the deep pockets" of Henry, overtly contending that more resources were what would improve the quality of the journalism.[11] According to *Globe* employees, Henry not only immediately began investing resources in the paper but also started a thorough evaluation of what worked and what did not. The way he and his team went about this, journalists say, is how his leadership began shaping the organizational culture of the newsroom.[12]

Henry's first big challenge in instilling a journalism-centric culture arose immediately on his purchase of the paper. Numerous members of the *Globe* staff felt apprehensive about Henry's purchase, considering that he also had an ownership stake in the Red Sox. "We have one of the most respected—and awarded—sports departments in the country. Really, we've had this since the 1970s," said one editor not in sports.

> And a large part of our readership comes to us for sports. Of course, especially in 2013, the Red Sox are the biggest, or maybe second to the

Patriots, game in town. How were we going to cover the team fairly with [Henry] owning the paper?

This seemingly major conflict of interest was a talking point throughout the newsroom once it became clear that Henry intended to bid on the news organization. However, every sports reporter interviewed for this chapter said that in his almost ten years of ownership at the time of this research, never once did Henry put any pressure on the *Globe* journalists to take any stance in coverage of the Red Sox. The paper continues to be very transparent about this potential conflict of interest, so transparent that it's become humorous to some journalists. "Red Sox Principal Owner John Henry, who also owns the *Globe*," laughed one reporter, reciting the disclaimer the sports department puts on every story about the Red Sox and Henry. They added,

> We've been doing that I don't know how long? I think he's owned the *Globe* for more than ten years now. And we still do that, which seems ridiculous to me. Like I think everybody understands he owns the paper. I don't know, but we always mention [it].

One journalist with a turbulent backstory concerning Henry's ownership believes the sale was one of the most positive things to happen in the *Globe's* history. After the ownership transfer and during the period when the Henrys were researching how the organization covered various places and subjects, this journalist and their entire team lost their jobs. "They eliminated my department, and so I was let go along with, like, [a significant number] of my colleagues. So I experienced [the ownership change] in that way, [through] this idea of, like, restructuring." They went on to note that in that way, the Henrys clearly dictate, on a large scale, "the priorities that our newspaper has, and so in that way they will shape the coverage that occurs down the line." But, they added, "In, like, the day-to-day of, like, picking stories or the editing of stories, or even having the tenacity to take on powerful people [in the newsroom], like, I don't see them exerting any kind of influence." Another editor echoed this sentiment, noting that although Linda Henry is the CEO, "she's so hands off, I'm not sure I've ever even seen or talked to her in person." Another longtime reporter who's been in the newsroom through three different ownership groups, said something similar:

> I'm appreciative of [the hands-off approach], and part of it, I think, has to do with this kind of laissez-faire management of the newsroom. Not that it's not managed. It's just done so in a way where the people like me have a lot of freedom, you know.

That sentiment implicitly connects the Henrys' management style with the management style already present in the newsroom. The overall idea is that because the Henrys provide ample resources and let people do their jobs, this attitude trickles down to department heads, who then treat their staff the same way, empowering reporters to do the journalism they believe is necessary in any given situation. Another longtime reporter recounted how the Henrys were able to implement this hands-off approach successfully. "There's a difference between being negligent and being hands off, because negligent is just not paying attention," they said. "But what the *Globe* needed, one of the things that happened when the Times sold the *Globe* to John Henry, was all the professional managers, the HR, the legal, they all left for the most part." The reporter explained that this allowed the Henrys to implement an organizational structure from the top down, eliminating the people who had propagated or at least strengthened the previous culture. The reporter added that after placing new people and implementing a new structure, the Henrys figured out exactly what they wanted to the paper to be. They said,

> And I think the big switch for the *Globe*, if you want to look at it from thirty thousand feet, is that we went from a business that was subsidized by advertisers—you know, there was your home delivery revenue, but that was a small percentage, and most of the money came from advertisers—and over time, that had to switch to being subsidized by the subscribers themselves. So [if the newsroom wanted] to do anything, if you're going to spend money, you've got to now show that it's going to get you subscribers, that they're going to be the kind of subscribers who last.... [They did this] from a classic business sense, operational sense, professionalizing the operational side while allowing the newsroom to do what it does best.

For this journalist and numerous other *Globe* employees, the Henrys' outside perspective, which allowed them to implement structures and initiate an uncommon culture in journalism, is the key to the success of the newsroom. Numerous interviewees talked about the advantages of an owner who does not own several news properties and how the Henrys' attention, at least in news, is focused on the *Globe*. To everyone interviewed, the mogul owner was the perfect type of leader for a newsroom, and they believed that the Henrys specifically deserved immense credit for the new organizational culture—and its attached subcultures—that permeate the *Globe*. "I do really believe that, you know, the billionaire owners . . . are the best ones to be the custodians of local journalism," said one reporter. They added,

It's because they do have the community in mind, and they have the institution in mind when they make decisions. I mean, the Henrys. We are making a profit, I know. The editor told us that. He's made no secret of that in company town halls and other things. But they don't really worry about the profit too much because they're obviously billionaires. But they also really do like the position the *Globe* holds in the community.

Socialization

One of the most important ways that the subcultures demonstrate power over the *Globe*'s organizational culture is in the socialization processes. Although there are some newsroom-wide socialization practices, each subgroup has its own practices. As one journalist explained, "Initially there was a formal HR onboarding as it pertained to training to use their content management system. I think there was something else about benefits, and we had a benefits training. But no, like, cultural onboarding" from a newsroom-wide perspective. Numerous other journalists who started during the Henry ownership were surprise at the lack of onboarding processes. "Honestly, at basically every other place I've been, whether it was formal or not," explained one reporter, "there was always something that basically said, 'This is what it's like to work here.' They don't have that here." In fact, journalists who predate Henry recalled more intentional newsroom socialization practices at the organizational level. "We definitely used to do things differently," explained one *Globe* veteran. "I remember a video that gave us the history of the place. It was a real hagiography, but it certainly kind of, sort of, told me what was expected in the big picture."

The one immutable element of the *Globe*'s overall organizational culture is, of course, related to the idea of a "writer's paper"; and, regardless of what team they join, new members of the organization learn about it quickly. "It doesn't matter what team you're on," laughed one editor. "At some point early on you're going to be told about our devotion to narrative reporting." Another journalist described their onboarding to their team as "different from what others in my hiring cohort went through if they were on a different team." But, they added, it was very quickly made known to the entire cohort that

> the *Globe* is very focused on compelling ways of presenting its journalism, so it's very interested in, like, narrative-style writing. It wants to tell regular news stories in a narrative way whenever possible. They are sometimes reluctant to use, like, hard news ledes even on hard news stories because they want the writing to be distinctive.

That journalist, who joined a team that publishes a significant amount of hard news, described how that overall culture of a writer's paper really took hold for them when an editor discussed how to write in a "distinctive manner," which really meant eschewing numerous norms such as traditional ledes when crafting a story.

Although new journalists become imbued with the overall culture, regardless of the team they join, each team or department's subculture becomes far more explicit in those early days of joining the newsroom. One journalist noticed this very quickly, explaining, "It depends on where you get assigned in the newsroom because even though you're part of the *Globe*, like, you end up spending a lot of time with the particular team that you're as assigned to." The journalist went on to say that almost all communication in their team occurs through electronic means such as email or Slack—made clear very early—whereas other teams are far more "of an in-person clique." In short, everyone in the newsroom has the same mission. According to this journalist. "You end up, like, sort of swimming in the same pond, I guess, so to speak," as the rest of the team. A few other teams in the newsroom have less overt socialization and more implicit practices. For example, multiple teams employ a "buddy system" whereby new employees are told to shadow a veteran for a specific amount of time. "I think this works really well for us," said one editor. "I could map it out, but inevitably some is going to go in one ear and out the other. But if they're just watching [a major journalist at the *Globe*] for weeks, they're going to see what to do." One journalist from a different department from that editor also was paired with a veteran journalist at the start. They said it was the "best thing" for them in those early days at the *Globe*:

> You're new somewhere and you don't want to mess up, you know. Other places I've been they give you a mentor, but it's, like, on an if-I-need-you basis. Here, I spent about three weeks doing absolutely nothing but shadowing [a veteran]. You know, you're told a lot at the beginning about what it's like to be a *Globe* reporter, but this [buddy system] made it really clear what I was supposed to do.

This journalist is articulating how some teams at the news organization have many new journalists in a newsroom learn the culture: through watching veterans. Decades ago, in his landmark study on socialization, the sociologist Warren Breed observed newcomers modeling the behavior of veterans to learn and aborb newsroom culture.[13] Regardless of how this process occurs, though, it seems obvious that the *Globe* takes seriously its need to socialize new entries in the newsroom into both the overall culture of the organization and the appropriate subculture. This goal was more explicitly discussed at the leadership level after the Henrys took over. One editor who predates the new ownership explained this clearly, recalling, "We had ways to get people to fit in when they started. After John and Linda came on, we were told to think about the ways to do that for the person as a *Globe* reporter and a teammate."

Technology

For generations of *Globe* reporters and readers, the news organization's headquarters was in Dorchester, a neighborhood on the outskirts of the city of Boston. Dorchester is not necessarily the most accessible part of the city and definitely not near downtown. Beginning in 1958, the headquarters was on Morrisey Boulevard. In 2017, the organization moved out of its celebrated headquarters and settled into a building in downtown Boston, near the historic Fanueil Hall, a move that the organization called "a symbolic gesture meant to show the journalistic institution will not retreat from its position near the center of civic life in Boston."[14] Numerous journalists called this move an important event; it was announced roughly two years into the Henry ownership. Multiple journalists said it illustrated the Henrys' commitment to caring about journalism; the move had a positive effect on the culture of the newsroom. One journalist explained,

> You know journalism, so you know what's happened a lot lately: newspaper owners keep selling the old building because the real estate is where the money is. I think some of these chains buy newspapers just for the real estate. So when [John] Henry took over and word started leaking out that they might sell the place on Morrisey, I got nervous. I wasn't alone. Obviously, that's a big building on a lot of land in what was then a real up-and-coming part of the city. At other places, from what I know, these newsrooms end up far outside of cities because cities are expensive. But here we are, right in downtown in a real expensive place. That shows commitment to the *Globe* and its place in the city. [Henry] earned a lot of respect around here for that.

Like many news organizations, the newsroom remained filled with "hustle and bustle," as one editor described it, until COVID, which forced most people to work remotely and made any journalistic processes reliant on technology. Even years after a vaccine rollout, most journalists are not back in the newsroom. Many *Globe* employees, particularly editors interviewed, believed that might become the norm. "People realized they could work from home, and now they're still very apprehensive about coming back in," said one editor.

This move toward remote work changed how the setup of the organization affected its workers. Some teams, such as sports, always had journalists working primarily outside the newsroom, but others had to make considerable adaptations. "I'm not sure if I spent ten minutes a week on Slack, pre-COVID, and now it's a clear part of my workday," said one reporter. Numerous other journalists agreed; technology became the key driver of culture. Although some teams are, at the time of this writing, essentially forcing journalists to come into the newsroom a relatively small amount of time each week, and a small number of *Globe* journalists have returned to the office full time, journalists still describe the newsroom as mostly empty compared with, say, 2019. "We don't *need* [stress theirs] a newsroom. But for me, and I think most journalists, the newsroom is what makes this job the most fun. It's got energy. We lose something when we don't use it," said one reporter. This lack of usage comes with a cost for the *Globe*, said multiple interviewees. That cost can mostly be felt when it comes to socializing new members. One editor said it now takes "two to three times as much time" for a new reporter to get a feel for the organization, or, in other words, to become socialized. Another editor explicitly fretted that the organization would lose some of what "makes the *Globe* the *Globe*." In other words, some of the place's organizational culture would erode through its innate reliance on technolgy. In short, when a news organization has a prominent headquarters/newsroom, that physical space plays a large role in the enabling and manifestation of organizational culture. As the newsroom becomes a less prominent part of news production, *Globe* journalists are noticing that it is becoming more difficult, but still possible, to maintain the culture.

Routines

As noted, in this post-COVID world, messaging platforms such as Slack became a much larger piece of the *Globe*'s ecosystem. However, the communication patterns between reporters and editors, and reporters and editors and upper management differ, depending on teams and their subcultures. Although virtually every team represented in this research utilizes Slack is some way, the intensity of that usage differs with each. One reporter explained the way they communicate with their editor in a fashion very similar to how others did. They said,

> Yeah, so [my editor and I] are in the office up to three days a week, usually it's more like two. And so [they] sit two desks from me, so if we're

in the office together, I will just talk to [them]. But mostly, though, our conversations are over Slack, and I think to a lesser extent email. So we're mostly talking on Slack, and then we have a weekly check-in over Zoom or in person just to kind of run through the gamut of projects [happening at the time].

This experience is very typical for most members of the newsroom. Reporters usually communicate with their editors through a variety of media that include Slack, emails, phone calls, and in-person meetings. Some teams utilize Slack far less than others and rely mostly on phone calls. Others have frequent—multiple times a week—Zoom meetings for the whole team. And for other teams, such as sports, rarely does the entire department come together. The overall communication patterns of a team seem to be heavily influenced by two main factors: the preferences of the department head and the size of the department. One sports reporter noted that frequent full-team meetings would be "useless" because of the size of the team's many reporters and the differences among the various beats reporters cover. Another reporter who has experience on multiple teams over the last handful of years summed it up thus: "The older your editor, the more prehistoric your interactions are," tacitly acknowledging the editor's own history in creating the communication patterns within each team.

Moreover, although the way teams communicate varies by department, the way communication occurs during the production of a story varies even more, depending on the team. Many journalists talked about complete freedom from communication during the production of stories, implying that they research, report, and file a story without any communication with the team. "I have the benefit of being basically allowed to do what I want at the *Globe* now, which is great," said one reporter. "It took me, like, seven years to get here, but we're here, so that's good. That's not to say that I don't get assignments," but there is very little communication, if any, during assignments. Although such a complete lack of communication is rare at the *Globe*, most interviewees described a process that they believe is more hands-off, in terms of editorial supervision, than at other similar news organizations. "It goes back to us being a writer's paper," said one reporter. "There is trust in us to know how to tell a story our way." Some team leaders, though, described a much more thorough process that still grants autonomy to reporters but gives editors a little more agency in stories. Describing their process, one editor said,

I mean ideally, there would be communication throughout the process of, like, how you're doing, when you think you can file, do you need another day, like, how long will it take you to do x or y? You know, . . . you should be communicating with your editor throughout the process, in my opinion.

These varying communication patterns are indisputably key pieces of each subculture within the *Globe*, but nobody interviewed felt that any pattern infringed on their ability to tell stories as they saw fit. Therefore, although it is clear that, for example, how often—and in what format—an entire team meets and how reporter-editor communication style clearly affects collegiality and overall subculture, it does not detract from the culture of the organization, which celebrates reporter autonomy. What's also clear, though, is that the extant subculture of each team does affect news-production processes. "You go from team to team," explained one longtime editor, "and you'll see a bunch of different ways to do the same thing. But I think if you investigate a little closely, you'll probably find the end result, the stories, look a little different from team to team."

Engagement

Although the idea of audience engagement is becoming more and more prevalent across the entire the journalism industry—so much so that numerous organizations have built all of their news production processes around the notion of engaging their audience—the *Globe* apparently builds its entire engagement strategy around audience metrics.[15] When asked about how journalists at the organization communicate or incorporate their audience into their news work, the explanation given by one reporter reiterates the attitudes of countless others. They said,

> When you put out a newspaper, you had no idea who read what or how much time they spent with a story, or which stories they skipped entirely. You could do surveys, but if you asked people what they wanted more of, they always wanted more of everything. But with digital, obviously you see what stories rise. You see what and how long people are engaged with that story. It's right there on your Chartbeat.

The messages inherent in that statement explain a significant amount about the way the *Globe* newsroom views its audience. Reporters have a clear and pervasive view of the audience as numbers and not partners in newswork. Journalists at the organization cannot sign in to the newsroom's content management system without seeing web metrics about both their own work and the work of the entire organization; all these metrics are provided by the technology company Chartbeat. Journalists are quick to acknowledge that news production decisions are made according to web metrics, but the organization attempts to balance the information with a clear understanding of what reporters believe is important to their communities. "Sure, we know, you know, a story about Tom Brady is going to get a lot of traction," said one journalist, "so we might do those more, but that is not common across the whole place." Another reporter echoed those thoughts, saying,

> What I appreciate about the *Globe* is we haven't turned into a clickbait machine by any stretch. There is a part of the operation that tries to do news quick, news that is going to be talked about a lot, that's, like, spreading virally on the internet, you know, and being part of that conversation. But we also continue to do big-term investigations, primarily.

Other reporters spoke about metrics as their relationship to the audience, noting that those numbers provide a small understanding of what the audience desires from journalists. But, many stressed, it is the job of journalists to understand their communities rather than relying on web metrics to determine what is important.

A reporter explained their relationship to the audience, and, more broadly, their role as a journalist by contending that every day, they need "to define what in this moment it's like to live in Greater Boston, to live in New England." If they do that, they said, they understand what's important to the audience far more than metrics can.

> You know, we have an awful housing crisis, our transportation system has fallen apart, the cost of living is going up, you know, Boston's middle class continues to be squeezed. So also you have a really hefty and significant history of racism and segregation in Boston and throughout the region in New England in general. So I think, you know, a lot of the job, it's as simple as that.

The journalists at the *Globe* clearly have a very traditional relationship with the public. Not once was there any indication of a journalist ceding any agenda-building agency to the audience. Metrics clearly influence and affect some news-production decisions, primarily across various breaking news teams, but they do not have much explicit power elsewhere. Journalists acknowledge that consistently viewing metrics may make some difference in their decisions, but they truly believe in the notion, arguably considered antiquated in journalism studies research, that journalists embedded in their various communities understand the issues important to those communities and should have the power to make those decisions and tell those stories.

News Production

In the years since the Henry ownership began, the way the *Globe* produces news changed considerably. Earlier in this chapter, a hypothesis by Dan Kennedy contended that the most important change the new ownership enacted was shifting the funding model from one that primarily relied on advertising to one where subscribers played the largest role—by significantly raising subscription costs. The effect of this funding-model change did not only include where the money to fund news production originated but also fundamentally changed how journalists did their jobs. As one longtime journalist described,

> It is a paper that has over the course of [the] years finally figured out how it works. Because we were your classic print newspaper for a long time. And the rhythm of the day was really [just like a] classic print newspaper. Come in at nine, ten a.m., you know, have a morning meeting, talk to some people, go to lunch for a couple hours, come back, write on deadline, and then go. And the whole news cycle has changed so much, and it's really changed the way that we work. So the internal clock at the *Globe* has changed and the metabolism has changed, I should say. And we just work in a different way. We work on building stories from the ground up. Like, you don't have to wait until you have breaking news now. You don't have to wait until you have a thousand words to put something online. You start with what you've got, and you update throughout the day. That's a big change, you know, that's a big change from when reporters would spend all day talking to people and then, you know, sometime in the afternoon, start writing.

Although the journalist is describing a shift in news production that manifested itself through most of the news industry in recent years, the *Globe*'s funding-structure change really allowed the newsroom to transform itself completely. Before, journalists explained, there was still a sentiment that certain things had to be saved for the print product. "That idea is kind of gone now," said one journalist. "People read stuff online mostly." An editor explained, "We just follow who pays the bills, so readers matter more than advertisers now. That's how it should be."

The new process of news production, unsurprisingly, affected the notion of the organization as a writer's paper. Dozens of reporters spoke happily of not worrying about word counts. Comparing working at the *Globe* with working at a Gannett paper in the past, one said,

> Gannett, especially towards the end, I mean it wasn't a burden, but, you know, you always heard things had to be shorter, [or] we didn't have

room to do this, we didn't have room to do that. And, um, with the *Globe*, that hasn't been the case.

Another reporter explained this freedom from word counts similarly. "The *Globe* is very much a writer's paper, and, you know, I don't think I've ever been told we don't have room for that or, you know, cut down on how much you're writing or anything." According to the journalists, the news-production process almost always begins with an idea proposed by a reporter. This does not mean the reporter themselves thought of the story—it typically comes from a source—but that the reporter proposed the piece, not an editor. "Maybe ten times a year I'll get assigned something," explained a reporter on a team where assignments would more than likely be common at other news organizations. "Maybe, I don't know, five times a year, maybe I might write something that somebody else [in the news-room] suggests," said another reporter, also echoing a common experience among journalists at the organization. Once a story is proposed and agreed upon, news-production practices vary by department subculture. As noted previously, some teams have far more communication between reporters and editors, whereas some teams have very little. One reporter on a team with very little communication explained the process as very "hands off." They said,

> Once I [propose a story] and [the editor says yes] there's, like, no contact at all. It's just, like, 'OK go do your thing.' In fact, sometimes I'm not even sure when the story's running, and I have to email [the editor when] I think something is running to double check. [The editor is] very laissez-faire in that way, hands off, which is great because I work well that way, too. But every once in a while, they'll email me when something is in progress, especially when it's a more reported piece with, like, photos.

A reporter is primarily left on their own in terms building stories. There is no policy, either in the organization as a whole or within certain teams, in terms of how to source stories. Reporters recalled previous jobs where, for example, a nonexpert or community member had to be included in a story, but the *Globe* seemingly offers complete freedom to reporters, implicitly telling them to produce a story in the way they think best, regardless of the sources. "It can get very clunky, a story, if you have to add a quote or anecdote that doesn't really fit just to make sure it fits some arbitrary standard," commented one journalist.

Even after reporters file stories, the notion of a writer's paper manifests itself. Several reporters described editors asking for additions to or subtractions from a piece, but rarely forcing the issue. Editors will fix obvious mistakes and ask questions, primarily about clarity issues, but rarely engage with anything more. One newer reporter said, "Once I file, occasionally [my editor] has questions or clarifications, but so far there's been no wholesale rewriting or tinkering or anything like that." In its totality, the news production process at the organization clearly leans on reporter autonomy by centering the reporter, not the editor or public, in all processes. The *Globe* provides reporters with the tools and, most important, the power do what they see fit—in the majority of cases—when working on stories. The only real exception to this description, according to journalists, occur on teams where journalists work more like a team. For example, in the famous—due to the Oscar-winning film—investigative unit Spotlight, reporters and editors work together on larger investigative projects. In these cases, rarely does one name appear in the byline. The *Globe* has other teams like Spotlight; journalists in those departments necessarily share agency over stories. According to interviewees, editors then need to wield more decision-making power. However, beyond these few exceptions, news-production processes at the organization overwhelmingly emphasizes reporter autonomy.

Conclusion

The benefits of what Dan Kennedy dubbed "mogul ownership" for news organizations becomes readily clear after talking to *Boston Globe* journalists. A single billionaire owner, particularly one without other news properties in their portfolio, immediately diminishes the sense of job precarity present throughout the industry.[16] When the Henry ownership took over the news organization, and after a period of extensive research into what was succeeding or not within the newsroom, John and Linda Henry began infusing the organization with resources and openly enabling a culture focused on quality, reporter-led journalism throughout. The perceived success, according to participants, of the manifestation of this revitalized culture can be clearly linked to the actions *not* taken by the Henry ownership.

In the early stages of mogul ownership for the *Globe*, lots of non-newsroom employees left the company, but, more saliently, the company laid off a significant number of journalists. This occasion did not catalyze as many negative thoughts and concerns across the newsroom as it may have if a company such as Gannett bought the paper and began a staff reduction plan because while the Henry ownership did not, almost unilaterally, trim departments here and there, but rather, almost exclusively, laid off whole teams. This macro-level change illustrated a reorganization of the newsroom, one that would better represent a new goal, a mission an aforementioned quotation described as a shift from a "paper of record" to a "paper of interest." This shift meant that certain types of reporters, primarily suburban town reporters and breaking news ones, would not be as necessary to the organization. Ownership and leadership explained these changes transparently, according to participants. This shift in structure absolutely began a shift in organizational culture, but more importantly did not attempt to change journalistic culture. Saliently, ownership never attempted to make micro-level change, the kinds of changes that would affect, in a perceived negative manner, how journalists did their jobs. In short, changes made to the *Globe* after the Henry ownership took over empowered journalists with more agency instead of the doing the opposite, regardless of initial staff cuts.

While a section of recent scholarship across journalism studies and, more broadly, media studies caution against centralizing power over the media to fewer individuals, particularly rich and powerful individuals, those fears do not seem to have materialized at the *Globe*. Yes, prior to the Henrys, under New York Times Company ownership, both a family, a board of directors and a large number of shareholders theoretically shared power over the *Globe*, a connection to the whims of the stock market clearly affected the newsroom in a negative manner. The Henrys, according to virtually everyone interviewed for this chapter, very overtly cared about turning the news organization into a profit-making enterprise, but are not concerned, as many public or vulture capital owners are, with maximizing the profits of the business. For a news organization to be successful, said one veteran journalist in the newsroom, it must take its role as a civic institution seriously. "I would never say we're perfect, not in a million years. And I have some opinions definitely different than what we're doing," they said, adding, "but there is no way that even really unhappy people here could say that we're not a better newspaper for the readers than we were before (John Henry) bought us. There is no way." While the *Globe* certainly does not employ as many journalists as it did in the financial heyday of newspapers in the 1970s-1990s, many in the newsroom believe it serves its community better now than maybe any other time. "A lot of things we used to cover, those things don't need covering in 2022," said one veteran. "What we do cover, we do in a way that's so much more readable, and I think that really makes a difference in the way readers are able to act on the information."

For a news organization with numerous subcultures within an overall organizational culture, the *Globe* clearly understood the potential downfalls of this. As previously noted, when the Henrys took over ownership, they told newsroom leaders to think far more intentionally about socialization processes. As a huge newsroom in terms of people, the emergence of various subcultures could be expected; it's one thing to have one culture in a newsroom of twenty, it's another in a newsroom with hundreds of journalists. However, the need to think intentionally about culture and the emphasis on the value of a "writer's paper" helps maintain an overall organizational structure that the various subcultures can align within. If the *Globe* did not make salient an overall cultural value, various subcultures could override any sense of culture that acts as connective tissue throughout the organization. The Henrys understood this, and a seemingly positive organizational culture permeates the *Globe*.

5

THE ATHLETIC

The Venture-Capital-Funded Newsroom

It was the middle of the season for the National Football League, and one team was about to make a change in the most important position on the field: quarterback. When it happened, "seismic change" would "ripple across the rest of the league," said a beat writer for the team. The journalist verified that the change would happen early in the day but did not immediately publish the information. "At first I thought this would really move on Twitter," they recalled, "but then I called my editor to see if I should do a short piece with just the news and come back later for the main story." The beat writer felt that given more time, a few more hours, they would have the necessary contextual information for publishing a "stellar" article that would be both illuminating and interesting. But the question remained: Take time away from gathering information to break the story? Or leave that to another journalist from another organization?

> My editor told me—and I kind of knew this is what we would do—to just not even think about breaking the story. Pretty much, the idea was that if I write this stellar story that truly provides all the background and decision-making thoughts that went into the benching [quarterback change] then that was what was going to matter to readers. Maybe I'd still break the story, you know? But probably not. And that's what happened. [A prominent football journalist] broke the news, but I like to think my story really gave fans what they wanted. It gave them the why, whereas [the prominent football journalist] just gave them a short tweet with the what. And just tweeting that so and so is happening sometimes makes people more confused. . . . Got to admit, though, it was tough sitting on that information.

As a one-year veteran beat reporter for this digitally native sports journalism website at the time, the beat writer felt they had to constantly squelch urges to behave like a traditional NFL beat writer for a newspaper. "Especially then [when this story broke]," they recollected, "I still considered myself a newbie at The Athletic, and it was hard to turn off, I don't know, my newspaper brain. I worked at newspapers for a long time, you know?" This "newspaper brain," as the beat writer describes it, symbolizes how for more than a decade, they internalized the culture of legacy news, the professional culture that typically transcended individual news organizations and permeated the journalism industry for decades.[1] For this journalist, in this situation, ignoring years of engrained normative routines felt difficult. "Honestly, if this happened a couple months before it did, when I was still really new, I'd probably tweet everything without even thinking about it," the beat writer hypothesized. "In this case, though, I think, I just kind of felt like that's not what they would want me to do." The "they" that the journalist mentions are their bosses, on both the journalism and business sides of The Athletic. "They," according to the beat writer, attempt to retrain journalists in some ways when they begin work at the sports news organization. "It's weird in that it's a balance," said the journalist.

> In the meeting where I was offered a job, it became really clear—and this is the case with so many of us hired away from newspapers to come here—they wanted me because they thought I was good at my job. I was told a few times in one meeting how my work was respected, how I did such a phenomenal job and how [this NFL team's] fans are lucky to have me covering everything. So I'm supposed to keep doing that, but when I got here, they kind of let you know the work will be different.

What the reporter means, and that numerous other Athletic journalists reiterate, is that frequently The Athletic hires journalists due to their prior success covering a team, encourages them to continue doing the same thing, but still establishes seemingly small changes to news production processes, minor alterations that run counter to traditionally recognized journalistic practice. "At [my last job at a newspaper], if we could have broken news before the Adam Schefters or the Jay Glazers of the world, we would have done it, and I would have been hypothetically treated like a hero." The reporter went on to describe how his former employer—a metropolitan newspaper—placed a premium on breaking news and being recognized as first in terms of delivering information to the public. This is why, they say, it felt "odd or counterintuitive" not to post on Twitter immediately after verifying the news of the quarterback change. "Even

before Twitter," they joked, "I would have wrote up a [short] story for
the web. . . . Really, they don't really care about that stuff here." The beat
writer said that at The Athletic, editors and the founders tell journalists that subscribers can get breaking news anywhere—sometimes at The
Athletic—but that is not why sports fans pay a fee to get behind the news
organization's paywall.

Covering this particular story, the beat writer declared, helped them
understand how working at The Athletic would be different. "I'd never
not worked at a newspaper before," they said, "and I knew it would be
different, but I'm not positive I knew how, if that makes sense." For them,
navigating a complex situation that tested their ability to ignore long-held-
sacred news production processes that prioritized breaking news over
telling contextualized and detailed stories truly made them understand
what their new employer expected. "I think I've got it now," they said, "but
it took some getting used to, you know? The Athletic might hire a bunch
of us newspaper [veterans], but we're not a newspaper. We're different."

Founded in January 2016, the digitally native, venture-capital-funded
sports journalism organization The Athletic currently employs more than
four hundred journalists.[2] The company's structure is rather unusual for a
news organization. Since its launch, The Athletic, which began by covering Chicago sports, opened more than forty verticals in cities across the
United States and Canada. For example, The Athletic Boston began in April
2018 with fewer than ten full-time journalists on staff.[3] Besides each local
vertical with journalists covering beats or specific teams in each city or
state, The Athletic also employs writers who cover sports at the national
level; for example, the renowned baseball writer Ken Rosenthal, the Hall
of Fame baseball writer Peter Gammons, and the celebrated professional
football journalists Tim Graham and Mike Sando write about those sports
in general. Inarguably, the main thing separating The Athletic from its
competitors in sports journalism is that all of its content sits behind a
paywall, implicitly communicating the belief of the organization's founders—Adam Hansmann and Alex Mather—that sports fans would pay for
quality.[4] In describing the formation of The Athletic, one of the founders
noted that both he and his cofounder grew up reading newspapers, which
have "as everyone knows, gone through a lot of change, some good, some
bad." He noted that reading the newspaper sports section made him realize
that sports news can bring people together, as long as quality is a salient
goal. "That was the point of view that for us, aligning the incentives, so
to speak, of people creating the content, doing the journalism with the
users' interests in actually consuming quality information, trustworthy

information," he said, noting that combining quality with an excellent user experience is expensive. "To bring those two things together in [the right] way is something that we didn't think was possible without that subscription model." For the founders, the user experience delivered through the website and especially the mobile application needed to be superlative; otherwise, it could catalyze subscription drops. But quality of journalism remains paramount, he said:

> Everyone's incentive here is around quality, because quality is the thing that people will pay for. So it's the, you know, the vision is really premium. "Premium" is a word I don't really like, but it works for the purpose of, like, [describing The Athletic], right? Think about what *Sports Illustrated* once was, the local sports section was, even some of the digital outlets, I should say, like Grantland or the FiveThirtyEight. We wanted to kind of blend some of those different editorial concepts that mix local and national. So this was really just about great storytelling and great journalism, great sports journalism. And that's it, and it's evolved because when we started, we were just in Chicago. And then we reached out and now we're sort of international in scope. It's a global sports page, if you will.

This single-minded focus on quality also comes from the founders' background as employees of Strava, an app and website for endurance athletes. Although many in journalism believed that a strict paywall-supported organization could never work in sports journalism when newspapers, blogs, and even behemoths such as ESPN offered much of their content for free, Mather and Hansmann saw Strava as a model for The Athletic. About Strava, one founder explained that "anybody can download a [free, GPS-supported app]. And if you go for a two-mile jog, there's a way to track that and time that, right?" He further explained, though,

> that the endurance athlete is looking for more. And what Strava gave avid endurance athletes was more. And when Strava gave avid endurance athletes more, they paid. And so, you know, even in a world like media, like journalism, where there's, like, plenty of free, we found at Strava that despite there being lots of free, if you focused on quality, the subscription model could work.

Numerous journalists at The Athletic agree that the one message most communicated to all employees, from the founders and others, involves quality. "People don't tell me what to write about. They trust me for that," said one national writer. They added, "But it's always about thinking about what kind of stories will people pay for? What will make my stuff different than other people covering [my sport]? Where is the quality I'm delivering to subscribers?" The journalists seem to think of quality as synonymous with unique and compelling. When asked to define what quality means to them, beat writers and national journalists overwhelmingly detailed delivering content that others do not, and delivering it in a way that makes people consume something for longer than expected. As one journalist explained, "When we think of today's readership or even public, it's all about a lack of attention span or people wanting to know everything right now." But, they added, "almost everything I've been told is that if you give people a piece of good journalism, no matter how long it is, they'll finish. I would say this country, in sports especially, lacks a glut of good journalism." Athletic employees repeatedly discussed thinking about what separates the work they do from what others on the same beat publish. "I'm always thinking about the competition and not because I want to beat them or something," one beat writer explained, "but I know, because I've been them, that they can't do what I'm allowed to do in terms of in-depth coverage. We lean into that. We're told to lean into that."

Organizational Culture

When beginning the process of initial hiring, the founders believed that trying to institute one cohesive organization culture or hierarchical systematizing operation would not be the way to go. In the ever-growing corporatization of journalism, with chains owning more and more properties, typically owners try to implement a consistent organizational culture throughout their individual newsrooms. Hansmann and Mather systematically disavowed that idea. "For us, like, we really built the first sort of operating model as really like a collection of local kinds of bureaus, if you will," explained one founder. He further explained,

> I think we worked hard and were intentional about preserving a kind of local sovereignty, the autonomy [of each vertical]. What have you [is different] within each of those cities and under each of those sort of respective editors. And so that was the idea, and I think we embraced the idea that what was the Bay Area sports media, or the Bay Area sports fan is different than, say, the Philadelphia sports fan or the Denver sports fan.

When they started the organization, the founders focused on hiring good editors. "We kind of weren't too prescriptive in the beginning," the founder said, "besides to say that if we hired great editors and recruited great people, the culture will sort of coalesce or just form itself." By celebrating the distinctive sports culture that each of the various verticals represented, the founders aimed to create truly local journalism. One beat writer, hired early in The Athletic's life span, noted that the idea of embracing localism in all ways surprised them more than anything. "I knew I was being hired because people in [my city] know my work and trust my work and, because of that, I would bring in an audience to The Athletic," they said, adding, "I thought I would have to adapt to a new corporate brand or culture or what have you. That wasn't the case at all. I was told, 'You're [my city], be [my city].'" A founder added that when The Athletic began "expanding so aggressively," they became far more intentional about communicating this idea to potential employees, to make them understand that they should continue doing what they already were doing, what got them noticed in the first place.

Maintaining local authenticity provided a focus for each individual vertical within The Athletic, but the founders also understood that establishing an organizational identification was paramount not only for recruiting and retaining journalists but also for overall success. To do this, the founders hold relatively regular all-staff meetings virtually. "It's really a way for them to kind of charge us up," said one journalist.

> They're very rah-rah-type meetings, but it's also a reminder of how we're all part of something bigger. One thing [the founders] really like to say in not so many words or differently or whatever is that we might be doing our things, but success comes to us together, if that makes sense.

The founders might not have studied organizational theory before creating their company, but they intuitively understood the importance of creating an organizational identification, a process by which "individuals link themselves to elements in the social scene," or in their organization.[5] Prior to the pandemic in March 2020 and later, when COVID received less attention, The Athletic would host events for its employees at various events specific to certain sports. For example, at the college scouting combine for the National Football League in Indianapolis each year, all the news organization's professional football writers would meet up for a variety of events. "You know, we would go to baseball winter meetings where every baseball writer has to be up there doing their job, and [we'd] actually create summits and, like, week-long sort of programming around those big events," explained one founder. "It also allowed us to get people sort of out of those local markets and into kind of a more of a cross-pollinated environment of people covering the same sport." He went on to clarify,

> We pick those spots where people are organically already kind of congregating and do workshops. I'll go and actually give updates and just

spend quality time there. So you know, that's something that is something unique to our culture beyond just, I think, the day-to-day.

Numerous journalists cited those events as making it implicitly obvious
that they work for a large news organization. "Most of the time, I just
kind of do my thing, only talking to a couple people and really never
seeing most in person at all," said one beat writer. "There are always
social events at [these types of things], but this is the first time I've ever
been to them with all coworkers. It's become like family get-togethers,
really." The founders and other company leaders use these events to
further distill organizational priorities, such as focusing on quality. But
they also believe these events can further a commitment to The Athletic, something implied by numerous journalists. "You forget this thing
is fucking huge," said one journalist. "We have like four dozen people
covering [my sport]. We're massive and when we're all in the same room
that's obvious." Another beat writer mentioned how when they cover a
game, they oftentimes will see their Athletic counterpart covering the
other team and they'll talk, but that it "is quite different than when we
are all together."

Before The Athletic published even one story, the original employees
created a stylebook, an obvious step toward enabling each vertical to produce a consistent type of work. The company also holds weekly calls for
all editors so ideas can be shared, concerns communicated. According
to one founder, "We can overcommunicate," which he said is important
because "we're so spread out to begin with, we're never in one building."
The founder also noted it took time for The Athletic's culture to take shape,
for the dozens of individual organizational cultures to coalesce into one
overall culture that does not infringe on local subcultures. He said that's
why he and the other founder did not hire a head of communications for
years; that person would not have known what brand or culture to communicate, since none had yet materialized. "You must trust the leaders
and journalists you put it place," he said, and an organic culture will follow. "It's tempting for modern or sort of digital publishers to skimp on
things like hiring the best, and [we did the opposite]. You really have to
trust your managers. You empower your managers to demand and manage
performance, to manage output, to manage the flow of information." But,
he added, you need to do it in a way that does not impede a journalist's
ability to "do their thing" and embrace the culture of their location.

Journalist after journalist at The Athletic, most of the time unprompted,
were effusive about the organization's ability to "stay out of the way,"
or make sure that journalists were given perceived complete autonomy.

"Nobody tells me what to do here," joked one journalist. "Maybe they should. But they don't. More sincerely, it's my [team I'm covering]. I know it better than anyone." Prior research illustrates the importance of autonomy in journalism, how it remains at the heart of journalistic authority or, more salient, journalistic professionalism.[6] In short, journalists believe that to do their jobs correctly, they must have authority over their decision-making processes. But recent years have seen the erosion of journalistic autonomy, both in favor of more audience input on the agenda and due to business decisions by nonjournalists aiming to make journalism more economically sound.[7] The problem with this loss of autonomy comes in the form of a negative culture in journalism, whereas organizations that provide journalists with more perceived autonomy tend to have a more positive organizational culture.[8] At The Athletic, journalists feel strongly empowered to embrace their autonomy. As one of the cofounders recalled, the idea to centralize the notion of autonomy within the culture was a conscious decision made very early in the organization's life span. He explained,

> We saw pretty early that there is a relationship between when someone on the staff is, like, "Oh, I've got this idea," and it's more self-directed. And the idea might be obviously really good or not obviously, but we don't know. It's, like, I'll give an example, it's less generic. But I remember in 2016, we're a four-person staff, one city. Scott Powers is our [NHL Chicago] Blackhawks writer. He said, "I want to go to Finland, and I want to go and have a conversation with this player. . . . " And we're, like, well, I mean, and maybe to you, that sounds like a fairly interesting but obvious angle, but, like, the fact that we weren't there telling Scott, like, "Nope, you need to cover, like, the waiver wire," or, "No, you need to write about these games." Like, unlocking that creativity nine times out of ten—or probably actually it is higher than that—[is something that works]. If someone on the staff comes to you and says to you, "I've got this big idea. I've got this weird idea," the fact that they're excited about it means your chances of that story being something that other people get excited about just go up exponentially, even if it's something that's different than what you'd expect.

Although this cofounder might not think that all ideas will work, giving journalists the chance to pursue them will benefit the organization in many ways: First, the journalist will have more attachment to The Athletic because they feel trusted. Second, the journalist's self-directed exuberance will almost always result in better stories than anything assigned. And third, the more the perceived autonomy Athletic journalists have, the better the organization's reputation in the field.

One journalist previously employed by a niche online sports analysis site said that they thought they had had autonomy before, but The Athletic provides something previously unimaginable: the total ability to do their job the way they see fit. When they hire people, the reporter recalled, "They'll tell us, like, 'We want you to be you. That's why we hired you.' And [The Athletic is] almost, you know, in terms of a brand, it's almost a collection of little mini brands," they said, adding that reporters can basically find where they fit because of this autonomy. "I think they made it a priority within the organization to tell us to do what we think is right, and to do what we want, and what we find interesting," said another journalist. A beat writer noted that you can see the organizational philosophy in action if you compare how leadership reacts to stories with very different subscriber metrics. "Every once in a while, I'll write something and I'll be like so proud of this story," they said, "and then only three negative people will read it. And I'll write another story that I know is, like, a C-minus and it'll blow up," but leadership celebrates the good story, not the one with more readership or the one that generates more traffic. "I've never worked somewhere like that. Everywhere I've been, I would have been told to keep doing the C-minus stuff because it's working." The spoken and unspoken trust The Athletic provides to its reporters clearly prompts their affinity for the organization. During the pandemic, The Athletic began incorporating more traditional short pieces of straight news, something it still does, if rarely. One reporter admitted that in the past, if a prior employer had done that, they might feel betrayed. "But [the founders]," the reporter explained, "I trust them to do what's right. They have my back, and I have theirs." When discussing journalistic autonomy, one communication scholar noted that "although in need of reform with respect to implementation, [autonomy] must be protected if journalists are to make a greater contribution to civic empowerment."[9] This normative idea—that journalists with autonomy can use it to contribute to a better society—might seem hyperbolic when discussing a digitally native sports news organization, but the journalists at The Athletic clearly have internalized a similar notion. They believe that the agency granted to them to control their own newsgathering is one of the most important drivers of the organization's success in terms of its subscriber base. Echoing numerous others, one journalist declared, "I'm in the field. I'm doing the dirty work. I know what stories to write. They trust me here. [At my previous employer], people who have no idea what's happening tell you what to write about." They added, "[My previous employer] is hemorrhaging money and subscribers, and we keep going up. Imagine that."

Routines

For the founders and leadership at The Athletic, culture-building exercises are at the forefront, because of one unique attribute of the organization: the lack of newsrooms. Obviously, with more than forty verticals spread out across the United States and Canada, one newsroom could not represent the totality of the organization, but a newsroom for each vertical would be standard for other journalism entities. "On the surface it could make sense," said one reporter. "We would basically have a bureau model. You know, a bunch of bureaus all over the country. That's got to be a waste of money, though." What that journalist and numerous others mean by a "waste of money" is that most reporters covering high-level sports at newspapers, for example, rarely spend time in newsrooms. "When I was at [my former employer, a metropolitan newspaper], I probably went into the office four times a year. You work out of stadiums or at home or a coffee shop, but mostly out of the pressroom at the stadium," explained a beat writer. In traditional journalism, the newsroom is at the center of socialization processes. When new journalists enter a newsroom, they implicitly and explicitly are socialized into both the organization and the overall field of journalism by viewing others who model successful behavior and, in general, consistently seeing how the newsroom operates.[10] Although journalists covering sports, with the exception of high school sports, often spend most of their time outside the newsroom, the existence of an actual, physical newsroom still affects the processes. "A lot of them are getting sold now," said one journalist,

> but [my old newspaper's] building is, kind of, a landmark in [its city]. Everyone knows that's where news is cooked up for serving. When I'd be there, it's when you really feel like you're part of the team. I work for [my old newspaper], you know? There's something to be said for talking, for interacting with people in person. I think that's been proven [during COVID-19]. When you go to a newsroom and look around, you can tell what the big shots will put up with. I can't tell that at [The Athletic] because I don't really see anyone, and I don't see the big shots.

What became clear when Athletic journalists discussed the lack of a newsroom is that although the effects may be minimal, they do exist. Journalists often talked about working out of newsrooms during their sport's off season or having semiregular in-person meetings with editors. According to the journalists spoken with for this chapter, rarely do the journalists within each vertical see each other in person. Some do arrange regular, in-person coffee meetings with editors, but that is exceptional.

The journalist quoted above acknowledged that visiting the newsroom allowed for understanding how "big shots" enforced rules, essentially articulating that newsroom observation could illuminate various normative behaviors at an organization. Without a newsroom, founders and leadership cannot enforce or introduce new norms easily. Organizational norms typically survive through group enforcement, which involves both vocal and silent processes.[11] Therefore, although The Athletic prioritizes each vertical's own local culture in terms of tone or subject of story, it also takes steps to install an organizational identification and overall culture. It would be a far more effective process with newsrooms. On the other hand, as numerous journalists (including one quoted earlier in this chapter), mentioned, the cost of renting real estate in large cities across the United States and beyond would drastically increase operating costs. Thus, although the absence of newsrooms might increase the difficulty of implementing some organizational culture elements, it no doubt makes it easier for The Athletic to hire veteran reporters with established reputations and audiences in each vertical. This presumably makes it far easier to maintain the quality at the heart of the organization's goals.

Without a newsroom and only semiregular meetings, communication between Athletic employees primarily takes place over the business communication platform Slack. As one founder explained, "Slack is sort of the go-to," and journalists cannot go "many minutes without mentioning that Slack is, like, vital. Like, you wouldn't be able to function as a member of our news wing" if not using the platform. He continued, "Slack is a place for communication, and for celebrating wins, for creating feedback loops, for coordinating on big projects and for even communicating at the story level." Essentially, despite not being an active part in news production processes or even, really, direct person-to-person communications with most employees, the cofounder could not understate the importance of Slack to the newsroom and, really, the overall operation. Every journalist interviewed discussed the importance of this platform for work flow and communication. Typically, unless actively reporting a story—and sometimes even then—journalists have various Slack channels open at different times. The Athletic's communication runs on numerous channels that have varied functions: for discussion about larger, company-wide projects; for awards and highlights; for editor-reporter conversations; for story idea threads, and much more. "It's everything," said one journalist about Slack.

> I could go on and on. It's basically the heart of the place. Think about [working] as a journalist in a normal newsroom. You might go from desk to desk, talking to editors and other writers. You might have

conversations about a story you're working on with your editor. You're definitely going to talk about story ideas and brainstorm that type of shit. You're going to have friends that you work with and just shoot the shit with. I'm probably forgetting, like, twenty more different ways people talk in newsrooms. All that happens over Slack here. I might talk to my editor over the phone occasionally, but, really, that's kind of rare. It's about Slack.

Journalists expressed the same sentiment over and over. One noted that at their previous job, even though they rarely set foot in a newsroom, phone calls with editors became the norm, sometimes as many as ten per day. They noted that at The Athletic, "Certainly I'm not getting phone calls every day. My editor and I probably jump on the phone once every couple of weeks or as needed." This change took some getting used to, they said. At first, not having direct, immediate communication about a story felt odd, as if "I was kind of on my own." However, the journalist noted that now, they think of it this way:

> If I need to talk to [my editor], then we talk about a story. You do that. But a lot of it, it's communicating over Slack. [My editor will] check in on what ideas I have and what I'm working on, you know, what timing we can expect with things. All over Slack.

Of course, mediated communication within organizations is nothing new in the twenty-first century. But The Athletic's lack of a newsroom and its unabashed, almost total dependence on Slack definitely differs from most newsrooms. Although the change to this form of communication took many journalists time to get used to, the vast majority now believe it is the optimum medium for newsroom communications. Research partly backs this up, with findings suggesting that "face-to-face communication has several perceived drawbacks compared to other channels: it is less accessible, indicating communication is more difficult to initiate; people feel less conversational control, so they may have difficulty avoiding unpleasant interactions."[12] In the past, when studying mediated communication within journalistic organizations, scholars found that journalists typically preferred a mixture of synchronous communication (for brainstorming and story discussion) and asynchronous communication (for progress updates and assigning tasks).[13] Although many studies reinforce those findings, the journalists at The Athletic would disagree. They perceived asynchronous, mediated communication via Slack as the best for their purposes and preferred it as a means of enabling far more productivity. "When you really get down to it," said one reporter, if I'm spending less time on the phone and moving my schedule around so I can make calls when [my editor and I are both free], then I have more time to do my job. I really think it's advantageous this way. It gives me an advantage over [the competition].

Much earlier research on organizational culture from the late twentieth and early twenty-first centuries suggests that nonmediated interpersonal communication is vital for the development of an organizational identity and, more salient, employee buy-in.[14] However, that may be changing as people become more comfortable with technology. Although the learning curve in adapting to almost uniform, asynchronous communication seemed steep for numerous journalists, they quickly accepted Slack as their principal form of communication. Everyone, from the founders on down to the newsroom and business personnel at The Athletic regards Slack as a mainstay of the company's organizational culture. In fact, Slack is an integral part of virtually every process essential to news production and beyond. According to journalists, Slack also catalyzes more communication than expected. "This might come as a shock or surprise to you," one said, "but I've never talked—even though we never really *talk* talk—to coworkers as much as I do now. It's all Slack, but we constantly talk." Due to their constant, universal connection via a communication platform, employees feel connected in a way that they did not in the past.

Engagement

One important reason that journalists today, across the industry, often feel as if they are losing autonomy is the changing nature of the audience-journalist relationship. Since around the turn of the twenty-first century, the industrywide focus seems to be on giving more and more agenda-setting power to the audience.[15] This shift in power comes in numerous forms, sometimes as engagement exercises truly meant to better the relationships between journalists and communities, especially marginalized groups, but also sometimes in ways perceived more as market-driven, such as comment sections, news analytics, and more. At The Athletic, journalists believe that the organization walks a fine line, valuing the audience and its wants and needs but not infringing on the near-sacred belief in autonomy. The comment sections on Athletic stories are one example. Typically, uncivil, racist, and wholly unproductive text populates comment sections.[16] Although comments originally were conceived, or at least marketed as, a new public sphere, journalists typically deride and often just ignore them.[17] At The Athletic, though, journalists find the comment sections not just a lively place for productive discussion with readers but also a spot to go to for story ideas, for understanding what their audience wants, and for community-building. "Never seen anything like it," said one national journalist. "When I was at [my last employer], they just shut off comments because they were so disgusting. Here it's amazing. I can't tell you how many ideas I get just perusing comments on my stories." One beat writer said comment sections after all their stories are like "neighborhood cookouts." They explained, "It's a bunch of good folks shooting the shit about [the team]. It's awesome. I get in there and mix it up with them, but, more truly, it's made me such a better reporter." No matter how journalists discussed this sentiment, though, it remained clear that they held authority over news decisions. However, the audience clearly had some power in this relationship, even it was not the ultimate authority on anything.

Because The Athletic is a relatively new start-up organization founded by former tech entrepreneurs, it is not surprising that it invested heavily in analytics. "We get all our numbers," explained one beat reporter:

> You know what how many people read, what percentage of subscribers read, how many comments, how many people subscribed to the paywall on that story, which is really, that's the ultimate metric. We've got goals for all sorts of different things, but that's the goal that everyone's kind of paying attention to, which makes sense. It's like any other business in that regard, right? Converting people to paying subscribers. So that's the big one, but I try not to think about it too much.

Many journalists communicated similar sentiments: that the organization relies on and distributes a significant amount of web metrics, but also tells journalists not to change what they do because of them. One journalist noted the implicit insincerity in the way leadership handles metrics but did not seem upset about it. "I'll say, truly, that nobody ever tells me what to do," they said,

> but we do have metrics in our system that we can follow. They tell us how many subscriptions we've gotten, how much engagement we're getting, stuff like that. But when we talk to [leadership] about it, they mostly say, "Don't worry about that, don't worry about that, don't worry about that. [Write] what you think is interesting. What do you think is interesting?" And I think it's really smart because you get that feeling of autonomy, and I do what I find interesting. But you also internalize the metrics. You have to.

Inherent in that comment is a key part of The Athletic's unspoken organizational culture: Leaders absolutely foster and encourage feelings of autonomy, specifically when it comes to the traditional journalist-audience relationship. On the other hand, it remains hard to ignore audience metrics, for example, when you cannot sign into the company's content-management system without seeing them. This is like comments; the company wouldn't make the number of comments a disseminated metric if all it cared about was fostering productive conversations or other normative engagement notions within that section. Despite this, though, journalists overwhelmingly did not feel that The Athletic's treatment of metrics forced them to engage in any market-driven rather than journalism-driven activities, something quite rare in the field of journalism.[18] The idea that The Athletic is, of course, a business and needs to do these sorts of things is prevalent at the organization. As one journalist explained, "When someone starts telling me to do something because some fan or subscriber says so, we'll have a problem. It can't hurt for me to know the numbers, though."

News Production

Without a newsroom and with the majority of interoffice communication happening over various Slack channels, the journalists at The Athletic accomplish news work primarily in public settings such as coffee shops, at home, or more often than not, in the pressrooms of stadiums, arenas, or fields. This inevitably results in much in-person communication with journalists from other organizations covering the same team or sport. Explained one journalist, "Even before I worked [at The Athletic], I always felt like I worked more closely with people you would consider [my competition]." Another journalist echoed this sentiment, noting, "Especially when you're a beat writer, the other traveling beat writers covering the same team, they almost become your family away from your family." This closeness among professionals covering the same teams often results in similar stories due to the constant discussions and similar access that teams grant to beat writers.[19] However, this outcome—many beat reporters publishing similar information—is counterintuitive to The Athletic's business model, which prospers only through providing subscribers with information and particularly storytelling they cannot get freely elsewhere. "I definitely have to think differently," said one reporter who's worked the same beat for more than a decade, for two different newspapers and now for The Athletic:

> You always want to beat everybody, for lack of a better word. You know, I want to get stories first, but now I have to be more intentional about presentation. . . . What I mean by that is I have to use the advantages

that come with working here. I'm not on a strict deadline. I have more [column] inches to play with. I can tell stories differently and that's what I always try to do.

The need to separate themselves from others covering the same teams or sports or geographic areas also extends to story selection, especially during and after the pandemic. During the beginning of COVID-19, when sports shut down, the news organization found itself in a predicament: Subscribers paid for content, but there were no sports to write about or produce content about. Journalists at The Athletic decided to create a Slack channel called "Let's Get Weird," dedicated to brainstorming story ideas that, in the past, would never have been necessary. One journalist recalled that "everybody, whenever they just had a weird-ass idea that was not even really that close to sports, posted in [the Let's Get Weird channel]. And really great pieces came out of that." The need for stories also encouraged journalists to think way outside the box, conjuring up ideas that arguably sit on the boundary of what is and what is not sports journalism. "I've worked hard to not compromise [on quality] during the quarantine, and I just needed to figure out how to do that at first," said one journalist. "Really, what I've learned, and I think a lot of us have, is that a good story is a good story and people come to The Athletic for good stories, no matter how weird they are." Journalists interviewed more than a year after the beginning of the pandemic, when fans returned to sporting events and times became somewhat more normal, noted that while the need to "get weird" might not be so pressing, The Athletic reporters learned a lot from having to brainstorm stories. As one journalist explained,

> Hopefully the worst is behind us, and we never have to go through something like this again, both as a company, but, I would say mostly, as a society. With that said, I think we learned a shitload about what makes us different, what makes us different during COVID. We're not bound by any 1995 idea of what sports news is. I don't have to file two stories a day. Our subscribers want good stories about sports and the people involved in sports. I'm always covering [my team], obviously, but now I know to be looking for any kind of story around [my team] and not necessarily front and center about them. People will read it if I tell it well. I think we all think like this now.

One key final element to news production at The Athletic comes in the form of story generation. Some content ideas happen due to collaboration across verticals. The majority of stories do not begin with an editor, but rather with individual journalists. "Me, [I've] never been anywhere where my ideas make the page more," remarked one beat writer. Another said that

> I am the coverage [of my team]. Almost anything you read on the site
> about [my team], that was me: I came up with the idea, did the report-
> ing and filed the story. [My editor] had very little to do with it unless I
> wanted [their] thoughts.

Over and over, journalists noted how a large part of their jobs revolved
around story selection. Many recalled that when they previously had
worked at newspapers, there was almost an unspoken schedule that said,
for example, for football, on Monday they would publish a game story and
an injury update, on Tuesday a story from press conferences, and so on.
"I didn't have to think much," said a journalist. But the need to provide
"value" to subscribers, as one of the founders called it, necessitates a need
to be different. "I still do a lot of the things I always did," explained one
beat writer, "but I do it in a different way. And I have to do a lot of different
things because I'm not [a journalist at a newspaper] anymore." The one
caveat in this way of thinking came from their national writers, the prominent names brought over from other national outlets. Those journalists
often remarked that they were recruited to The Athletic because they did
something well and had a kind of brand within the industry. "I'll give you
an example," said one well-known columnist. "When I was at [nationally
known website], my most read thing each year was my [prominent feature
article]. I'm here because of that, so of course I'm going to do [that]." So
although The Athletic hired beat writers because of their past work, those
beat writers needed to adapt their news production to an organization that
sits behind a paywall and relies on subscribers, whereas national reporters
continue doing the very same things that made them prominent originally.

One of the most important ways that The Athletic's news production
processes differ from those at many other sports news organizations, specifically legacy media, is time. For example, one historic mainstay within
sports journalism practice is the production of the same-day game story,
a recap or summary of a game that happened that day, written for the
web that night or for the paper the next morning.[20] Although The Athletic began incorporating more traditional, event-focused coverage over
time, the amount it publishes pales in comparison to the amount at most
sports news organizations. Journalists at The Athletic typically enjoy the
freedom to produce stories that are more analytical and less summariz-
ing. "That's definitely what separates us," said one beat writer. "While
everyone else is off hurrying to finish a story by deadline, I can try to get
more quotes or, really, think about what I want to say. It makes my stuff
less cookie-cutter, I think." Most subscribers, journalists say, do not rush
to The Athletic's website or open its app immediately after a game for a

summary of what they just watched. "That's what Twitter's for," laughed one beat writer. Instead, journalists believe that subscribers come to the site or open the app for intelligent commentary and analysis on the game, not for the summaries that most other beat writers are forced to produce on deadline.

Journalists at The Athletic, as so many noted over and over, are not beholden to traditional deadlines or traditional stories, so they believe they can concentrate on doing their best work, as opposed to just cranking out, as one journalist called it, "carbon-copy, petrified shit that everyone does, including myself before." Another beat writer explained,

> It's not 1982 anymore, you know? People can get a summary of a game they missed from almost anywhere. People can see clips of press conferences themselves. They don't need me taking a couple lines here and there and regurgitating. I do that sometimes, of course, but I'm talking about as a rule. Anyway, people can also just watch games on their phones; they don't need a TV and a couch. My point is there is very little value in that old type of bare-bones, kind of boring summation journalism anymore. People want real analysis, something they can't get on their own.

Many Athletic scribes also noted that more time is afforded to them not due only to the business model of the organization and the lack of a daily newspaper or newscast but also because of the sheer size of the journalistic staff at the organization. For example, numerous participants noted that at prior jobs, where sports department staff did not amount to even 10 percent of The Athletic's staff, they frequently needed to publish numerous stories a day because the sports section of the newspaper or website needed content. Even at large metropolitan newspapers, a sports section might feature the work of five or six journalists on a given day, said one reporter. "That's not at all what happens here." Interviewees noted that the size of The Athletic's staff meant reporters could publish content when it was ready, not necessarily when it was needed. "Just because we're so huge," they said, "we still have plenty of stories every day. It gives me time to make my stuff the best it can be." Journalists consistently reiterated the idea that although content remained vitally important to the organization's economic outlook, staff size made it possible not to rush journalism. "The mission of this place isn't to produce crap just to produce crap. It's about quality, long-form work. And pandemic or not, we're still able to do that because, just like before, we have enough people that we don't have to sweat if stories are ready on any given day." Staff size is hugely important for producing news on a daily basis. Journalists admitted that of course they still needed to produce content about each and every game on a given schedule, but the extra time they had helped them produce "much better" content. More salient, numerous journalists talked about how that extra time, "even if it's just a couple hours" as described by one beat writer, helped them craft a far more readable story. "When you're on autopilot and just writing a [game] recap," explained one beat writer,

> it's like paint by numbers. The piece can be informative, but it's boring. When you do what I do now, with more time to use, I can really think about the story and how to tell it. I can have more important details. I can really think about quotes, angles, framing, character, really all the things you don't have time for on a tight deadline.

Due to technological innovations and disruptions, the field of journalism, as an industry, lacks creativity, something journalists often lament.[21] The journalists at The Athletic, though, contend that creativity can flourish if they are given the time to produce better stories, something they argue is a vital byproduct of the organization's paywall-fueled market model.

Due to its unique structure of dozens of separate verticals, dozens of national writers, and numerous niche reporters such as data journalists, The Athletic provides its journalists with a framework for flourishing collaborations. Discussing the company's need for unique journalism that provides value, specifically during the pandemic but really for all times, one reporter said, "You need something different. And with limited access, everyone's writing the same stuff. We have such a huge and varied company, though, that there is an overwhelming opportunity for partnering on stories." For example, one reporter discussed writing a story about COVID-19 testing protocols for the sport they covered. Instead of concentrating on that sport, they reached out to others in the organization covering other sports and came up with a comprehensive piece about all sports. "That's not necessarily something I couldn't have done [at my old job]," said the journalist, "but it was so much easier here." Numerous reporters discussed taking advantage of both the time provided and the numerous staff to produce stories that were simply not possible almost anywhere else. One data journalist, comparing The Athletic with their old job at a digitally native site, said, "It's kind of cool. Usually, I just find trends and write about them myself, but now I'm helping others with stories." Another data journalist mentioned that reporters keep reaching out with potential ideas. "And because I come from a certain perspective," they said, "a collaboration will start with a question. . . . And then I'll look it up and I'll say, 'Whoa, you know, there's something kind of interesting here; let's broaden this out.'" Over and over reporters discussed reaching out to colleagues for help with story ideas. One beat writer, discussing their inability to get a source on the phone, said, "Who else can just text [a very prominent national writer] to help get a source?" They added, "I was honestly struggling to iron out the piece and within maybe ten minutes, I had [the source] on the phone. That wouldn't have happened if it wasn't for [prominent writer]." This type of collaboration came up over and over again. The ability to utilize the organization's large stable of journalists to help get a source on record, to help flesh out a story, to help with news work would not be possible in a typical editor-reporter relationship. "At my last job [at a newspaper], I was a beat writer covering [the same team I do now for The Athletic]," a reporter recalled:

> But it was just me covering [the team]. We had [a big-name columnist] who used to cover the team, so they were helpful sometimes. But here I have a . . . virtual Rolodex of people covering [the same sport] that I can call on for help.

Numerous reporters recounted how, before arriving at The Athletic, they often would stop working on certain stories because of dead ends in the reporting process, sources not coming through, or simply lack of verification. At The Athletic, that still happens, but not so frequently because of collaboration.

The other, more common collaborations that happen at The Athletic, also due primarily to its large staff size, are overtly collaborative stories. "We do more roundups now than we used to," said one reporter. Roundups are stories that examine a professional league as a whole. For example, during any given week during the National Basketball Association season, The Athletic might publish a story that highlights a particular player on each team whose performance is not garnering enough perceived attention. For a roundup, a beat writer for each team will identify a player and write a relatively short blurb explaining the choice. That blurb will be collected with all the other blurbs for a larger, more macro look at the entire league. "I guess it's one way for us to do national reporting" without a national reporter, explained a beat writer. These types of stories "are really similar to what ESPN does with its football coverage, but we do it with all sports," said one reporter. Another noted the benefit to these types of stories:

> Sports fandom is provincial, if you get what I mean. People are fans of teams, not really leagues. It might be different, sort of, with football because of the popularity of fantasy and, now more lately, gambling, but people like their teams and not other teams. The thing is though that their teams play [within] a larger circle, the league, and they play other

teams, obviously. So the types of stories that take work from all of us help people learn about the entire sport they love.

Journalists also noted the overall potential, or at least perceived, monetary benefit of doing these types of stories: they take very little time to produce but are long, easy to read, and "jam-packed with info" that subscribers cannot get from many other organizations. One editor, talking about collaboration in general, made the overall benefit of the trend clear. "When we started, or at least the early days when I got here," they said, "we didn't do it much. But it's silly not to leverage our heft. We have resources, people included, that nobody else ultimately does. We should use them." Therefore, the benefits of collaboration come in many forms, both definitive and perceived. Reporters can collaborate on stories in ways not possible at other places, because coverage topics overlap in ways not evident at, for example, cash-strapped legacy media. The sheer size of the staff allows for collaboration in the form of help in a variety of different manners. Finally, according to the company's metrics, less organic collaboration can lead to stories that subscribers read but are easy to produce in terms of time for individual reporters.

Epilogue: After The Sale

As noted in the introduction, in January 2022, the *New York Times* announced its intention of purchasing The Athletic for $550 million in cash with the explicitly stated plan of allowing it to continue operating as an autonomous news organization, wholly separate "from The Times's newsroom and its sports section."[22] At first, Athletic journalists felt guardedly excited about joining arguably the most prestigious news organization in the United States, if not the world, but they quickly noticed a lack of transparency from the *New York Times* leadership, a lack of communication that left Athletic employees doubting the *Times*'s stated intention of letting The Athletic operate as it had.[23] In reality, within months, the *Times* altered the travel budgets and travel approval processes for Athletic journalists—diminishing their perceived autonomy over their jobs—and enforced rules about utilizing social media, policies aimed at making sure Athletic journalists do not discuss anything political on social media platforms.[24] One journalist explained how changes were implemented but not communicated. They said that during companywide meetings, many questions were asked of new management, but

> they knew [the answers] but wouldn't tell us. I get it to a point, but it was like I was no longer working for The Athletic. Everything changes.

Nothing was the same. The way this was handled was not like where I'd been working for [years].

This quote reflects the newsroom's perception that transparency and clear communication no longer existed within the organization. Regardless of whether Athletic journalists agreed with company leaders, these elements were entrenched in the culture. Once they were removed, journalists felt as if The Athletic was no longer the place where they had worked before the purchase.

Conclusion

Prior to its sale, as a for-profit, venture-capital-funded, digitally native sports news organization, The Athletic relied on its ability to increase subscribers for its long-term viability. The organization boasts more than 1 million subscribers and generates more than $77 million in revenue, but due to a multitude of investments over the years (in technology, infrastructure, etc.), The Athletic lost roughly $95 million between 2019 and 2020.[25] However, the organization would have become completely profitable if it had doubled its revenue, which would happen if it doubled its subscriber base.[26] It seems, though, that The Athletic's founders, intentionally or not, internalized the current economic crisis enveloping the journalistic field and doubled down on valuing quality journalism. Perhaps due to their background in mobile applications rather than journalism, the founders zagged when most other journalism organizations relying on subscriptions zigged; instead of trying any of the many market-driven approaches to making journalism that have been popular since roughly the 1980s, they prioritized the opposite approach by continuing to embrace journalistic autonomy.[27] The founders also might have taken this stance because they never truly desired profitability but rather the sale of the company, which eventually did occur. The decision to embrace autonomy generated an organizational culture and identification such that journalists perceived a symbiotic relationship with the founders and the business side of The Athletic; they felt trusted and appreciated and encouraged to do their jobs in the way they believed optimal. Moreover, this positive culture manifested itself late in the pandemic, when The Athletic made minor changes to its content vision, deciding to start producing some traditional journalism and breaking news. In the past, as scholarship illustrates, making such a change to newsroom processes could lead to overwhelming complaints if not near mutiny.[28] However, at The Athletic, because of the goodwill built up through its embrace of autonomy, journalists believed the company's changes must necessarily be positive. Since the company was not publicly traded, and since they did not have to show immediate positive economic metrics, the founders believed they could take the time to create a positive organizational culture that would nurture quality journalism.

However, what happened after the news organization's purchase by the *Times* indicates the importance of cultivating a positive organizational culture at all times. The founders of The Athletic might have acted in ways that strengthened the quality of the journalism and the perceived autonomy of the journalists, primarily because all along, their goal was not to make The Athletic profitable but to make it attractive to potential buyers. Once the *Times* expressed interest, the founders may have assumed, incorrectly, that the *Times*'s positive reputation throughout journalism would engender goodwill from the Athletic journalists. This situation illustrates the need always to think about goal alignment. For a merger such as this to be a success, the parties involved need to understand how any planned change aligns with historical organizational goals.[29] The *Times*, itself reporting by proxy at The Athletic, either erroneously believed that infringing on journalistic autonomy would not matter or simply did not care that Athletic journalists, through years of public expression, regarded the perceived autonomy granted by the organization as tantamount to their professional identity.[30] For any organizational change to succeed, for any organization to navigate a disruption, nonleaders must feel that their voices are heard and that their opinions matter.[31] Over and over, the *New York Times*'s lack of transparency negatively affected the journalists' perceptions of their new employer. All of this could have been avoided through simple measures that at least would have made the Athletic journalists feel valued as they had been in the past. In this case, several Athletic journalists left the organization after the merger, one saying, "It wasn't the same Athletic anymore, and I did not want to be at the new one." That quote is incredibly powerful, denoting a perception of drastic change, despite evidence of only slight actual change. It demonstrates the importance of leadership and transparent communication, something that the Athletic journalists felt had evaporated after the merger.

Although the current Athletic operates in a different manner than the venture-capital-funded version examined in this chapter, the venture-capital-funded model is instructive for future research. With venture-capital-funded newsrooms becoming more and more prevalent across the journalism ecosystem, and with The Athletic's successful return on investment more than likely providing an impetus for more venture-capital investors making funds available for journalism, the way The Athletic operated before the merger could be informative. First, the organization's overwhelming embrace of journalistic autonomy illustrates how much journalists value it, how it makes for a positive work experience, and how it can lead to a symbiotic trust between the editorial and business sides of a news organization, something relatively rare in today's journalism industry. Second, a top-down culture that makes everyone perceive both individual agency and a clear organizational mission created a transparent, positive organizational culture in the newsroom, where journalists felt that leadership both respected and valued them.

6

THE *DENVER POST*
The Hedge-Fund-Owned Newspaper

During the holiday season in 2021, Colorado faced some tragic news across the state's Front Range, comprising both the Denver and Boulder metropolitan areas with their large populations. Just after Christmas, a shooter killed five and wounded others in a spree that hit both the city of Denver and its suburbs. "It was horrible," said one *Denver Post* reporter who did not cover the story. "The mood in the newsroom was really bad. Some of us had just come back from Christmas and then this happens." The newsroom came together to cover the shootings in a manner befitting a large metropolitan daily. "It was this crazy huge, breaking news thing where we covered the breaking news, and then we covered, you know, there were multiple victims' stories, there was the shooter's story, and here was the police response story," explained another reporter. Journalists at the paper estimated that across the staff of the paper, more than a dozen stories about the horrific incident ran in print and online. An editor explained, "It was one of those stories that we, at the time, felt like needed to be blanket covered. And I would put that breaking news coverage up against anything we've done recently." The paper tackled the coverage with a minimal staff, since it was the week between Christmas and New Year's, a popular time for vacations. "So that happened at the beginning of the week," explained a journalist, "and then at the end of the week, the Marshall Fire happened."

The Marshall Fire was a significant wildfire that began on December 30 in towns surrounding Boulder. Besides killing two people, the fire became the most destructive in the history of the state in terms of the economic impact of the damage. "We're talking about a wildfire in the middle of the winter, a wildfire that happened in sleepy suburbs," explained one reporter. "First, it's like, 'How is this even happening?' Then, you're like, 'Well, here's another huge story.' In retrospect, you know, minus sports championships, we're talking about maybe the story of the decade." Once again, an already small newsroom had to unite to tell a hugely significant, traumatic story in a way that resonated with readers. "I mean it was one of those weeks where you're like, 'I don't even know how we did that. I don't remember. I don't remember certain parts of it," explained one reporter. Another journalist recalled the newsroom "working insanely hard to do the shooting" but having to tamp down coverage because, "Wait, Boulder is on fire? What?" With essentially the same small staff covering both events, the job of covering Colorado became even more difficult for the journalists involved. "It's like deeply traumatic work that happened in a span of seven days," remembered one reporter, adding, "If our newsroom wasn't as understaffed and we had had more people to disperse, that would have been nice."

While dealing with many of the same economic disruptions faced by all media in the twenty-first century, but particularly legacy media funded primarily by advertising revenue, the *Denver Post*'s journalistic staff—once close to three hundred—dipped to around seventy by the end of 2021, when both the mass the shooting and the Marshall Fire occurred.[1] Owned by the notorious—in the journalistic world—hedge fund company Alden Global Capital, a company once called a "hedge fund vampire" by *Vanity Fair* and "journalism's biggest bogeyman" by *Mother Jones*, the morale inside the *Post*'s newsroom is not nearly so positive as it was prior to the beginning of the new century.[2] However, during this tumultuous time, when a small group of journalists extensively blanket-covered two traumatic events, the camaraderie in the newsroom became palpable. "When you think about most of the people in this newsroom," said one editor, "many of us have been together for at least a few years. We've been through a lot together and, I think, that week demonstrated how much we rely on each other to get through hard times." Another journalist echoed those thoughts, explaining, "I would say we're each other's therapists in a way. It's hard working through horrible events, but also living through a perpetual state of maybe losing our jobs. It brings us together, deeply."

Organizational Culture

A feeling of necessary unity permeates the *Denver Post* newsroom. This does not mean that everyone gets along or that everyone is on the same page. As is common in Alden-owned newsrooms, the overwhelming pervasiveness of job precarity brings everyone close together. As illustrated in the opening anecdote, *Post* journalists rely on each other not just to get work done but also for the emotional support that is needed to continue working for a company that, as one journalist put it, "could[n't] give a shit if I die tomorrow, or could give a shit if I can provide for my family." The unity in the *Post* newsroom arises from a general feeling that everyone must come together to produce the highest quality journalism, regardless of whether or not Alden cares about the quality of journalism.

Founded in the last decade of the nineteenth century, the *Denver Post* began life as a politically minded newspaper run by supporters of the twenty-second and twenty-fourth president of the United States, Grover Cleveland. Like many political newspapers of the time, the *Post* professionalized and become a commercially driven general newspaper during the early twentieth century.[3] During the middle of the twentieth century, the *Post* began to enjoy a reputation as one of the finest metropolitan newspapers in the country; the newsroom took home nine Pulitzer Prizes between 1964 and 2013, including an impressive run of four years in a row (2010–13). "It was absolutely a destination newspaper in those days," said one journalist who spent decades at the *Post*, leaving only in the 2020s. "The newspaper had a reputation as a place you worked your way up to, and then retired from because you didn't need to go anywhere better, since that was basically only the [*New York*] *Times* or something like that." According to staffers, that all changed in the early 2010s, right around the time Alden Global Capital took over in 2011. Describing the modus operandi of Alden, *The Atlantic* wrote in 2021,

> What threatens local newspapers now is not just digital disruption or abstract market forces. They're being targeted by investors who have figured out how to get rich by strip-mining local-news outfits. The model is simple: Gut the staff, sell the real estate, jack up subscription prices, and wring as much cash as possible out of the enterprise until eventually enough readers cancel their subscriptions that the paper folds, or is reduced to a desiccated husk of its former self.[4]

This model is essentially exactly what happened to the *Post*. When describing how Alden dealt with any problem that arose in the entire news organization, a journalist at a different Alden paper recalled that the "answer was always cut, because you don't have to spend money to do that. They had this brutal phrase they called rightsizing. But we never seemed to get to the right size."[5] The belief that Alden just eviscerates the newspapers it buys is widespread. Nieman Lab wrote that Alden is "now known far and wide as the news industry's ever-more-engorged leech, a cost-cutting omnivore that makes every newsroom it touches worse, King Midas in

reverse."[6] Many people outside of journalism did not have a true understanding of Alden's history as a destroyer of quality journalism until the
Denver Rebellion, a series of editorials led by the former *Post* editorial editor Chuck Plunkett that explicitly criticized Alden.[7] *Vanity Fair* noted that

> Alden didn't really become a synonym for evil until 2018, when the
> *Denver Post* made national headlines for openly revolting against its
> hedge fund overlord. Prompted by yet another painful downsizing in the
> nine-time Pulitzer Prize-winning *Post*'s newsroom, which had already
> dwindled to under a hundred journalists, the fierce but futile uprising
> brought journalists out of their offices and into the streets. The ensu-
> ing publicity threw Alden's draconian playbook into sharp relief: buy
> distressed newspapers on the cheap, cut the shit out of them, and reap
> the profits that can still be made from print advertising.[8]

Of course, not only the *Post* faced these dire consequences. Although
it is arguable that Alden deservedly owns the worst reputation of any
owner in American journalism, in some ways the overwhelming success
of journalism in the twentieth century was the direct cause of the ills that
many legacy media newsrooms currently face. By the early 1980s, the business of journalism was booming, so much so that its profit margins across
the industry exceeded those of almost every other industry. Newspapers,
especially, became attractive to many corporations, which began buying
newspaper properties across the country; many of these newspapers had
been family owned for roughly a century. As described by the late journalist and media critic Professor Ben Bagdikian, the result was a "majority
of Americans with artificially narrowed choices."[9] Corporations started
buying up legacy media, instituting corporate policies, making news stories look similar no matter where they were happening and, of course,
prioritizing the economic bottom line over quality journalism.[10] By the
late 1980s, the journalism industry first started experiencing slower profit
growth. Many corporate owners began experimenting with what many
scholars called "market-driven journalism," or the type of work that places
a premium on audience size and not necessarily news quality, that "values
the attention of the wealthy and young over the poor and old because news
selection must satisfy advertisers' preferences."[11] In many ways, an owner
such as Alden buying a legacy newspaper such as the *Denver Post* could be
considered easily predictable: as profit margins decreased, money-hungry
companies would do whatever they could to squeeze every last dollar out
of newspapers.

Gareth Morgan explained that organizations with a lack of strong,
present leadership and a workforce characterized by "group illusions

and perceptions that have a self-sealing quality," or groupthink, could be described as having a culture of a "psychic prison."[12] This is not necessarily a negative thing but rather explains how, whatever the situation, overwhelmingly pervasive ideas about an organization can result in groupthink; the group never seriously questions or challenges its beliefs or assumptions about what is happening. At the *Post*, the idea of the organization as a psychic prison is obvious; an immense and formidable belief persists that Alden is horrible, negatively affects the journalism done, makes working at the *Post* traumatic in some way, and generally does not care about the people or product of the *Post*. One reporter said,

> At first when I got here, I thought it was a good job. I mean, it was better resourced than my last paper. But then I started talking to people [here], and I realized just how bad Alden was and how what they were doing affected me.

Inherent in that recollection is the idea that although working at the *Post* might have negative aspects, this reporter did not immediately notice most of them until, after speaking to other journalists, they realized the overwhelming view that pervades the newsroom. The principal way these views manifest themselves within the organization is through the precarity that looms over everyone. One editor explained, "It really is like a million cuts over time. It contributes to burnout. If we had, you know, ten more reporters, would I feel as exhausted as I do every day? Probably not." They added, "I'm used to it. I came into the journalism industry at a time when it was already bad, so I don't have like a baseline to be like, 'Oh, remember when things were great?'" Another, more senior, journalist recalled, "The paper got smaller while our staff also got smaller. So, you know, the paper got smaller [in two ways], literally" through layoffs and the shrinking print product. Throughout the newsroom, there is a feeling of, as one reporter called it, "dread—dread that this could be the day the next cut comes and we're out on our ass."

Although groupthink pervades the newsroom due to the effects of Alden's ownership, that ownership also contributes to the camaraderie evident across the paper. Alden's financial decisions have a clear effect on the staffers, but the owners make no decisions about news production. This gives the newsroom a feeling of autonomy and thus the us-versus-them attitude. One editor explained that "on a day-to-day basis, it's not like I ever hear from Alden, and neither does my boss, and neither does their boss. It's not like they are involved in our coverage in any way." Another journalist said about Alden, "They really, you know, couldn't give less of a shit about what we're covering or our journalism or anything like that.

They're not interested in the news." Beyond the absolute lack of interference from Alden in journalistic decisions, the other way the owner's
absenteeism—and ownership priorities—contributes to the culture comes
through the decision to leave the *Post*'s historic downtown building for a
new newsroom outside the city in early 2018. "If the owners were here,"
said one journalist, "there is no fucking way we would have moved to
where we are now." Another staffer described the move as bad not only
for company morale but also for social capital in the city of Denver. They
explained,

> I think being downtown in the heart of Denver, you feel [like it implies]
> importance. Like being able to go out and just look at the capitol building
> and be able to just look at the rallies that were happening downtown and
> look at the stuff, being able to cover something downtown and then just
> immediately be in the newsroom. And so that was there and it just like
> it felt like you're in a prominent place in the city. Like that's the *Denver
> Post*. That's where I work. Like it's cool, right? I work downtown at the
> *Denver Post* building that's across from the capitol. When I first started
> working, it's like that's cool. Then being moved out to the [new location]
> is just so far removed. But then also it's just gross. It's just not like if the
> [location] was somewhere else in Denver, maybe it wouldn't have been
> so bad. But it just smells awful. They're like sticking you in this place
> with literally zero windows and that really affected me as a person. I
> just need light to function. So, it's like being in a casino for, you know,
> nine hours a day. It just messes with your brain.

After the move, many journalists started going to the newsroom less often,
which clearly affects the culture of the place. The new location, nowhere
near the center of the city, was one more thing that brought the journalists
closer in shared hatred of the owners, but also gave them a clear, focused
mindset of doing quality work "just to spite [Alden]."

"The *Denver Post* is known for just being really supportive and friendly
within its reporter ranks. And I love that," said one reporter. "My best
friends work there and like I love my coworkers. . . . It's just been super
helpful, I think, to have that kind of collegiality." An editor with many years
at the *Post* explained that there is almost a feeling of "survivorhood" in the
newsroom, as those remaining feel connected by the fact they somehow
have made it through so many layoffs unscathed. "The people who stayed,
the people who remained, you know, stayed there because they had a really
strong passion to do good work," they said.

> There was a point there where that worked really good for us. You know,
> the four straight years of Pulitzers. You see that sort of drive and that

sort of passion for the work that we were doing during that period where we still had enough staff to kind of break off to do important projects. [There are still] important projects now, but it feels like all of a sudden [you look at the] paper and it'll be, you know, four staff-written stories in the whole edition. And that's where you can see the trade-offs that they've had to make in order to do some of those bigger, more important projects.

The other manner that this "psychic prison" organizational culture manifests itself is through the notion, rampant throughout the newsroom, that everyone is doing their job without even close to the resources necessary to do it well. According to staffers, despite this predicament, the newsroom comes together to overcome the odds and produce good work, primarily because the journalists see their work as a calling, rather than a job. As one reporter explained, "There is no one else who would be in this job. There is no sane person who would do this for the pay, the hours, for the mental anguish, for the abuse that you get from readers and everybody." They added that you cannot work at the *Post*

> unless it is [part of your] core. I also understand that people use the phrase, like, "Oh, it's a calling as a way to take advantage of you. People know that they can just keep piling on and keep not [providing] resources and all of these things and that you're just so dedicated to the cause." And I don't think it's the only job like that. I know that there are a bunch of other jobs like that, but [this is] one of those jobs.

One longtime journalist noted the change in work climate from when they started at the paper to when Alden took over. "You could basically work a forty-five-hour week and feel like you were doing your job really well, and get recharged and come back ready to go," they recalled from the time before Alden.

> And, you know, you could be taking care of yourself and taking care of your family and having the kind of work-life balance that I would think a reasonable person would want you to have. You would think, 'Yeah, you know, I could go try to work at the *Washington Post* or the *New York Times*, but I would have to lose what I have here because I work about forty-five hours a week, and I do have time where I go home and it's my time. Whereas after Alden, it just seemed like we were all working all the time. It was almost impossible to get any time away and even on your vacation, you felt guilty all the time and you'd be fielding messages at times and stuff like that. Anyway, once it got down to a hundred [journalists in the newsroom], we felt like we were just barely keeping our chins above water. . . . So when they said that they were going to

cut another 30 percent and we were going to down to seventy or fewer, we just thought that that was the end of the paper [even if it wasn't and we clearly survived].

Leadership

Inside the *Post* newsroom, there is a disconnect among journalists on where leadership sits within the organization. Organizational scholars consider leadership one of the most vital influences on organizational culture, regardless of what theory they apply. This disconnect creates a noteworthy dynamic within the *Post*.[13] Some journalists point to the absentee owner, Alden, as the leader of the organization; others believe that the paper's editor, Lee Ann Colacioppo, is the clear leader of the newsroom. Colacioppo became the first female editor in chief of the newspaper in 2016. The faction of journalists who believe Alden should be considered the organizational leader clearly have significant respect for Colacioppo and all she must navigate in her position, but they believe her hands are completely tied by ownership. "Lee Ann is a great journalist, and she is a mentor here. She's a mentor for young women journalists in particular, but a mentor for everyone, really," explained one editor.

> But let's be serious for a second. If deciding what goes in the paper is what our leader does, she's that. But I don't think that's true. A leader makes essential and important decisions across a paper. My last editor [at my prior employer] did that. Lee Ann cannot do that. She plays in a sandbox that is constantly getting smaller and smaller, which limits her ability to decide much of anything beyond what stories we cover.

A reporter echoed those thoughts, agreeing that everyone at the *Post*, not just Colacioppo, is boxed in because of Alden's seemingly random economic decisions. "We'll have a good period where subscribers go up and that means, I assume, revenue goes up, or we can have a bad month or two. It doesn't matter. A layoff or budget cut could come." They added that the feeling that things could change at any moment "really is the only leadership we have. We know we need to do the best we can [right then] because tomorrow we might have to recalibrate our best. Lee Ann can't help that." The people in the newsroom who follow this line of thinking overwhelmingly appreciate the autonomy over news production that Alden provides—"It's the fucking least they can do, right?" joked one reporter—but they believe that the economic decisions that Alden consistently makes and then forces on the newsroom are the main choices affecting journalists. "Some people will say, and I agree, that I have control over what I cover," said one reporter, "but I only have that control inso-much as I have the resources, whatever those may be, to do the job I want to do. Alden decides that."

Despite Colacioppo's inability to affect Alden's decision making, many in the newsroom see her as the clear leader of the organization. One journal-ist, noting the absenteeism of Alden, wondered how anyone could think otherwise. "She's the one here. Every day, she's here. Lee Ann is, in every sense of the word, our leader. She makes every decision that affects our work." An editor said likewise, noting that

> Lee Ann has somehow survived for [several] years as the top dog. That takes leadership. We've been through a lot on her watch and yet, some-how, I think we're still a collaborative, positive work environment. That's a testament to her ability to run this thing well.

Many at the *Post* believe that Colacioppo puts the newsroom in the best position to succeed. One reporter said, "While I'm not in those conversa-tions, every time we face a hiccup, it seems like she makes important deci-sions that provide us a with way forward, and we continue doing pretty well." One journalist recalled the Denver Rebellion as a clear example of Colacioppo's leadership and "calming effect" on the newsroom:

> You remember. I mean, we're talking about a bunch of people who didn't tell Lee Ann what they were going to do, publishing this whole section that is basically a "fuck you" to ownership. This is all happening as layoffs are looming. Some people quit. Some people didn't get fired, but basically couldn't have come back to work, you know? And here's Lee Ann, really acting as a go-between, protecting us from Alden and figuring out how we can all continue really hating our owner with a passion while still doing an awesome job despite Alden.

Numerous journalists remembered the Rebellion as a standard of exem-plary leadership:

> She got us through that. She got us through what came before and what's come since. I think we're doing the best work we've done in the last five years, right now. That's a testament to hiring decisions and, also, decid-ing what we should be doing when.

In general, the presence—or lack thereof—of Alden, which seemingly makes decisions based only on cutting resources from the newsroom on a regular basis, places the *Post* newsroom as an organization in an awkward spot. Although it would make sense for all to consider Cola-cioppo the unequivocal leader of the organization, the need to model an us-versus-them mentality that pits the newsroom against its "leader" in Alden means that many cannot consider Colacioppo as separate from the rank and file of the organization. "She's one of us," explained one journalist. "It's not like she can be spared from what [Alden] does to us. We're all in the same big old boat, a boat that's springing leaks that we're all frantically trying to patch day in and day out." What's clear is that regardless of who should be considered the leader of the *Post*—Colacioppo or Alden—there are clear reasons that it is difficult for the entirety of the newsroom to agree. This makes it difficult for any overall culture to diffuse throughout the organization, resulting in the psychic prison described earlier, an organization imbued with groupthink without a clear, focused charge in terms of its mission as a news organization in the 2020s.

Socialization

The *Denver Post* does not have a standard protocol for socializing new members into the organization. Depending on the supervising editor of a new employee, the process can vary wildly. Most editors provide incoming journalists with what one editor dubbed the "lay of the land." They explained when a new journalist joins their team, "We want to make sure they know where to go for answers and, really, know who does what at the paper." This can be informative, but it does not really explain to incoming journalists exactly what the job entails. One reporter who started at the *Post* within the past few years explained the socialization process at the organization as vital but lacking in some ways. "It's good I had some journalism experience before I got here," they explained, adding,

> My editor really went out of [their] way to make sure I really got the place in terms of who everyone was. If I had a problem, I knew where to go, you know, and there was a welcome wagon of people who, you know, became some of my best friends early on in my time here. But if I'm being honest, what I think was missing is like, "What does it mean to work here?" Does that make sense? Like, nobody really told me what stories should look like, or how we're different in some way here. Like I said, I had to kind of rely on my [previous journalism experience] to actually understand the day-to-day of my actual job.

This sentiment was echoed, in various ways, by everyone interviewed who had joined the *Post* in recent years. When asked why there seemed not to be a "*Post* way of doing journalism that is shared with new hires," one veteran editor agreed:

Man, when I got here, I was put under [a longtime reporter's] wing and I learned what it meant to work at the *Denver Post*. If I could explain it, it meant that I really started to understand the community, the types of issues important to them, the sources I should make contact with and the ones to avoid. I learned the ropes, you know? To get a job here, you used to need, like, a decade of experience in other papers. Now, you know, a lot of them are great, but we're hiring people just out of school or with a couple years or less of experience. They'll come for the peanuts we pay. We just don't have the staff size and the experience necessary to really train people on what we want. Really, what we want now is decent copy and it doesn't matter about much else.

The most important aspect of socialization that new hires learn, despite no real planning by the *Post* staff, is the clear understanding that Alden is a problem and is to blame for every dilemma facing the *Post*, within reason. "You take this job with your eyes open," said one reporter. "Everyone knows the reputation, you know? But when I got here, my eyes got opened real quick to how much hatred—rightfully so—there is for [Alden]. They're just awful." Participant after participant who began at the *Post* following the 2011 merger with Alden shared similar recollections of understanding that the problems lay with Alden—and its predecessor, Digital First Media—and the newspaper business in general but were initially surprised by the vitriol toward Alden in the newsroom. These explicitly negative views are omnipresent at the *Post*, and this is where the organization's most effective socialization occurs. New people start and rather rapidly, they get brought into this us-versus-them, groupthink-filled culture. One editor explained how this happens.

You know, people who come on to that staff who are then, I think, that they're indoctrinated, which is the wrong word because that has a negative connotation. But it is definitely that sense of where they just they get to feel like this is, you know, "You have a huge role to play in this organization, and we are so glad that you're here to help us go through this." You know it's that level of care and understanding, I think, that's really important to how you do your job, and that having somebody who is going through it with you. It's kind of like, you know, there's a band of brothers, and [the *Post*] definitely has that.

Implicit in that statement is the trauma that remains pervasive in the newsroom. The idea that new people will "help us get through this" implies a constant struggle for existence, a constant fight against ownership. The idea of a "band of brothers" that are "going through it with you" signals an ongoing fight with an absentee ownership rather than a healthy newsroom.

Therefore, although the *Post* indisputably continues producing quality journalism, the all-encompassing, consistent labor precarity that looms over the newsroom creates the psychic-prison-style organizational culture whose socialization process obliquely depends on making sure new employees understand that they are going to be part of a traumatic experience but that their fellow journalists are also experiencing it, and they'll get through it together. Once a new journalist gets completely socialized into this culture, they can then motivate themselves to do the best possible work as a way to fight back against ownership. "It's weird, I know, to think of doing my job well as a big 'Fuck you' to the people who profit from me doing my job well," explained one reporter, "but it's true. [Alden] doesn't care about what we do, and I think, I mean, I know, we all think us excelling despite the circumstances is really a 'Fuck you' to them." This feeling absolutely is espoused throughout the *Post* newsroom, all in a culture whose focus is a single-minded, cohesive hatred of ownership, a hatred socialized into all new entrants to the newsroom.

Routines

Many of the embedded routines of news production at the *Post* seemingly began once the newspaper moved its offices from downtown Denver to a location outside the city in 2018. The global COVID pandemic forced most newsrooms to depend more on remote work and less on the physical workplace than ever before, this process began at the *Post* before COVID, when the move happened. In this way, Alden's decision to maximize profits by shedding its downtown Denver real estate significantly affected news production, primarily through the altering of routines. One editor explained:

> You know, we are still essentially remote. The newsroom is open if people want to go there, but, you know, after we moved out of that downtown building into the printing plant, no one was really fond of that newsroom anyways. It has no windows. It's like a bunker. So there has not been a charge of people wanting to go back. There are a handful who do; there's a reporter on my team who basically just got sick of working at home and so [they go] in pretty much every day. But that's not the case normally, so we learned to do these kind of virtual meetings [that have become part of our everyday schedule]. Our corporate email is through Gmail, so we use Meetups [*sic*] or Hangout[s], whatever they call it these days. We use that or our calendar for a lot of that.

The lack of a heavily populated newsroom significantly changed the way the *Post* schedules its day. One longtime reporter recalled that his routine

used to include "basically harassing the old timers on the staff for help
with basically everything," but now they lament that without a vital newsroom culture, journalists do their jobs without being able to draw on that
newsroom experience. "And that changes things because, you know, a
newsroom is really the focal point of what happens at most places, but
not here anymore, since nobody wants to go to that hellhole of an office."
Reporters not working on breaking news have the autonomy to generate their own story ideas without much assistance from editors, but now
there are fewer touchpoints for the entire staff, fewer opportunities for
department-level meetings or the unscheduled editor-reporter meetings
that would happen regularly if most of the staff worked out of the newsroom. "Now we, the editors, have a meeting at nine-thirty every morning,
just to get things going," explained one editor. "And then [after that], I do a
team meeting that is voluntary to the point if you can't make it, you don't
need to tell me. Whoever's there is there and sometimes I just cancel it."
Unspoken in that statement is that for this editor, as for many others at
the *Post*, there are mandatory meetings every day, but the reporters and
other journalists have very few, if any, routinized processes each week that
are dictated to them. Another editor, discussing how often they meet with
their staff, explained, "It's voluntary, but we end up meeting four to five
times a week, and sometimes we talk about very serious things and other
times we just kind of shoot the shit and talk." Even this level of habit is
rare at the newspaper; the editor noted that these voluntary meetings are

> pretty helpful to the point where I've had reporters on other teams
> ask if they could come. I'd like to start doing more things back in the
> newsroom. We've had some meetings. I was going in occasionally, but
> there just were not ever that many people in there. I do think it would
> help. You know, for election night last year, we basically had everybody
> who was involved in election coverage in the newsroom. Just made it
> easier to be able to yell across the room while we're all on deadline, that
> kind of thing.

Therefore, as with the processes surrounding news production and
story selection for all non-breaking-news journalists, there are very few
structured, organizationwide routines in news production processes for
journalists to follow when working on breaking news. This results in a very
individualized approach to news production. Of course, journalists at the
Post have a very clear understanding of what is news for the *Denver Post*,
but how that news is produced varies depending on the journalist. Some
enterprise reporters spoke about completely determining the routinized
practices they follow and how those processes are completely independent

from the rest of the newsroom. "I barely check in with my editor beyond the, you know, 'Here's what I'm doing today.' It's like that old commercial about being a truck driver where the guy says, 'I'm my own boss.'" Another reporter, though, did not talk about communication routines with their editor but rather the way that they and other reporters will brainstorm ideas together and rely on each other for support through the process. In general, the lack of routines reflects the bigger culture of the *Post*, one characterized less by an organizational philosophy or mission or espoused values but rather on the one consistent, unifying belief that having Alden as an owner is a traumatic situation.

Technology

Since the acquisition by Alden, the *Post* newsroom's relationship with technology has fluctuated, illustrating some clear market forces affecting news production. Journalists at the *Post*, like those at many newsrooms in the early decades of the twenty-first century, found themselves experimenting with technology in pursuit of economic growth. In journalism in the 2000s, it was not uncommon to encounter newsrooms "pivoting to video" as a way to increase revenue while also reaching audiences in a way that seemed sensible.[14] The *Post* was no different in that the newsroom pivoted hard to video. "We moved a lot of our budget, I can't tell you how much exactly, over to video because it seemed like a place we could make money," explained one journalist. "At that point, there was this idea that Alden would let us spend whatever we made in extra revenue, and video seemed like an untapped resource. But it's expensive in an up-front kind of way." Over and over, journalists spoke of the mid-2010s—a period the newsroom still has not recovered from, according to many participants—as a time when the company allotted significant resources to the production of video. Journalists spoke of the paper creating video products that sometimes aligned with journalism, but not always. This gave rise to the impression that the newsroom cared more about revenue than about informing the community. "For a while we were really trying hard to push video and create shows that were sellable, basically," explained one journalist:

> And I think we did that. Like, I don't know the cost of production versus how much money it made for the paper versus how that went. But I think that it did seem like we were actually bringing in extra revenue streams that the paper didn't have before. But I don't think that it was sustainable in the long term, because it was never set up correctly. So, for example, [at one point] we were like, "Okay let's create shows that

we can sell. Basically." So [we made] a cooking show, right, which is kind of journalism but it's not really, right? It's really just how to cook something.

Another journalist contended that the newsroom hired the right people and became fluent in producing quality video content, but it could never figure out exactly how to monetize the content. "Really, they never figured out how to sell ads on the video stuff. So, it kind of backfired because we sort of set ourselves up as we have the potential to make money and then we couldn't." The journalist went on to note that the *Post* had invested quite a bit in hiring a group of employees focused on producing these videos and then ended up laying most of those people off when the monetization never came. "So we spent a lot of time and money hoping for something to work that we didn't know if it could, instead of investing in the, you know, journalism." Looking back on this period, one longtime editor spoke about how much energy in the newsroom went into producing video content, all under the auspices of making more revenue, but Alden never really had a clear plan and was not generous with the resources needed to make the transition work.

> And so, then it just became a lot of effort, a lot of resources, and it's not something we can afford to keep doing. And then, plus, you know, at that point, well, I mean, everybody in the industry talks about that there was a whole move to pivot to video, because everybody had said that's where you can find that profit. You can find the profits there, and Facebook was going to promote them and none of that came to pass. So whether that was folly or not, I still think it was something that was really smart to do. But it needed some time, and it needed a better launching structure. I mean, I think that Advertising never really got their feet under them in order to be able to sell it better. And then from there, it was just, you know, it was just a tough situation.

Beyond this temporary focus on video, the *Post*, as a newsroom, does not rely on technology in a significant way. Most of the staff that did specialize in various technologies—photo, video, visualizations, and so on—did not survive the numerous layoffs over the last decade or so. At least according to the journalists, technology usage in the newsroom is minimal. The other piece of technology, if you can call it that, that repeatedly was mentioned as integral in the newsroom was Twitter/X. The vast majority of *Post* reporters and editors rely on Twitter for multiple processes, from connecting to the audience to, following what is happening in the area. "I would say there's no, like, 'You have to do x, y, z.' There's no quota of number of tweets or whatever that we are told to do," explained one reporter.

It's just that so many places like the police department, that's the first place you're going to find out about a shooting is [the Denver Police Department] tweeting it. So if you're covering police, you have to follow them on Twitter, and there are so many agencies and people in administrations that tweet out their stuff first now. So if you're, like, covering certain things, you just are on Twitter because that's where the news is.

Engagement

Whether speaking explicitly or considering the implicit meaning behind sentiments, the *Denver Post*, as a whole, considers its audience more as customers than citizens. This does not mean journalists do not see their jobs as primarily informing and advocating for the community, but there is a clear distinction between audience and journalist. Even the most audience-centered journalist at the *Post* thinks of citizens as potential sources, as people who might provide story ideas, but definitely not as coproducers or partners in building stories. Beyond normal on-the-ground reporting and talking to community members, when the *Post* journalists discuss engagement, the information they share comes through analytics. The *Post* does not have quotas for page views, nor does it apply web analytics in particularly complex ways, but the newsroom absolutely makes decisions based on the data gleaned from analytics. The main analytics focused on throughout the newsroom are page views and subscriptions—that is, which stories generate subscriptions. "They're both important for different reasons," explained one editor. "Subscriptions are now certainly more important, and a story, you know, you can have a random story that just gets just huge page views, and that's not necessarily going to get you any subscriptions." Another editor talked about a particular football-related story that, at the time of the interview, had generated almost a million page views. They noted that story's importance for digital ad rates, but also commented on its limited impact on the paper.

> It boosted our traffic way over goal for, like, four straight days. And nobody saw it coming, but I don't know that it generated a single subscription. [The traffic] was all coming in through Google, and I'm still not sure why people clicked. I mean, I'm not a big Broncos fan. I didn't recognize the name. . . . [B]ut a story that doesn't do huge page views but gets us subscriptions is going to be more valuable. So we are to the point where we have over, I don't know what the number is right now, over fifty or sixty thousand pure digital subscriptions with no print part, too, because all the print subscriptions come with digital. But the goal is to have enough pure digital subscriptions to support the budget of the

newsroom, and we do have that now. That doesn't mean we're getting rid of the print product anytime soon.

According to that editor, the value of clicks is minimal compared with that of online stories that result in subscriptions. The *Post* does not give reporters quotas, but it does have goals for its journalists, and despite the focus on subscriptions, these goals revolve around page views. "We do have goals for reporters, although honestly we don't track or even enforce [them]," explained an editor. "We probably should, because they're our goals, but there is, you know, there's sort of this innate repulsion to narrowing it down to just page views because they just tell you literally this is what people want to read." And that quote underscores the tension of working in a newsroom while dealing with the reality of economic precarity.

Since the *Post* does not have much choice but to consider its audience customers or potential customers first, web analytics are much discussed in the newsroom. And even though all the journalists will admit that page views matter very little to the economic bottom line, they are tracked. If you're a reporter and someone tells you these numbers, it could affect how you conduct your news-production processes. "It's impossible not to think about it when you know [Alden] absolutely thinks about it and they are determining if people get the boot next." The *Post* is experimenting with an oversight board made up of community members that, ideally, will give the community a feeling of more ownership over its news, but this is in the early stages of development, and nobody interviewed could really pinpoint the clear goal of the board. "I mean, ideally I hope it helps marginalized people feel like we care," explained one journalist, "but it might also just be another way to build subscriptions. I don't know."

News Production

At the *Post*, everyone interviewed basically agrees on a focus: news in Colorado. What exactly that means varies depending on the journalist. Each one essentially makes their own decisions on how to go about news-production processes. One reporter explained that "there's no editorial directive we're getting from anyone." That reporter meant that neither newsroom leadership nor Alden provides a blueprint in terms of scope of coverage. The *Post* newsroom is, essentially, broken into two different camps: a breaking-news team and an enterprise team. The breaking news team has a clearer understanding of their roles. One reporter explained that "it's not rocket science, really. If big stories happen, we cover it. Our goal is to cover every breaking story and be the best in the state. That's really what it boils down to." Therefore, when an event such as the Marshall Fire or the mass shooting occurs, the *Post* will cover it. However, major, breaking stories that that occur beyond the Front Range are covered less frequently. Due to staffing cuts, the *Post* seldom covers news far beyond the Denver and Boulder areas. But journalists understand that most breaking news coverage is augmented or, in many ways challenged, by social media. "Think about the Marshall Fire, remember? Where were you getting your information from?" asked one editor. "I'm a journalist and I was following Twitter. Oh, sure, some of those people were journalists, but it's not like I waited for the next day's paper or even a news website for the info." The staff understands that whereas breaking news is a key component of what the *Post* provides for its audience and the citizens of Colorado, the enterprise stories are where the collective skill of the paper comes through. "We still do amazing work in that area," said one veteran editor. But this is also where the individual interests and skills of journalists manifest themselves in coverage. One reporter explained,

> You know, I think as far as story selections kind of go, it is that case of what do we feel like people are interested in? And I don't think that's changed at all. What's the conversation? Where's the conversation going? And so, you see people who are a lot more adept and smart about how they recognize the conversations that are happening mostly online and address those in their stories in really smart ways.

That statement illustrates how much autonomy—or, in other words, lack of overt direction—the *Post* journalists receive. Editors clearly assist with nurturing and improving stories, but reporters really are, for the most part, on their own in terms of coming up with story ideas. As this reporter implies, quality of idea and execution will vary according to the skills of the journalist. As another reporter explained,

> Yeah, so typically if you're not a breaking-news reporter, you kind of have to come up with your own stories generally. So I will, you know, have a story idea, and will pitch it to my editor, and [they] have never told me no on anything I've ever pitched, so that's really nice that [they're] just, like, "Yeah, whatever. Do it." So, I mean, depending on what it is, we will, like, talk about it more if I feel like I need more help or more guidance or whatever.

An overall news-production process that provides reporters the autonomy to listen to the community and then make decisions about what should be covered is not rare and is celebrated in journalism, but many editors or veteran reporters identify the *Post* staff's lack of experience as a potential reason that these processes might not work so well as they did, perhaps, two decades ago or at least prior to Alden's ownership. One longtime editor explained,

> You know, I think people forget this, but the *Post* is still publishing a paper, and it still has some of the most talented journalists in Colorado working for it. And so there are days when the *Post* really shines. Usually, every week there are stories that are fine or better, you know, [ones that] are well done that we're proud of. But one of the obvious ways that [we] degrade our news coverage is simply by not having enough of the best journalists in Colorado. So, you know, [the newsroom] had about a hundred at the start of 2018, one hundred journalists, and that's reporters and editors. That's, you know, when you say "journalists," you mean reporters and editors, but that's also photographers and photography editors. That's the very small number of copy editors that were left, which was practically nil. And there's support staff, digital producers, the people that make it look pretty and pop on the internet. And so, a hundred people isn't really that many reporters when you boil it all down. More people means more ideas and that's inevitably better.

That editor is fundamentally implying that although a staff of roughly seventy journalists—or a hundred a handful of years ago—might seem large to the outside world, when you count everyone involved in the news-production process, particularly photojournalists and editors, it does not leave many reporters. And when many of these reporters are less seasoned and almost all are left to their own devices for story generation, it could result in fewer stories that "shine" on a regular basis. "Again, it's just every time we would lose [veteran] people, it's, like, you're left with a very green staff, who through no fault of their own, don't know what's happened before at that granular level," explained one editor.

> You're never going to be able to replicate [that experience]. You can step into a newsroom and start reading a bunch of past stories and getting boned up on your beat and make good sources and, over a period of time, do surprisingly well and understand a lot of what came before. But there's nothing like having a seasoned hand that you can go to. And the *Post* used to be filled with them. They were all over the place. And, you know, we just don't have that anymore.

So although the newsroom wholly believes it still produces what one editor dubbed the "best journalism in the state, bar none," it struggles with comparing itself to its own past. Regardless of how well the remaining staff does it job, a newsroom of seventy cannot produce journalism at the same level of quality as a newsroom of roughly three hundred. Therefore, with the *Post* consistently dwelling on its own past successes, it sets up a culture of news production that embodies a "We're great, but . . . " mentality.

Conclusion

Ownership affects everything in the *Denver Post* newsroom. Rarely, if ever, will a member of the Alden leadership team set foot in the newsroom, and the hedge fund may not provide any input at all into newsroom decisions, but Alden—its reputation, its past actions—always looms over the organizational culture of the newsroom. Without doing much of anything directly, Alden feels omnipresent. Although all *Post* journalists interviewed extensively discuss succeeding despite a lack of resources—and awards and local reputation back up this claim—a conversation cannot pass roughly the five-minute mark without Alden receiving a mention. Moreover, a strong sense of precarity pervades the US journalism industry as a whole, but it is unmistakably obvious at the *Post*. As previously mentioned, even when new journalists start at the *Post* knowing that they will be working for bad ownership, the notion of horrible ownership is amplified through an unintended socialization process. The resulting groupthink positions the newsroom in direct opposition to the ownership group. Because the newsroom leadership is unable to establish its own organizational culture, a culture with an undergirding, omnipresent us-versus-them credo results.

The history of the *Post* also affects the mindset of journalists, who continuously discuss doing more with less. Owners such as Alden continuously cut back resources in newsrooms; nevertheless the *Post* journalists still talk about how the paper "covers the entire state," even though that is not true in any real way. But this, however, *was* true when the newsroom staff numbered almost three hundred. This means that journalists see their organization as partly failing because it simply cannot do what it used to do. If the *Post* were a new organization, it would intentionally implement a mission and goals that would be attainable. The idea of the *Post* and its place in the state of Colorado has not changed in the newsroom, even though it cannot possibly be what it used to be in terms of its prior status as a state newspaper.

Due to the combination of this organizational culture, the perception of failure, and the overwhelming sense of precarity, the *Post's* newsroom is filled with trauma, more than the trauma that regularly comes with working as a journalist.[15] As previously mentioned, when a new *Post* journalist starts, as one editor explained, the message to them is, "You have a huge role to play in this organization, and we are so glad that you're here to help us go through this." Whether implied or explicitly stated, the trauma throughout the *Post* newsroom affects the way each and every journalist works, regardless of whether they are still doing high-quality work. There is a general feeling of not doing enough, primarily because the paper cannot simply accomplish what it did in, say, the 1990s, when the newsroom was essentially four times larger. And even though Alden does not directly infringe on newsroom decisions, the looming precarity absolutely affects journalists. For example, the decision to move from the downtown office lowered morale and indisputably altered news-production routines. The perceived economic crisis within the newsroom forces journalists to make economic decisions, such as the failed "pivot to video" phase, and finds the newsroom making decisions based on data gleaned from analytics. The journalists know these decisions make very little sense in terms of the mission of delivering quality news, but they do it anyway. In short, Alden's ownership looms over everything that happens in the newsroom and definitely is the primary influence on a psychic prison organizational culture consumed by groupthink around trauma.

CONCLUSION

The Organization and the Deprofessionalization of American Journalism

Through the case studies highlighted in these chapters, the increasing power of the organization in journalism, at the expense of industry professionalization, cannot be questioned. This book opened with an anecdote from the scholar David M. Ryfe, a narrative from an ethnography he conducted roughly fifteen years ago. The anecdote highlighted how organizations could attempt change, but unless that change aligned with normative notions of journalism, failure would more than likely follow.[1] My use of Ryfe's work is intentional, since it played a prominent role in my own maturation as a scholar; I read that article as a graduate student and found it instrumental in the way I think about the profession of journalism. However, nothing Ryfe found would have been surprising to any journalism studies scholar—or any professional journalist, for that matter—during the first decade of the twenty-first century or before. In some of the most influential works in the field, countless media sociologists, from Herbert Gans to Gaye Tuchman to Mark Fishman—and even scholars from non-media fields, such as the management theorist Chris Argyris—conducted rigorous research into the intersection of organizations and journalism practice. All came away with similar conclusions: organizations have minimal power over journalists' work because of the significant influence and undergirding of journalistic practice vis-à-vis the norms and routines of the industry as a whole.[2] In short, the professionalization of journalism, particularly since the early twentieth century, provided the foundation for the work done by journalists for roughly a century; if an organization tried to infringe on those norms, which the profession held so sacrosanct—as the organization in Ryfe's work attempted—it would fail, often spectacularly. However, the case studies from this book demonstrate, at best, a fraying professional culture across American journalism, an ecosystem with a variety of ethics, norms, and processes partly connected to some industry-wide beliefs, but also partly attributed to the various unique organizational cultures throughout the field.

In his doctoral dissertation, written more than thirty-five years ago, the journalism scholar Randal A. Beam contended that professionalism in journalism could be partly considered an organizational concern, arguing that "if the occupational group is the controlling agent at the organization, the occupationally articulated expectations of behavior and standards of work should prevail at the organization."[3] Beam's overriding assertion was based on the idea that each journalistic organization existed on a continuum of professionalism; depending on where an organization landed on the continuum, the level of professionalism in the newsroom would follow. Beam's dissertation posited that when individual journalism organizations attempt to dictate norms, they fall into a constant tug-of-war with the field of journalism, because a stringent professionalization process—such as those in medicine or law, for example– is lacking. This, too, does not deviate from what work in this area previously argued: organizations can exert some control over journalistic practice, but overall industrywide norms and belief systems linked to professionalism drastically limit such agency. Recent work—including this book—should provide new relevance to much of the argument Beam delivers in his dissertation. The assertion that an individual organization can control factors if the "customs of the organization" are "consonant with those expectations and standards articulated by the profession" made sense then—and still make sense.[4] The only difference, this book argues, is that the profession's expectations and standards are no longer obvious. Furthermore, any professional body—such as the Society of Professional Journalists or the Accrediting Council on Education in Journalism and Mass Communications—that previously would have dictated those standards across the field no longer have anywhere near the influential reach to do so. The field is left with individual newsrooms that are far more isolated from each other. Now, instead of dictating standards and expectations, journalism resembles most other American business organizations, whose norms, or core values, are determined by organizational culture and, therefore, the espoused values of the organization; this is what unifies an organization around its mission and goals.[5]

This book argues that an individual newsroom's organizational culture is the "rationale for people's behavior, a guideline for action, a cause for praise and condemnation, pride and despair" and that culture effectively distinguishes one newsroom's practices from another's.[6]

The case studies in this book illustrate six newsrooms, each with a different funding model, each essentially defining and enacting journalistic practice differently. Beyond the publishing of truthful information, there are few key similarities between, for example, the *Denver Post* and Defector. Beyond notions of accuracy and truthfulness, not much connects The Athletic, the *Boston Globe*, the Colorado Sun, Defector, the St. Louis Beacon, and the *Denver Post*. This is true even when considering the two traditional, legacy media organizations researched at the *Boston Globe* and the *Denver Post*. The *Globe* defines itself as a "paper of interest," making the explicit decision to cut coverage of suburban areas and most traditional city hall beats; instead it focuses on narrative and telling engaging stories, fulfilling its belief that the organization is a "writer's paper." The *Globe* effectively redefined itself under the ownership of the billionaire mogul John Henry, transforming from the traditional metropolitan newspaper ubiquitous during the twentieth century to a streamlined, storytelling-focused enterprise that concentrates primarily on text-based narrative. It eschews many of the technology-driven flourishes that many legacy organizations espoused in the "pivot to video" era of American journalism. The *Post*, on the other hand, continuously has shed journalists over the past couple of decades but never explicitly adjusted its mission or its espoused beliefs. Instead, the organization adopted a culture of precarity and failure. Despite the continued excellent work of its staff, the *Post* inhabits a demoralizing environment where journalists feel that they are constantly failing the public because the newsroom no longer covers the entire state of Colorado as thoroughly as it did in, for example, the 1990s. The key distinction here is that both the *Post* and the *Globe* shrank their coverage areas considerably in the twenty-first century. It is arguable that the *Globe* now covers even less of the state of Massachusetts—a much smaller state in geographic area—than the *Post* does of Colorado. However, the *Globe* now considers itself the paper of interest, not the paper of record. That rhetorical shift in mission leads to an explicit alteration in espoused beliefs in the organization, which then catalyzes a change in underlying assumptions among its journalists. We have seen that *Globe* journalists focus on telling interesting stories and feel successful at that mission, whereas *Post* journalists do quality work, but because their mission has never altered for decades, they consistently assume failure, a failure that manifests in a culture that focuses on an us-versus-them mentality about ownership. Each organization's market model directly affects the organizational cultures in its newsroom. At the *Globe*, where John Henry is perceived as an owner who wants to make a profit but primarily owns the newspaper as part of what many employees believe is a civic obligation, there is a belief that resources are distributed fairly. Thus journalists, particularly report-ers, are motivated to do the best work possible. At the *Post*, though, the hedge-fund owners consistently treat the newspaper as a glorified piggy bank, a line item where financial cuts can boost the hedge fund's bottom line. These market model differences distill themselves into different lead-ership styles, different missions, and different ways of doing and defining journalism, although some macro-level norms such as accuracy and truth remain consistent across the organizations.

Understanding Organizational Culture in Journalism Studies

The fundamental assertion of this book concerns the need for a more thor-ough understanding of the effects of organizational culture in journalism, a demand for a more determined exploration of how funding models beget market orientation, which then shapes organizational culture, which ulti-mately determines journalistic practice. Each funding model has its own systematicity; with each model comes a generally cohesive set of governing principles that ultimately shape all facets of news work at an organization. For researchers, this means a need to identify conclusively—or operational-ize—the elements of organizational culture that affect journalistic practice. As illustrated throughout this book's six case studies, researchers should examine at least six significant foci when studying organizational culture in journalism studies.

First, the *leadership* of a news operation, as in any organization, is the most fundamental element influencing culture.[7] Today, depending on the organization, leadership can arise in the newsroom or beyond—a signif-icant concern. In the case studies presented here, when the perceived absolute leader of an organization is a journalist, the culture is distinctly more positive. This is primarily because journalists seem to trust that a journalist-leader will make decisions with the quality of journalism rather than the business of journalism in mind. When those in the newsroom believe the leader is "one of us"—as one journalist at the Colorado Sun described the operation's editor—they can move beyond decisions they disagree with more easily, without resentment. When leadership comes from beyond the newsroom, as at the *Boston Globe*, it remains essential for leadership to make only those decisions that do not affect journalistic practice. Journalists will see that as an infringement on their autonomy; ultimately, it will have a significant negative impact on journalists' per-ceptions of organizational culture, as seen at The Athletic after the *Times* merger.

The *mission* of the organization—either its explicit mission or journalists' rhetorical narratives—is also fundamental to culture, making up much of the undergirding of the culture's espoused values. The mission sets the goal of the organization and implicitly tells organizational members what decisions they should make. For example, one clear detriment to the culture at the *Denver Post* is its unchanged mission. It is still focused on covering the entire state of Colorado, something no longer achievable with the newsroom's significantly diminished resources. Or take the differences between the Colorado Sun and Defector, two newsrooms with different models but both having employee ownership. Both places espouse missions based on collaboration and shared decision making, but the Sun's decision to create a de facto division between founders and nonfounders makes that mission difficult to align completely with underlying assumptions about that collaboration. Defector, on the other hand, does not have the same problem because the alignment between mission and model is clear.

An essential element of organizational culture involves how organizations socialize new journalists into the newsroom. *Socialization processes* must be investigated. This is especially important in an era of the disappearance of physical newsrooms. The findings presented in the preceding chapters overwhelmingly elucidate the essentials of an intentional, robust, explicit, and formal socialization process. While writing about the dearth of physical newsrooms across the field of journalism for the *New York Times*, the columnist Maureen Dowd quoted veteran journalists who argued that they "can't think of a profession that relies more on osmosis, and just being around other people, than journalism" and that "the best journalism school is overhearing journalists doing their jobs."[8] Although this 2023 column undoubtedly romanticizes a past time in journalism when organizations earned healthy profit margins and newsrooms were filled to the brim with what many veterans would euphemistically label "characters," the quotes above implicitly detail the way the field of journalism relics on socialization processes for its newsrooms to function optimally. In chapter 6, newsroom veterans and newcomers alike lamented the *Denver Post*'s nonexistent or haphazard socialization processes. Veterans specifically discussed how, due to cost cutting, so few in the newsroom boasted experience, and the thinning out of the veterans made the osmosis described above nearly impossible. The *Post*'s entire socialization process involves a makeshift buddy system and an informal, general education detailing just how awful employees perceive their ownership to be. None of this tells new employees what it means to work for the *Denver Post* as opposed to any other news organization. Neither the *Boston Globe*, the Colorado Sun, the St. Louis Beacon, nor The Athletic have much more of a formal socialization process, either. But all four of those organizations have key differences from the *Post*: Each one's organizational culture is built around an explicit mission or philosophy that permeates the operation, allowing them to circumvent some of the disadvantages of not having a robust socialization process. At the *Globe*, reporters are elevated for being the primary embodiments of the "writer's paper"; prior to its sale to the *New York Times*, The Athletic started implicitly socializing in the hiring process by making explicit in interviews that the organization values "old-school" or "traditional" journalistic values, as one reporter put it, based on ideas of journalistic autonomy; the Sun espouses a collaborative nature built around journalistic quality; and the *Beacon* immediately indoctrinates new journalists into the mindset of covering only "news that matters." Each of those newsrooms offers a buddy system, distributes an employee handbook, and most important, has a clear, strong mission that guides journalistic practice. In her column, Maureen Dowd laments that at the *Times*,

> remote work is a major priority in contract negotiations for the *Times* union, which wants employees to have to come into the office no more than two days a week this year and three days a week starting next year. Management, which says one thing it is worried about is that young people will stagnate and see the institution as an abstraction if they work remotely too often, has committed to a three-day-a-week policy this year but wants to reserve the right to expand that in the future.[9]

The assumption in that statement is that without a newsroom, journalists do not perceive themselves as working for an organization but rather as journalists not necessarily connected to a specific business. Hence, the need for socialization processes that initiate journalists and other employees into the specific organizational culture they are entering. The obvious takeaway, then, is that once an organization settles on a culture it aims to attain, it must make sure that culture's mission is embedded in all aspects of organizational life, that the culture begets the infancy of the organization, and that members are properly socialized into this culture.[10]

The fourth focus for studying organizational culture in journalism is the *routines of news production*. These routines not only help us understand and decipher how journalists attempt to fulfill the mission but also illuminate the underlying assumptions of the newsroom. Essentially, understanding the routines of news helps scholars ascertain whether journalists at an organization are actually doing what they say—or think—they are doing:

are they actually living the espoused beliefs of the organization? This book illustrates, for example, how the way in which reporters experience the entire news-production process surrounding a particular story tells us a great deal about power dynamics within a newsroom. For example, the newsrooms at the *Globe* and The Athletic allow individual departments, or verticals, the ability to set distinct routines. But whereas The Athletic had overall editors and reporters not linked to various teams, which made for a more unified set of routines, the *Globe* did not, which made a subculture emerge.

The fifth focus is *engagement*. In this book, engagement does not pertain solely to practices such as those described in the significant body of literature on engaged journalism but also a larger-scale understanding of how an organization conceptualizes its audience. In effect, an organizational culture is significantly influenced by, for example, whether journalists see the audience as a group to which news content is disseminated, partners in production, or some combination of the two. The conceptualization of an audience overtly affects not only journalistic routines but also the mission of the organization. The case studies in this book illustrate how journalistic practice differs when the audience is simply the group consuming journalism (Athletic, *Globe*, *Post*) or an integral part of news production processes (Defector, Beacon), or a combination of both (Sun).

The last element of culture this book clearly advocates for studying is the use of *technology* in the organization. This does not mean just the technology used discretely in news-production processes but also the tech that provides the structure for the entire organization. For example, in case study after case study in this book, how an organization uses Slack or another similar organizational communication platform can have robust effects on overall culture. The decision of the Defector founders, for instance, to use Slack as not only a tool for doing collaborative work but also to foster team building unequivocally had a positive effect on its newsroom culture. The further decision to create a glossary to allow new members to understand better the organization's shared history and vocabulary proved integral for creating a sense of belonging. Technology can also have significant effects on how an organization practices engagement—or does not.

In short, although this book focuses on six foci that definitely affect organizational culture, it's important to recognize that these are not the only influences, or even the six most significant influences. However, these six, independently and overlapping each other, provide a vital framework for the organizational culture of a news organization. If a market model determines market orientation, which generates an organizational culture, these six influences provide the nuanced—but important—differences we can see when studying organizational culture.

What This Means for the Future of Practice

The case studies in this book illustrate the inner workings of six market models and the ways in which funding structures directly and indirectly affect organizational culture, which filters down to influence journalistic practice. The future of journalism in America indisputably will include an ecosystem populated by a variety of divergent market models. Thus it seems significantly important to understand how individual organizations can create positive organizational cultures that would support quality journalism. What this book's findings demonstrate, though, is that the steps to forming these cultures at existing and new organizations will differ.

In the chapter on The Athletic, one of the journalists discussed covering a story when they first arrived at the organization. They almost reflexively wanted to cover the story a certain way because, they recalled, "It was hard to turn off, I don't know, my newspaper brain." That idea of a newspaper brain signifies the strength of what could be called twentieth-century professional journalism culture. For most of the mid- to late-twentieth century, newspapers produced an outsized amount of the original reporting published in America.[11] The vast majority of these newspapers covered their geographic areas in a very specific manner; they were general news organizations that prided themselves on covering all aspects of their regions. The problem with this mission can be seen easily in the *Denver Post*, whose newsroom is filled with journalists who believe the organization is not doing as much as it should. This aura of failure comes from the newsroom's inability to cover the state of Colorado as it once did. The *Post* and other legacy media organizations, particularly large metropolitan newspapers, are no longer large enough to cover effectively what they had earlier. In contrast, the *Boston Globe*, under new ownership when John Henry purchased the paper, transformed its mission, not only by implementing the espoused value of a "writer's paper" but also by transforming the underlying assumption about what the *Globe* covers. One reporter explained this implicit change:

> When [Henry] started, there was a period of, I would call it, trepidation. He basically was studying the place, and some of us didn't know what would happen. There were a lot of layoffs at first, but when it was over, I don't think we really cut staff, because we then hired a lot of people, too. The idea, as far as it was told to me, was to figure out what we were going to be in the future. That meant a lot of our suburban staff, for

example, got laid off because we now cover the suburbs less and, when we do, basically through freelancers. But we beefed up staff where we wanted to, also.

The idea inherent in that quote is that the *Globe* underwent a period of self-evaluation that helped leadership understand what the newsroom should be moving forward. Existing news organizations need to follow the *Globe*'s example.

At the St. Louis Beacon, organizational leadership changes inevitably alter the mission and the practice of journalism. In contrast, the *Post* remains committed to a mission from 1995 or so—impossible to accomplish now—which makes it a failure to some corners of the newsroom, regardless of the *Post*'s good work. When the *Globe* underwent change, it did not simply keep operating as before while incorporating alterations to the newsroom; instead, it took a step back and completely redefined the mission of the newsroom. It pivoted to being a "writer's paper" and a "paper of interest," each a rhetorical device and an espoused value that the paper has achieved. The Beacon's entire culture revolved around its editor and its cofounder. When a change in leadership eventually occurred through a merger, this completely upended the journalists' sense of professional identity; they did not know how to navigate the change right away and felt a little, as one reporter recalled, "lost for a few months there until I figured out" the new organization. At The Athletic, something similar happened. The *New York Times* bought the organization, publicly promised no changes, but implemented slight changes. The culture was transformed in a decidedly negative manner. Neither the Beacon and The Athletic had an organizational culture built to withstand change. More than likely the situation at the *Globe* was similar. However, at the *Globe*, all changes aligned with newly espoused values. At the Beacon and The Athletic, the espoused values of "news that matters" and total autonomy did not change, but the new leaders implemented changes or underlying assumptions that did not align with the newsroom's prior espoused values. This led to organizational turbulence and, in a sense, identity crises, as journalists felt they no longer worked at the same establishments, even though little changed in terms of their day-to-day work routines.

This book's findings suggest five key best practices for an optimal organizational culture moving forward:

1. **Navigating Change:** As we have seen in Ryfe's study, abrupt changes in journalistic culture do not translate into buy-in from journalists. Regardless of market model, ownership must

understand that it can make macro-level changes to journalistic
practice but must communicate those changes with transparency.
For example, the *Globe*'s elimination of most full-time suburban
reporters did not change the way the remaining journalists do their
jobs, especially because those cuts did not result in more work for
the remaining reporters.

Any changes that alter journalistic routines must come from
newsroom leadership, which allows journalists to maintain a perception of autonomy over practice. Once the Beacon reporters
began to understand how things would change after the merger
with St. Louis Public Radio, a new culture emerged, and journalists remained positive about their employer. This occurred because
the journalists believed they still had autonomy over their jobs,
even though those jobs changed slightly, simply because the radio
station had a marginally different mission from the Beacon's. We
see a counterexample in the *Times*'s purchase of The Athletic. The
Times Corporation attempted to make micro-level changes from
outside the newsroom. For example, it changed The Athletic's
travel policy, which indisputably altered journalistic practice and
the perception of autonomy in the newsroom. The *Times* also
reformed social-media policies, which made journalists feel that
people beyond the newsroom controlled their work practices.
Therefore, any change must be navigated carefully, with particular
attention to whether a change will alter any perceptions of autonomy or will affect journalist practices in the newsroom.

2. **Shared Decision Making:** It is unrealistic for any organization
to share decision-making responsibility across all elements of the
organization, but personnel need to believe that everyone contributes to the major choices faced by a newsroom. For example,
a key part of Defector's mission is equality across the news organization, so the newest addition to the staff wields just as much
power as the founders and the editor in chief of the site. Of necessity, the editor in chief makes decisions such as content, budgets,
and hiring that do not always involve everyone. However, through
numerous committees and organizational votes, everyone at
Defector effectively shares decision-making power. Although the
Denver Post's organizational culture is not optimal, its newsroom
is another example of shared decision making. When the *Post*
decided to pursue a "pivot to video," this choice came from the
newsroom, not ownership. Because the reporters shared in this
decision making, journalists interviewed years later still defended
the decision despite its failure. The journalists did not blame
Alden for this miscalculation, which absolutely affected the newspaper's quality for some time.

When decision making is shared throughout an organization, it creates a perception of a goal alignment and does not make individual journalists feel like cogs in a machine. Another example of this can be seen at the Colorado Sun, where the founders all share most decision making and feel strongly connected to the organization. However, nonfounders are not included in most decisions beyond their own coverage, making them feel decidedly less connected to the Sun.

For the most productive culture, news organizations first should define the exact parameters of decisions that come from within the newsroom, then set up processes that allow for a form of shared decision making to arise. The boundaries around newsroom decisions can vary from organization to organization—Defector accomplishes this goal by having everyone make decisions about all major matters, whereas the *Globe* does it by focusing only on journalistic issues—but once those parameters are set, everyone needs a voice.

3. **Engagement:** Over the last decade at least, the idea of journalistic engagement has gained significant traction in both the journalism industry and with journalism studies scholars. Of course, defining engagement is not easy.[12] In a recent book on the subject, the journalism studies scholar Sue Robinson explores engagement by articulating its principal goal: building trust with various stakeholders (e.g., sources, audiences, communities, etc.).[13] This trust cannot happen, though, unless all parties believe in the sincerity of this engagement. In chapter 1 on the St. Louis Beacon, the organization's general manager defined engagement as

> an exchange of information. Somebody at a conference last year was talking about cross-cultural engagement, and she said it's not enough to say, "I invited you." Or "I invited you, and you didn't come." Or "I reached out, I invited you, I engaged you." You have to be able to say, "I invited you, you said no. I asked you why you said no. And then I changed my invitation, and you came. And that's the idea of it being an ongoing conversation that isn't even two ways, but sort of like a partnership toward a shared goal of understanding.

That definition really encapsulates how journalists and communities can engage in a manner that make all parties feel trust rather than like part of some economically driven activity. Each organization needs to define how it sees its audience's role in journalistic processes, then create engagement activities around that role. For example, the Beacon wanted to give its community and audience some type of agenda-setting activity and story construction, then held news-storming gatherings, the Public Insight Network, and more. All of these processes granted the community a voice in the journalism, even before reporters understood what they were covering and how it should be covered. The *Post* and the *Globe* barely took part in engagement activities, primarily because, at these legacy organizations, journalists did not place a premium on audience input beyond traditional sourcing, story tips, and whatever information could be gleaned from analytics. It is easy to contend that these metropolitan newspapers lose some trust and credibility with audiences by not engaging more. The Athletic, on the other hand, has a culture very similar to many legacy news organizations but places a premium on engagement through a robust commenting platform, a consistent social media presence, frequent question-and-answer sessions with subscribers, and more. At The Athletic, journalists believe they should have power over agenda setting, but do earnestly engage with the audience to better understand its wants and needs.

Defector, though, should be considered a model of how to engage audiences. First, the organization hosts frequent virtual events that make subscribers feel like part of the organization: "because they are," as one journalist noted. These events are not aimed at earning more subscribers or even improving the content of the site. Instead, events such as staff trivia nights or video game presentations are simply fun and targeted toward building a sense of community and trust between organization members and their specific audience. This type of engagement aligns directly with the definition of engagement provided by the Beacon's general manager, a definition that implicitly highlights the need for engagement practices that do not simply ask questions of the community.

4. **Journalism as a Job:** With its low pay, long hours, and strong sense of precarity, journalism is often regarded as a calling by its professionals, a way to explain why people would intentionally embark on a career with so many potential disadvantages.[14] For many in the field, such as those at the *Denver Post,* this means connecting their identity to their profession in significant ways. This may never change, considering that on the whole, professionals do enter the field with a desire to do civic good rather than for personal economic enrichment or job stability. However, the case studies in this book illustrate the value that organizations accrue when making separating jobs from personal lives an explicit part of their culture. The way to accomplish this goal is through a mixture of explicit policies, but also seemingly indirect measures. For example, both Defector and the Sun boast different—but positive— organizational cultures. Both organizations have enacted policies explicitly aimed at ensuring that employees can enjoy their lives outside of work. Both have strict work hours, with exceptions for

breaking news or engagement activities. They each also have more indirect policies meant to restrict overuse of communications platforms such as Slack, something that Defector employees especially believed was necessary for a quality work-life balance. The other key decision that indirectly promotes this separation comes in the form of a living wage. Most of the organizations studied here (Defector, the Sun, The Athletic, and the *Globe*) have made paying employees/journalists a living wage a key part of their mission. Although potentially difficult for these organizations' focus on the bottom line and attention to market realities, this decision frees journalists from having to rationalize their career choices; this separates their personal identities from their professional identities, creating more allowance for a work-life balance.

5. **Leadership.** Obviously, leadership is the primary driver of organizational culture, but how journalists perceive leadership is vitally important to a newsroom. First, as seen in many of these case studies, if journalists regarded another journalist as the organization leader, they were more likely to believe that decisions were made with the civic mission in mind. Over and over, even when decisions were more problematic, participants across organizations would consider those decisions necessary or just a disagreement, not something definitively negative. But when some at the *Post* or at the postmerger Athletic felt that leadership came from outside the newsroom, even the most innocuous decision—such as a slight change in a travel policy—was perceived a violation of autonomy. Decisions made by newsroom leaders essentially never felt threatening to interview participants. The need for leadership to originate in the newsroom is vital. It is also important to recall events at the Beacon as a cautionary tale of leadership becoming too connected to one specific person. After the merger with St. Louis Public Radio, the Beacon went through a period of uncertainty because so much of the organization mirrored the priorities of its editor and cofounder. During the researching and writing of this book, the *Globe* also experienced a leadership change when its main editor departed the organization for a role at a local university. But because the *Globe*'s culture was not one person's vision, the transition seemed seamless to the journalists interviewed, because the new editor did not make major changes. A newsroom leader needs to align mission and practice, but must not let the mission be an extension of themselves. One founder at Defector anticipated a day when the organization would make its first leadership change. "At some point, Tom [Ley] is either going to have enough and just want to be another guy here or maybe he'd leave, though I doubt it,"

explained the founder. "But while Tom's great at his job, it won't really matter, because we know what we are." That statement implicitly separates the mission of the organization from the editor himself, making it clear there would not be a crisis of organizational identity if the founding editor decided he just wanted to be a regular staff member at some point.

Journalism Studies and the Deprofessionalization of American Journalism

In his book about the numerous deleterious factors facing the traditional press in the United States, the media sociologist Stephen Reese ponders the future of the profession amid numerous funding models for journalism. He questions whether "through the different forms of support for journalism," will the "resulting field hang together with shared values and operate with a sense of shared purpose?"[15] Reese's thought-provoking work deals primarily with theoretical questions and does not include the empirical data to answer such a question. Through the case studies included in this book, the answer becomes clearer: unless those "shared values" and "shared purpose" can be considered something as simple as truth, the answer is no.

Writing for the *New York Times*, the paper's then media columnist Ben Smith quoted the then dean of Columbia University's journalism school as saying about the field of journalism, "The church is gone, and there's no orthodoxy left.... There's many journalisms, and that's kind of liberating."[16] The piece goes on to assert that "much of the shift has to do with the changing nature of the news business."[17] This hypothesis mirrors the argument put forth by this book: that the disruptive changes experienced by the American news business—changes that led to a spate of funding variations—caused a destabilization process across the field of journalism. The results of this destabilization could be summed up as "there's no orthodoxy left" in the field or, more broadly, American journalism is in the late stages of deprofessionalization.

The central guiding definition of professionalism is that "certain occupational groups are seen as possessing, among other things, special power and prestige."[18] Scholars in journalism studies and across media sociology operationalize professionalization as a four-tenet concept, arguing that to be a profession, (1) it must be distinct from other occupations; (2) the job must have a core knowledge and set of abilities; (3) professionals must utilize a formalized set of processes; and (4) there must be a concept of autonomy over entry into the field and internal accountability.[19] In the past, evidence supporting journalism's long-standing distinction as a profession could be illustrated very easily across all four tenets:[20]

1. The first tenet of professionalization is a distinction from other occupations, which could be seen through the publication of newspapers or broadcast journalism. The field of journalism wielded overwhelming power to disseminate news through these media platforms; their power could not be infringed on easily.

2. A profession necessitates core knowledge and a set of abilities. Journalism established these principles through the growth of journalism schools and standardized education goals. The massive, cohesive development of journalism schools and departments, along with accreditation bodies, throughout the twentieth century instilled this core knowledge and these abilities.

3. The third component involves the concepts of perceived autonomy over entry into the field and internal accountability. Over time, both of these precepts were promoted through hiring practices, gatekeeping abilities, and the establishment of media accountability systems predominantly controlled by the industry itself.[21] Accountability is intrinsically linked to perceived autonomy in that journalistic organizations uniquely controlled dissemination through platforms, but they also controlled who became a journalist by hiring journalists. They also became accountable through the introdution of ombudsmen or public editors, letters to the editor, and other mechanisms.[22]

4. The last component is a formalized set of normative processes. Walter Williams, the founding dean of the University of Missouri School of Journalism, argued that objectivity should be the "most critical component of professionalism" in American journalism.[23] The establishment of norms, particularly objectivity, allowed the journalism profession "to endow their occupation with an identity they can count as worthy."[24] Over the course of the twentieth century, American journalism became imbued with a set of normative processes, particularly objectivity, that permeated the entire nationwide journalism ecosystem.

If establishing a field as a profession necessitates fulfilling each of these four tenets, this book's case studies demonstrate how American journalism finds itself in a process of deprofessionalization. This process started during the early portion of the twenty-first century, when the internet began making the dissemination of what external audiences would call journalism more possible for nonlegacy media. The broad public adoption of the internet and anybody's ability to acquire a web page and turn it into a news site gave people who wanted to build a news organization, cover

news topics, or create a news blog the capacity to start a news organization without the historically needed funds to acquire a printing press or
receive a government license to operate a television station or radio station.
Like many of this book's nonlegacy examples, something as successful
as Defector could not have existed before the twenty-first century. The
founders would have had no option but newsprint, which would have
made the organization cost prohibitive. Furthermore, these new entrants
into journalism do not consistently conform to the historical norms of
journalism.

1. As we have seen, the first tenet of professionalization is a distinction from other occupations, as in the publication of newspapers
   or broadcast journalism. This is no longer the case. Web sites such
   as Defector or the Colorado Sun do not appear too distinct from
   other similar looking—to audiences—sites for clearly nonjour-
   nalistic political mouthpieces such as Breitbart or The Gateway
   Pundit. Without control over the dissemination platforms, journalism is vulnerable to imitators that do not conform to its norms or
   missions. Therefore, to a significant portion of the public, there is
   barely a slight distinction between a legacy journalism organization adhering to norms versus a right-wing website dedicated to
   propagating falsehoods. This situation is due primarily to the dis-
   solution of journalism's distinction from other occupations.

2. The second component of a profession involves core knowledge and a set of abilities. As noted, journalism established these
   through the growth of journalism schools and standardized education goals. However, as noted by much research and portions of
   this book, many organizations do not exclusively hire people with
   journalism degrees, or even people with journalism experience.
   This is not atypical, even in the past. As noted consistently across
   the case studies, this core knowledge and set of abilities would
   be inculcated into new journalists through intentional and unin-
   tentional socialization processes—primarily through the implicit
   socialization that occurs within a newsroom. Now, as also shown
   in the case studies, socialization does not consistently occur in an
   era of vanishing physical newsrooms. Whatever socialization does
   occur often does not focus on instilling a set of abilities or knowledge of the profession—independent of news organization—to new
   journalists.

3. The third tenet involves the concepts of perceived autonomy over
   entry into the field and internal accountability. As we have seen,
   these tenets were promoted through hiring practices, gatekeeping
   abilities, and the establishment of media accountability systems
   predominantly controlled by the industry itself. As previously

noted, autonomy and accountability could be fulfilled by owning the means of production and dissemination. Although these concepts still prevail within the journalism ecosystem in America, the press's gatekeeping ability is severely diminished at best, or has simply vanished.[25] Without gatekeeping, it has become increasingly difficult for journalism to actually uphold these tenets. This says nothing of the elimination of most forms of internal accountability such as ombudsmen or public editors.

4. The final component of a profession involves a formalized set of normative processes. In the past, many in journalism studies would point to objectivity and other norms as proof of this tenet. However, simply examining these case studies makes a clear argument against the proliferation of objectivity across the field. The case studies also unmistakably demonstrate few, if any, consistent normative processes. Although all the organizations valued truth and verification and accuracy, the processes they employed to attain those goals varied wildly across organizations. This is even more apparent when considering the myriad news organizations not considered in this book.

These findings and the notion of a fraying profession should be considered in future studies of organizations in journalism. In the past, this has not been the case. In his famous and influential studies of journalistic organizations adopting digital tools, Pablo J. Boczkowski examined multiple news organizations just after the turn of the twenty-first century.[26] His work emphasizes how organizational decisions surrounding the transition to web publishing and multimedia tools altered journalistic routines. However, like much research from that time, it seemingly overemphasizes the amount of lasting change these alterations caused. The journalists in the case studies, though, never seemed to notice changes in the profession, just more alterations to practice as digitalization begins, matures, and normalizes. Similarly, more recent ethnographic work surrounding journalism's quantitative turn—specifically the embrace of web metrics in news production—illustrate the power of certain decisions to fundamentally affect professional identity and the very way journalism is done, but this work focuses on the field of journalism rather than the organizations studied.[27]

In an edited volume published in 2022, Scott A. Eldridge II asked if when scholars study journalism, they are actually studying the current discursive conceptualization of journalism, because the institution is "in a constant state of becoming."[28] That volume ends with a contention that the "field of journalism is now more of a constellation of normative ideals dispersed."[29] The main takeaway concerns whether what we think of as journalism is actually something relatively stable across the media ecosystem. The present book asserts the answer is no, due to a process of deprofessionalization. In their book *After Broadcast News*, the scholars Bruce A. Williams and Michael X. Delli Carpini argue that the field of journalism is essentially always in flux and that it is possible to describe what journalism looks like now and how it is produced as a new media regime.[30] The book contends that during a period of transition, when one media regime transforms into the next media regime, it becomes obvious to practitioners and scholars alike that something is afoot; when the new media regime stabilizes, it is "naturalized until the next disjuncture occurs."[31] In a sense, Williams and Delli Carpini might argue that we are in one of those periods right now, when a new media regime is stabilizing. In fact, in a recent piece, Jacob L. Nelson avows that the journalism industry of the 2020s is in one of these disjoined periods because a new media regime focused on audience engagement is upon us.[32] Although that argument does make a lot of sense, it falls apart when actual journalism practice is considered. Yes, engagement is becoming more and more popular across journalism, but three of the organizations studied here—the *Globe*, the Sun and the *Post*—essentially do very little audience engagement beyond some use of web metrics. And both The Athletic and Defector, though practicing more engagement, almost never provide agency over the news agenda to the audience, something essential for true engagement. No, the media regime we are currently witnessing is deprofessionalization.

Systems theory, still a theoretical framework for journalism studies, is a functionalist approach to thinking about how society, or an organization, is part of a complex system that is influenced by numerous factors.[33] When systems theory is applied in journalism studies, journalism is typically is defined as the system. This conceptualization, of course, remains the antithesis of this book's contention: that journalism in the United States should not be considered a profession or a monolithic enterprise.

However, in organizational communication research, many scholars conceptualize an individual organization as the system, because the "term system denotes any set of interrelated elements that form a unified or complex whole."[34] When considering any system, it remains vital to note that every system has a different level of openness; this is true of journalism organizations as well. When conceiving systems theory, Talcott Parsons contended that, for an organization to survive and thrive, it must be capable of solving four functional problems. That is, it must have the capacity to adapt; the capacity to attain goals; the capacity to integrate new elements into the system; and it must have the capacity to maintain itself in the face of change. In a way similar to understanding the biological and physiological aspects of the human body, systems theory contends that any change to the overall system in which the organization exists will affect the organization itself. When studying organizations from a systems theory approach, researchers must understand that "social organizations do not occur naturally in nature; they are contrived by man" and that the actions of actors inside and outside the organization "cannot be separated from the processes" of the organization.[35] Therefore, in studying a journalism organization, it is vital to consider all levels of the organization and all the outside forces influencing it.[36] Overlapping this book's contention that there is a systematicity related to a news organization's market model, systems theory concludes that if we can know the structure of the organization—in this case the market model—then "one can know many of the system's properties (e.g., relatively stable distributions of hierarchical authority) without having to observe the system itself."[37] In effect, knowing the market model of a news organization allows us to know many of the organization's attributes and many of the inside and outside forces affecting the system's stasis. This helps us understand power within an organization.

In past journalism studies, numerous scholars have illustrated how organizational structure and leadership impact journalistic practice. Warren Breed famously argued that organizational policies, more than professional standards, oriented how journalists did their jobs.[38] Whereas Breed contended that power dynamics with individuals in the newsroom wielded this influence, others have cautioned that the organization itself is "a source of constraints, influencing or determining media production," that although professional norms do impact people in the organization, the actual structure and policies of the organization can also significantly influence how journalists do their jobs.[39] For example, an organization's decision to adopt or not adopt technology alters not only news practices but also journalists' professional identity.[40] Therefore, it makes sense to argue that organizational policies and structure should be studied to understand completely why journalistic practice happens the way it does in a specific newsroom.[41] Moreover, today's media ecosystem suggests that the organization is actually the fulcrum of influence.[42] The contention from a systems perspective is that although influence most definitely comes from outside a news organization, the organization's own policies and leadership have the biggest impact on practice. However, journalism studies research, like much work on various professions, often finds that "at the individual (or group) level of analysis, the systemic or 'macro-social' consequences of filtering most of life through organizational lenses remain undeveloped."[43]

The point being made here is that systems theory of the organization—or a reworked model of influence that centralizes the organization—provides a framework for studying how organizational culture and overall structure impact newswork.[44] For media sociology work, this allows researchers a theoretical umbrella for analyzing how an organization decides—intentionally or unintentionally—on what outside influences to let in but also for better understanding organizational change catalyzed by internal or external forces. For example, if an organization is the system, journalism culture—or the remnants of professionalization in American culture—can be considered one outside entity impacting the organization, akin to various institutions such as foundations, advertising, the audience, universities, and so on. This approach centers the organization in the study of journalistic practice, allowing for a more nuanced understanding of how the organization and its elements are foundational to how the work of journalism happens but also acknowledging the constellation of other influences affecting practice. This theoretical undergirding, considering this book's findings, is more useful for studying influence than the most-used practices in media sociology. As noted in the introduction, the hierarchical theories or those that situate journalism as a monolithic field, puts the organization into a meso level that often results in its influences being overlooked in favor of more macro- or micro-level forces. The organizational communication scholar Timothy Kuhn contended that applying these types of theories often results in a myopic focus on "boundedly rational actors at the micro level, influenced by inducements and punishments and internalizing" forces at the macro level.[45] This removes any focus on the organization and very clearly decenters the organization in journalism studies research, often minimizing the power of the organization. Systems theory of the organization, though, centers the organization in all study of journalism practice, something essential with so many market models and cultures directly shaping practice.

However, from a purely conceptual perspective, systems of theory of the organization should be a sort of container framework for the study of journalistic practice from an organizational perspective. But, the functionalism at the heart of systems theory provides little utility for describing organizational culture. In essence, if we agree on David Ryfe's argument that the economics of journalism—and he focused on nonprofit organizations—effectively determines differences in journalism practice, then systems theory of the organization allows for a robust understanding of the types of systems within which individual news organizations can be situated.[46] But the question then becomes: How do researchers specifically theorize about the various models of journalism identified as systems?

Well, the idea is that the study of how economics affects journalism practice needs to move beyond the social-system-focused myopia prevalent in current research. Of course, it is useful to understand, for example, the political-economic view of journalism in America, how a system overwhelmingly undergirded by capitalism can produce a democratically driven press. However, to truly understand the effects of market models on how journalists do their jobs, the field of journalism studies needs to incorporate more of what the sociologist Robert Merton called middle-range theory.[47] He described middle-range theories as "theories that lie between the minor but necessary working hypotheses that evolve in abundance during day-to-day research and the all-inclusive systematic efforts to develop a unified theory that will explain all the observed uniformities of social behavior, social organization, and social change."[48] Popular and important theories in journalism studies such as the hierarchies of influences and field theory view journalism as a singular entity, a united profession despite the various intricacies and nuanced differences it contains. These theories often minimize organizational forces or occasionally simply ignore them. A middle-range approach to studying journalistic organizations would allow for theorizing without seeing the field as a single entity. When discussing middle-range theory, Merton contended that sociologists should study without attempting to explain the totality of the social world. In journalism studies this could be extrapolated to argue that we should stop attempting to study or theorize about the entirety of the field of American journalism and instead focus on the middle range, theories that explain portions of the field, because any implication of vast similarities across the field will lead to substandard theorizing. Merton predicted that with more and more studies of the middle range, scholars would formulate powerful theories to elucidate much that we do not know. The middle range allows for the systematicity that this book explores. Each model is its own system, one we can theorize about rather than theorizing about journalism—or more specifically, American journalism—as a whole.

Final Thoughts

We are living in scary times for journalism. If we were to ask scholars or practitioners to define journalism, the answers could be innumerable. Across the journalism ecosystem in America, it is easy to see fissures exposing disagreements concerning the field's importance and focus. We can see a population—across ideologies—that cannot figure out what journalism is and what it is not, which inevitably leads to increasingly hazy understandings of truth, forcing journalism to try to earn back that trust. This is an unrelenting cycle. In late May of 2020, the killing of George Floyd by a Minneapolis police officer catalyzed a wave of protests across the United States. The brutal way an officer knelt on Floyd's neck for almost nine minutes, killing the forty-six-year-old man without ever attempting to treat him, motivated and marshalled an already thriving protest movement concerning racial injustice in America. Floyd's murder and the ensuing protests became dominated mainstream news, according to the Pew Research Center.[49] Roughly one week after Floyd's death, as American cities became stages for protests both large and small, US Senator Tom Cotton, a Republican representing Arkansas, wrote an op-ed for the *New York Times* that argued, among other things, that "rioters have plunged many American cities into anarchy," that "nihilist criminals are simply out for loot and the thrill of destruction, with cadres of left-wing radicals like antifa infiltrating protest marches to exploit Floyd's death for their own anarchic purposes," and that "many politicians prefer to wring their hands while the country burns."[50] This polarizing editorial ultimately called for the United States to invoke the Insurrection Act of 1807 by deploying the National Guard to forcefully put an end to the primarily peaceful protests. The fallout the *Times* received for publishing the editorial was quick and predominantly consistent, with even the newspaper's staffers calling the editorial dangerous and a viewpoint not fit for publication.[51] Writing about the editorial for Vox, Ezra Klein argued that "there have always been boundaries around acceptable discourse, and the media has always been involved, in a complex and often unacknowledged way, in both enforcing and contesting them."[52] This sentiment, in effect, matched that of a columnist in the *New York Times* about a week after Cotton's editorial ran. In this response, Kara Swisher contended that "The *New York Times* is not a public square."[53] In essence, Swisher articulated that although Senator Cotton might have a "view" on an issue of public interest, and although he may take a "side" on said issue, it is not a news organization's responsibility to publish all opinions or represent all sides. Some views, Swisher maintained—such as the dangerous ones Cotton presented—should not be granted publication. The point here is that the economic model within which the *Times* operates prioritizes increasing readership numbers. Many regarded the Cotton editorial as a way to increase subscriptions from the politically conservative people who often abandon legacy media for cable news.[54] But all it did was lead to more distrust and negative publicity, resulting in disapproval from the *Times*'s core audience. This is the cycle journalism finds itself in. And news organizations are making these decisions on the basis of numerous organizational factors.

The focus of this book's chapters is to illustrate how market models have significant impact on practice. This does not imply that each market model is discrete and has a different type of influence on practice. But what the findings do illustrate is that many of the decisions about production, about staffing, about funding are dictated by the market model, which means that model will affect how journalists do their jobs.

Journalism sits at inflection point: Is this deprofessionalization period a media regime in itself? Or do we remain in the period of disruption that Williams and Delli Carpini contend occurs right before a new media regime becomes stable? In his book *The Crisis of the Institutional Press*, Steve Reese writes about the numerous disruptions affecting the institutional press.[55] But the question remains: Is there currently an institutional press? In a recent book, Matthew Powers and Sandra Vera-Zambrano describe journalism as a "declining profession," contending that their data illustrate that "what is imperiled is less journalism per se than the capacity of journalists to secure a personally acceptable balance of rewards from journalism." They argue that because people are still willing to be journalists, "journalism in some form persists."[56] But does journalism in some form, or some forms persist? If journalism is in "some form," is it still actually journalism? Are we just assuming that there is a journalism, and not just a bunch of differing processes that results in news? Powers and Vera-Zambrano even hypothesize that this declining version of the profession of journalism could not "necessarily accord with the various normative expectations so often ascribed to journalists."[57] But if there are no normative expectations across a field, then it is not a declining profession but a profession no more. And if is not a profession, we as scholars need to rethink the way we research journalism, and that starts with a renewed focus on the organizations of journalism.

NOTES

Acknowledgments

1. Patrick Ferrucci and Timothy Kuhn, "Remodeling the Hierarchy: An Organization-Centric Model of Influence for Media Sociology Research," *Journalism Studies* 23, no. 4 (2022): 525–43.

Introduction

1. David M. Ryfe produced two important pieces very salient to this introduction through this ethnography. They are "Broader and Deeper: A Study of Newsroom Culture in a Time of Change," *Journalism* 10, no. 2 (2009): 197–216; and "Structure, Agency, and Change in an American Newsroom," *Journalism* 10, no. 5 (2009): 665–83.

2. Ryfe, "Broader and Deeper," 198.

3. Ryfe, "Broader and Deeper," 212.

4. Michael McDevitt, "In Defense of Autonomy: A Critique of the Public Journalism Critique." *Journal of Communication* 53, no. 1 (2003): 155–64.

5. Ryfe, "Broader and Deeper," 198.

6. Ryfe, "Broader and Deeper," 198.

7. Ryfe, "Broader and Deeper," 212.

8. Eric Klinenberg, "Convergence: News Production in a Digital Age," *Annals of the American Academy of Political and Social Science* 597, no. 1 (2005): 48–64.

9. Stephen A. Banning, "The Professionalization of Journalism: A Nineteenth-Century Beginning," *Journalism History* 24, no. 4 (1999): 157.

10. Betty Houchin Winfield, *Journalism 1908: Birth of a Profession* (Columbia: University of Missouri Press, 2008).

11. Silvio Waisbord, *Reinventing Professionalism: Journalism and News in Global Perspective* (New York: Wiley, 2013).

12. See Herbert J. Gans, *Deciding What's News: A Study of CBS Evening News, NBC Nightly News, Newsweek, and Time* (New York: Pantheon, 1979); and Gaye Tuchman, *Making News: A Study in the Construction of Reality*. (New York: Free Press, 1978).

13. Gerald J. Baldasty, *The Commercialization of News in the Nineteenth Century* (Madison: University of Wisconsin Press, 1992).

14. For a full understanding of levels of analysis and the hierarchy of influences model I'm discussing, see Pamela J. Shoemaker and Stephen D. Reese, *Mediating the Message in the 21st Century: A Media Sociology Perspective*, 3rd ed. (New York: Routledge, 2014).

15. Timothy Kuhn, "Negotiating the Micro-Macro Divide: Thought Leadership from Organizational Communication for Theorizing Organizatio," *Management Communication Quarterly* 26, no. 4 (2012): 545.

16. Ferrucci and Kuhn, "Remodeling the Hierarchy."

17. David Manning White, "The 'Gate Keeper': A Case Study in the Selection of News," *Journalism Quarterly* 27, no. 4 (1950): 383–90.

18. Obviously, there were exceptions to this norm, but the average journalist was a liberal arts graduate, according to works such as Bill Kovach and Tom Rosenstiel, *The Elements of Journalism: What Newspeople Should Know and the Public Should Expect*, 1st rev. ed. (New York: Three Rivers Press, 2007); and Michael Schudson, *Discovering the News: A Social History of American Newspapers* (New York: Basic Books, 1978).

19. Dale Maharidge, "What Happens to Journalists When No One Wants to Print Their Words Anymore?" *The Nation*, March 21, 2016.

20. Patrick Ferrucci, "Joining the Team: Metajournalistic Discourse, Paradigm Repair, the Athletic and Sports Journalism Practice," *Journalism Practice* 16, no. 10 (2022):1–19.

21. Bryan Pirolli, "Travel Journalists and Professional Identity: Ideology and Evolution in an Online Era." *Journalism Practice* 11, no. 6 (2017): 740–59.

22. See, for example, how Fox News does this: Kerwin C. Swint, *Dark Genius: The Influential Career of Legendary Political Operative and Fox News Founder Roger Ailes* (New York: Union Square Press, 2008).

23. Sue Green, "When the Numbers Don't Add Up: Accommodating Data Journalism in a Compact Journalism Programme." *Asia Pacific Media Educator* 28, no. 1 (2018): 78–90.

24. Jane B. Singer, "Journalism and Digital Technologies," in *Changing the News: The Forces Shaping Journalism in Uncertain Times*, ed. Wilson Lowrey and Peter J. Gade (New York: Routledge, 2011), 214–29.

25. Kovach and Rosenstiel, *Elements of Journalism*.

26. Daniel C. Hallin, "The Passing of the 'High Modernism' of American Journalism," *Journal of Communication* 42, no. 3 (1992): 14–25.

27. Mark Deuze, "The Professional Identity of Journalists in the Context of Convergence Culture," *Observatorio (Obs*)* 2, no. 4 (2008): 103–17.

28. Maarit Jaakkola, Heikki Hellman, Kari Koljonen, and Jari Väliverronen, "Liquid Modern Journalism with a Difference: The Changing Professional Ethos of Cultural Journalism," *Journalism Practice* 9, no. 67 (2015.): 811–28.

29. Jaakkola et al., 814.

30. Jaakkola et al., 824.

31. Tim P. Vos and Patrick Ferrucci, "Who Am I? Perceptions of Digital Journalists' Professional Identity," in *The Routledge Handbook of Developments in Digital Journalism Studies*, ed. Scott Eldridge II and Bob Franklin (New York: Routledge, 2018), 47.

32. For this work, see Patrick Ferrucci, Ross Taylor, and Kathleen I. Alaimo, "On the Boundaries: Professonal Photojournalists Navigating Identity in an Age of Technological Democratization," *Digital Journalism* 8, no. 3 (2020): 367–85; Patrick Ferrucci and Tim P. Vos, "Who's In, Who's Out? Constructing the Identity of Digital Journalists," *Digital Journalism* 5, no. 7 (2017): 868–83; and Vos and Ferrucci, "Who Am I?"

33. Ferrucci and Vos, "Who's In, Who's Out?" 880.

34. Waisbord, *Reinventing Professionalism*.

35. Claude-Jean Bertrand, *Media Ethics and Accountability Systems* (New York: Routledge, 2018).

36. Deirdre Carmody, "*Time* Responds to Criticism over Simpson Cover," *New York Times*, June 25, 1994.

37. Thomas H. Wheeler and Tim Gleason, "Photography or Photofiction: An Ethical Protocol for the Digital Age," *Visual Communication Quarterly* 2, no. 1 (1995): 8–12.

38. Patrick Ferrucci and Ross Taylor, "Blurred Boundaries: Toning Ethics in News Routines," *Journalism Studies* 20, no. 15 (2019): 2179.

39. Ryfe, "Broader and Deeper."

40. Michael Schudson, "The Objectivity Norm in American Journalism," *Journalism* 2, no. 2 (2001): 149–70.

41. For just a couple examples of this, see Patrick Ferrucci, "Murder Incorporated: Market Orientation and Coverage of the Annie Le Investigation," *Electronic News* 9, no. 2 (2015):108–21; and Patrick Ferrucci, "Primary Differences: How Market Orientation Can Influence Content," *Journal of Media Practice* 16, no. 3 (2015): 195–210.

42. Patrick Ferrucci and Kathleen I. Alaimo, "Escaping the News Desert: Nonprofit News and Open-System Journalism Organizations," *Journalism* 21, no. 4 (2020): 489–506.

43. See Patrick Ferrucci, "It Is in the Numbers: How Market Orientation Impacts Journalists' Use of News Metrics," *Journalism* 21, no. 2 (2020): 244–61; and Ferrucci and Edson C. Tandoc Jr., "A Tale of Two Newsrooms: How Market Orientation Affects Web Analytics Use," in *Contemporary Research Methods and Data Analytics in the News Industry*, ed. William Gibbs and Joseph McKendrick (Philadelphia: IGI Global, 2015), 58–76.

44. See Edson C. Tandoc Jr., "Journalism Is Twerking? How Web Analytics Is Changing the Process of Gatekeeping," *New Media and Society* 16, no. 4 (2014): 559–75; Tandoc, "Why Web Analytics Click: Factors Affecting the Ways Journalists Use Audience Metrics," *Journalism Studies* 16, no. 6 (2015): 782–99; and Tandoc, *Analyzing Analytics: Disrupting Journalism One Click at a Time* (New York: Routledge, 2019).

45. C. Edwin Baker, *Advertising and a Democratic Press* (Princeton, N.J.: Princeton University Press, 1994).

46. Oscar Gandy, *Beyond Agenda-Setting: Information Subsidies and Public Policy* (Norwood, NJ: Ablex, 1982).

47. Patrick Ferrucci and Scott A. Eldridge II, eds, *The Institutions Changing Journalism: Barbarians Inside the Gate* (New York: Routledge, 2022).

48. See Patrick Ferrucci and Jacob L Nelson, "The New Advertisers: How Foundation Funding Impacts Journalism," *Media and Communication* 7, no. 4 (2019): 45–55; and Martin Scott, Mel Bunce, and Kate Wright, "Foundation Funding and the Boundaries of Journalism," *Journalism Studies* 20, no. 14 (2019): 2034–52.

49. Rebecca Coates Nee, "Social Responsibility Theory and the Digital Nonprofits: Should the Government Aid Online News Startups?" *Journalism* 15, no. 3 (2014): 326–43.

50. Erin E. Schauster, Patrick Ferrucci, and Marlene S. Neill, "Native Advertising Is the New Journalism: How Deception Affects Social Responsibility," *American Behavioral Scientist* 60, no. 12 (2016): 1408–24.

51. See Valérie Bélair-Gagnon and Avery E. Holton, "Boundary Work, Interloper Media, and Analytics in Newsrooms: An Analysis of the Roles of Web Analytics Companies in News Production," *Digital Journalism* 6, no. 4 (2018): 492–508; Bélair-Gagnon and Holton, "Strangers to the Game? Interlopers, Intralopers, and Shifting News Production," *Media and Communication* 6, no. 4 (2018): 70–78; and Scott A. Eldridge II, *Online Journalism from the Periphery: Interloper Media and the Journalistic Field* (New York: Routledge, 2017).

52. Bélair-Gagnon, Valérie. "Web Analytics in Journalism," in *The Institutions Changing Journalism: Barbarians Inside the Gate*, ed. Patrick Ferrucci and Scott A. Eldridge II (New York: Routledge, 2022), 153–64.

53. Wilson Lowrey, Lindsey Sherrill, and Ryan Broussard, "Field and Ecology Approaches to Journalism Innovation: The Role of Ancillary Organizations," *Journalism Studies* 20, no. 15 (2019): 2131–49.

54. Baker, *Advertising and a Democratic Press*.

55. Tim P. Vos and Frank Michael Russell, "Theorizing Journalism's Institutional Relationships: An Elaboration of Gatekeeping Theory," *Journalism Studies* 20, no. 16 (2019): 2331–48.

56. Christine Larson, "Live Publishing: The Onstage Redeployment of Journalistic Authority," *Media, Culture & Society* 37, no. 3 (2015): 440–59.

57. See Lili Levi, "The Weaponized Lawsuit Against the Media: Litigation Funding as a New Threat to Journalism," *American University Law Review* 66 (2017): 761–828; and Jonathan Peters, "Staying Abreast of the Law: Legal

Issues Affecting Journalism," in Ferrucci and Eldridge, *The Institutions Changing Journalism*, 46–58.

58. J. David Wolfgang, "Taming the 'Trolls': How Journalists Negotiate the Boundaries of Journalism and Online Comments," *Journalism* 22, no. 1 (2021): 139–56.

59. See Magda Konieczna, *Journalism Without Profit: Making News When the Market Fails* (New York: Oxford University Press, 2018); and Magda Konieczna and Elia Powers, "What Can Nonprofit Journalists Actually Do for Democracy?" *Journalism Studies* 18, no. 12 (2017): 1542–58.

60. Daniel C. Hallin and Paolo Mancini, Comparing Media Systems Beyond the Western World (Cambridge: Cambridge University Press, 2011).

61. Michael Schudson, *Watergate in American Memory: How We Remember, Forget, and Reconstruct the Past* (New York: Basic Books, 1992).

62. Heloiza G. Herscovitz, "Brazilian Journalists' Perceptions of Media Roles, Ethics and Foreign Influences on Brazilian Journalism," *Journalism Studies* 5, no. 1 (2004): 71–86.

63. See Dani Madrid-Morales and Herman Wasserman, "Chinese Media Engagement in South Africa: What Is Its Impact on Local Journalism?" *Journalism Studies* 19, no. 8 (2018):1218–35; and Emeka Umejei, "Hybridizing Journalism: Clash of Two "Journalisms" in Africa," *Chinese Journal of Communication* 11, no. 3 (2018): 344–58.

64. Sara García Santamaría, "The Sovietization of Cuban Journalism: The Impact of Foreign Economy Dependency on Media Structures in a Post-Soviet Era," *Journal of Latin American Communication Research* 6, no. 1–2 (2018): 135–51.

65. Edson C. Tandoc Jr. and Joy Jenkins, "Out of Bounds? How Gawker's outing a Married Man Fits into the Boundaries of Journalism," *New Media & Society* 20, no. 2 (2018): 581–98.

66. James W. Carey, "A Short History of Journalism for Journalists: A proposal and Essay," *Harvard International Journal of Press/Politics* 12, no. 1 (2007): 3–16.

67. Alfred McClung Lee. *The Daily Newspaper in America: The Evolution of a Social Instrument*. (New York: Routledge, 1990).

68. Baldasty, *The Commercialization of News*.

69. Erik Barnouw, ed., *Conglomerates and the Media* (New York: New Press, 1997).

70. David Ralph Spencer and Judith Spencer, *The Yellow Journalism: The Press and America's Emergence as a World Power* (Evanston, IL: Northwestern University Press, 2007).

71. C. Edwin Baker, *Advertising and a Democratic Press*.

72. See Mark Fishman, *Manufacturing the News* (Austin: University of Texas Press, 1980); Gans, *Deciding What's News*; and Tuchman, *Making News*.

73. See Henrik Örnebring, "Professionalization of Journalists: Historical," in *The International Encyclopedia of Journalism Studies*, ed. Tim P. Vos and Folker Hanusch (New York: Wiley, 2019); and Waisbord, *Reinventing Professionalism*.

74. Chris Argyris, *Behind the Front Page: Organizational Self-Renewal in Metropolition Newspapers* (San Francisco: Jossey-Bass, 1974), x.

75. Simon Cottle, "Ethnography and News Production: New(s) Developments in the Field," *Sociology Compass* 1, no. 1 (2007): 1–16.

76. See Patrick Ferrucci, *Making Nonprofit News: Market Models, Influence and Journalistic Practice* (New York: Routledge, 2019); and Konieczna, *Journalism Without Profit).*

77. Numerous citations illustrate this both implicitly and explicitly. For example, see Mark Deuze and Tamara Witschge, "Beyond Journalism: Theorizing the Transformation of Journalism," *Journalism* 19, no. 2 (2018): 165–81; Lian Jian and Nikki Usher, "Crowd-Funded Journalism," *Journal of Computer-Mediated Communication* 19, no. 2 (2014): 155–70; or Miguel Franquet Santos Silva and Scott A. Eldridge II, *The Ethics of Photojournalism in the Digital Age* (New York: Routledge, 2020).

78. Bryan C. Taylor, Jamie McDonald, and James Fortney, "But Fade Away? The Current Status of 'Organizational Culture' in Organizational Communication Studies," in *Faces of Culture and Organizational Communication: Metatheoretical Perspectives*, ed. Massimo Marchiori and Sergio Bulgacov (São Caetano do Sul, Brazil: Difusão, 2013), 78–111.

79. Obviously, there are some studies that do examine the intersection of journalism and organizational culture, but they are few and far between for a discipline that, essentially, studies work emanating from organizations. See C. Ann Hollifield, Gerald M. Kosicki, and Lee B. Becker. "Organizational vs. Professional Culture in the Newsroom: Television News Directors' and Newspaper Editors' Hiring Decisions," *Journal of Broadcasting & Electronic Media* 45, no. 1 (2001): 92–117.

80. Jonathan Groves and Carrie Brown, *Transforming Newsrooms: Connecting Organizational Culture, Strategy, and Innovation* (New York: Routledge, 2020).

81. Joanne Martin, "The Style and Structure of *Cultures in Organizations: Three Perspectives*," *Organization Science* 6, no. 2 (1995): 230–32.

82. Joanne Martin, *Cultures in Organizations: Three Perspectives* (Oxford: Oxford University Press, 1992), 45.

83. See Gideon Kunda, *Engineering Culture: Control and Commitment in a High-Tech Corporation* (Philadelphia: Temple University Press, 2009); and Edgar H. Schein, *Organizational Culture and Leadership*, 3rd ed. (San Francisco: Jossey-Bass, 2006).

84. Schein, *Organizational Culture*, 5.

85. Thomas Hanitzsch, "Deconstructing Journalism Culture: Toward a Universal Theory." *Communication Theory* 17, no. 4 (2007): 367–85.

86. Ferrucci and Taylor, 2019. "Blurred Boundaries."

87. Timothy Kuhn, "A Communicative Theory of the Firm: Developing an Alternative Perspective on Intra-Organizational Power and Stakeholder Relationships," *Organization Studies* 29, no. 8–9 (2008), 1228.

88. Karl E. Weick, *Making Sense of the Organization*, vol. 2, *The Imperma-nent Organization* (New York: Wiley, 2012).

89. Kuhn, "A Communicative Theory," 1229.

90. Gabriel Yiannis, *Organizations in Depth: The Psychoanalysis of Organi-zations* (Thousand Oaks, CA: Sage, 1999), 1.

91. Schein, *Organizational Culture*.

92. Schein, *Organizational Culture*, 1.

93. Timothy Kuhn and Jared Kopczynski, "Organizational Structures, Pro-cesses, and Agency," in *Movements in Organizational Communication Research: Current Issues and Future Directions*, ed. Jamie McDonald and Rahul Mitra (New York: Routledge, 2019), 14.

94. Gregory S. Larson and Phillip K Tompkins, "Ambivalence and Resis-tance: A Study of Management in a Concertive Control System," *Communica-tion Monographs* 72, no. 1 (2005), 2.

95. Keith Grint and Darren Nixon, *The Sociology of Work*, 4th ed. (Malden, MA: Polity, 2015), 13.

96. Schein, *Organizational Culture*.

97. One very interesting study along these lines is an older work that did not examine the totality of organizational culture—because it assumed a similar organizational culture across newsrooms—but that did focus on leadership. See Cecilie Gaziano and David C. Coulson, "Effect of Newsroom Management Styles on Journalists: A Case Study," *Journalism Quarterly* 65, no. 4 (1988): 869–80.

98. Ferrucci, *Making Nonprofit News*, 65.

99. See Warren Breed, "Social Control in the Newsroom: A Functional Analysis," *Social Forces* 33, no. 4 (1955): 326–35; and Stephen D. Reese and Jane Ballinger, "The Roots of a Sociology of News: Remembering Mr. Gates and Social Control in the Newsroom," *Journalism & Mass Communication Quarterly* 78, no. 4 (2001): 641–58.

100. Randal A. Beam, "What It Means to Be a Market-Oriented Newspaper." *Newspaper Research Journal* 19, no. 3 (1998), 2.

101. David Ryfe, "The Economics of News and the Practice of News Pro-duction." *Journalism Studies* 22, no. 1 (2021): 60–76.

102. Ryfe, "The Economics of News," 73.

103. To see recent research on the effects of organizational market orien-tation, recent work from myself includes: Ferrucci, "Murder Incorporated"; Ferrucci, "Money Matters? Journalists' Perception of the Effects of a Weak Market Orientation," *Convergence* 24, no. 4 (2018): 424–38; Ferrucci, "It Is in the Numbers"; or Patrick Ferrucci, Chad E. Painter, and Angelika Kalika, "How Market Orientation and Ethics Affected Coverage of Marijuana Legalization," *Newspaper Research Journal* 40, no. 3 (2019): 391–404.

104. Ferrucci, "It Is in the Numbers."

105. John H. McManus, *Market-Driven Journalism: Let the Citizen Beware?* (Thousand Oaks, CA: Sage, 1994).

106. Schein, *Organizational Culture*.

107. Robert Stuart Weiss, *Learning from Strangers: The Art and Method of Qualitative Interview Studies* (New York: Free Press, 1994).

108. Schein, *Organizational Culture*.

109. Timothy Kuhn, Karen Lee Ashcraft, and François Cooren, *The Work of Communication: Relational Perspectives on Working and Organizing in Contemporary Capitalism* (New York: Routledge, 2017), 189.

110. Jacques Hamel, Stéphane Dufour, and Dominic Fortin. *Case Study Methods* (Newbury Park, CA: Sage, 1993), 3.

111. Joe R. Feagin Anthony M. Orum, and Gideon Sjoberg. *A Case for the Case Study* (Chapel Hill: University of North Carolina Press, 1991).

112. Hamel, Dufour, and Fortin, *Case Study Methods*.

113. Kathy Gilsanin, "The St. Louis Beacon: 'News That Matters' for St. Louis," *Columbia Journalism Review*, December 29, 2010, https://www.cjr.org/news_startups_guide/2010/12/the-st-louis-beacon.php/.

114. Ferrucci, "Follow the Leader: How Leadership Can Affect the Future of Community Journalism," *Community Journalism* 4, no. 2 (2015): 19–35.

115. Margaret Sullivan, "Defector.com's Journalistic Experiment Began with a Staff Walkout. It Might Actually Be Working," *Washington Post*, February 21, 2021.

116. Ben Markus, The Colorado Sun to Launch with Former Denver Post 'A-Team' Stars and Tech Cash, Colorado Public Radio, June 17, 2018, https://www.cpr.org/2018/06/17/the-colorado-sun-to-launch-with-former-denver-post-a-team-stars-and-tech-cash/.

117. About Us, Colorado Sun, https://coloradosun.com/about-us/

118. Erwin D. Canham, *Newspaper Story: One Hundred Years of the Boston Globe* (Cambridge, MA: Harvard University Press, 1972).

119. Ben Koo, The Athletic Is Worth $300 Million, But Can It Become a Billion Dollar Company? Awful Announcing, September 23, 2019, https://awfulannouncing.com/athletic/the-athletic-is-worth-300-million-but-can-it-become-a-billion-dollar-company.html; and Alex Sherman, The Athletic Says It Hits 1 Million Subscribers after Surviving Sports Shutdown, CNBC.com, September 9, 2020, https://www.cnbc.com/2020/09/09/the-athletic-hits-1-million-subscribers-after-enduring-sports-shutdown.html.

120. Aaron Gordon, The Sports Pages' New Clothes, Slate, September 6, 2018, https://slate.com/culture/2018/09/the-athletic-is-poaching-from-local-sports-pages-and-reading-like-them-too.html.

121. Kevin Draper, At The Athletic, A Hiring Spree Becomes a Story in Itself. *New York Times*, August 24, 2018, https://www.nytimes.com/2018/08/24/sports/the-athletic-netflix.html.

122. Sara Fischer, Scoop: New York Times in Talks to Buy The Athletic. Axios, May 25, 2021, https://www.axios.com/2021/05/25/new-york-times-nytimes-acquisition-athletic.

123. Ferrucci, "Joining the Team."

124. Ken Ward, "America's Last Newspaper War: One Hundred and Sixteen Years of Competition between the *Denver Post* and *Rocky Mountain News*" (PhD diss., Ohio University, 2018).

125. Ward, "America's Last Newspaper War."

126. Margaret Sullivan, "Is This Strip-Mining or Journalism? 'Sobs, Gasps, Expletives' over Latest Denver Post Layoffs," *Washington Post*, March 15, 2018.

127. Joe Pompeo, "The Hedge Fund Vampire That Bleeds Newspapers Dry Now Has the Chicago Tribune by the Throat," Vanity Fair, February 5, 2020, https://www.vanityfair.com/news/2020/02/hedge-fund-vampire-alden-global -capital-that-bleeds-newspapers-dry-has-chicago-tribune-by-the-throat.

Chapter 1. The St. Louis Beacon

The ethnographic research that provides the foundation for the bulk of this chapter took place between January and April 2013. During this time, I spent hundreds of hours in the newsroom with editors, shadowing reporters, and attending meetings. I also analyzed documents related to all processes at the Beacon. Most important, I conducted in-depth interviews with almost every single employee of the organization. In 2022, I did follow-up Zoom interviews with six journalists who worked for the Beacon before its merger and for at least a handful of years after.

1. For a more thorough inquiry into the power of leadership at the Beacon, see Ferrucci, "Follow the Leader."

2. For a full recounting of this anecdote, see Ferrucci, *Making Nonprofit News*.

3. The first time I saw the acronym DNNN was in what I consider a formative and brilliant study on nonprofit journalism, conducted by Rebecca Coates Nee at San Diego State University: "Creative Destruction: An Exploratory Study of How Digitally Native News Nonprofits Are Innovating Online Journalism Practices," *International Journal on Media Management* 15, no. 1 (2013): 3–22.

4. For an almost complete list, see the Institute for Nonprofit News' website: https://findyournews.org/campaign/inn-network-directory/.

5. To get a better understanding of this phenomenon, see both Ferrucci, *Making Nonprofit News*, and Dan Kennedy, *The Wired City: Reimagining Journalism and Civic Life in the Post-Newspaper Age* (Amherst: University of Massachusetts Press, 2013).

6. Serena Carpenter, Jan Boehmer, and Frederick Fico, "The Measurement of Journalistic Role Enactments: A Study of Organizational Constraints and Support in For-Profit and Nonprofit Journalism," *Journalism & Mass Communication Quarterly* 93, no. 3 (2016): 601.

7. Ferrucci, "Public Journalism No More: The Digitally Native News Nonprofit and Public Service Journalism," *Journalism* 16, no. 7 (2015): 904–19.

8. Magda Konieczna, "Do Old Norms Have a Place in New Media? A Case Study of the Nonprofit MinnPost," *Journalism Practice* 8, no. 1 (2014): 49–64.

9. Schudson, "The Objectivity Norm in American Journalism."

10. Konieczna, *Journalism Without Profit*, 61.

11. Kunda, *Engineering Culture*.

12. Gareth Morgan, *Images of Organization: The Executive Edition* (Thousand Oaks, CA: Sage, 1998), 150.

13. Deborah Linnell, "Founders and Other Gods," *Nonprofit Quarterly* 11, no. 1 (2004): 11.

14. Leona English and Nancy Peters, "Founders' Syndrome in Women's Nonprofit Organizations: Implications for Practice and Organizational Life," *Nonprofit Management and Leadership* 22, no. 2 (2011): 159–71.

15. There are many mainstream media and trade magazine descriptions of the merger. For a scholarly inquiry featuring participant observation from before, during, and after the merger, see Patrick Ferrucci, Frank Michael Russell, Heesook Choi, Margaret Duffy, and Esther Thorson, 2017. "Times Are a Changin': How a Merger Affects the Construction of News Processes." *Journalism Studies* 18 (3): 247–64.

16. Roy Malone, "Beacon, KWMU Join Forces for the Better in St. Louis." *Gateway Journalism Review*, Winter (2014): 10.

17. Amber Hinsley, "Developing New Organizational Identity: Merger of St. Louis Public Radio and the St. Louis Beacon." *Journal of Radio & Audio Media* 24, no. 1 (2017): 144–60.

18. See Schein, *Organizational Culture and Leadership*, particularly, ch. 8.

Chapter 2. Defector Media

The interviews and participant observation for this chapter occurred between September 2020 and August 2022. A total of fourteen in-depth interviews were conducted for this chapter. The participant observation for this case study occurred virtually over roughly twenty hours with multiple participants.

1. Alexia Fernandez Campbell, "What the Mass Resignations at Deadspin Tell Us About Work in America," Vox, November 1, 2019, https://www.vox.com/identities/2019/11/1/20941677/deadspin-resignations-writers-workers-quit.

2. Campbell, "Mass Resignations."

3. Caleb Pershan, "'We Have the Simplest Business in the World': A Conversation with Defector Media, *Columbia Journalism Review*, March 23, 2022, https://www.cjr.org/q_and_a/defector-media-coop-deadspin-gawker.php.

4. "About Us," Defector, 2022.

5. Sarah Scire, "Defector's Most Successful Promo Email Was Too 'Creepy' to Repeat," NiemanLab, October 22, 2022, https://www.niemanlab.org/2022/10/defectors-most-successful-promo-email-was-too-creepy-to-repeat/; and Mark Stenberg, "How Defector Media Turned Its Hit Podcast into a 7% Bump in Subscribers," AdWeek, October 27, 2022, https://www.adweek.com/media/defector-media-normal-gossip/.

6. Sullivan, "Defector.com's journalistic experiment began with a staff walkout."

7. Ian Casselberry, "Six Months In, Defector Looks Like a Sports Media Success Story," Awful Announcing, February 22, 2021, https://awfulannouncing .com/online-outlets/six-months-in-defector-looks-like-sports-media-success -story.html.

8. Morgan, *Images of Organization*, 132.

9. Rafael Grohmann, "Media Workers Co-Ops: Possibilities, Contradictions and Argentinean Scenario," Intercom: Revista Brasileira de Ciências da Comunicação 42, no. 3 (2019): 78, 80.

10. Leona Achtenhagen, "Media Entrepreneurship—Taking Stock and Moving Forward," *International Journal on Media Management* 19, no. 1 (2017): 1–10.

11. Monica Chadha, "What I Am versus What I do: Work and Identity Negotiation in Hyperlocal News Startups," *Journalism Practice* 10, no. 6 (2016): 697–714.

12. Nathan Schneider, "An Internet of Ownership: Democratic Design for the Online Economy," *Sociological Review* 66, no. 2 (2018.): 321.

13. Nathan Schneider, "Broad-Based Stakeholder Ownership in Journalism: Co-ops, ESOPs, Blockchains," *Media Industries Journal* 7, no. 2 (2020). https:// doi.org/https://doi.org/10.3998/mij.15031809.0007.203.

14. Yehiel Limor and Itai Himelboim, "Journalism and Moonlighting: An International Comparison of 242 Codes of Ethics." *Journal of Mass Media Ethics* 21, no. 4 (2006): 265–85.

15. Schein, *Organizational Culture and Leadership*.

Chapter 3. The Colorado Sun

I began collecting data for this chapter in June 2018, when I participated in some working groups before the establishment of the Sun. I conducted a small number of interviews at this point. The majority of this chapter's data, though, comes from in-depth interviews, textual analysis, and participant observation that occurred between April and November 2022. I did more than a dozen interviews and more than thirty hours of participant observation. The participant observation happened both virtually and in person.

1. Sydney Ember, "Denver Post Rebels Against Its Hedge-Fund Ownership," *New York Times*, April 7, 2018.

2. In the interest of full transparency: Chuck Plunkett is now a teaching assistant professor in the Department of Journalism at the University of Colorado-Boulder, the department where I currently serve as chair. I was also on the search committee that hired Plunkett to oversee our capstone course for both undergraduates and graduate students.

3. Mario Nicolais, "Five Years since the Denver Post Rebellion, Colorado Journalism Has Had Its Ups and Downs,"Colorado Sun, 2023, https://colorado sun.com/2023/02/26/colorado-journalism-news-opinion-nicolais/.

4. Corey Hutchins, "The Colorado Sun Pits Civil-Backed Startup Against *The Denver Post*," *Columbia Journalism Review*, July 18, 2018, https://www.cjr.org/united_states_project/colorado-sun-denver-post-civil.php.

5. Along with colleagues from the Departments of Journalism, Media Studies, and Information Science, I was one of the people that participated in a couple of these early meetings about the Sun's possible business model. After a couple of meetings and two phone calls with Sun's leadership, I left the working group.

6. Ben Markus, "The Colorado Sun to Launch with Former Denver Post 'A-Team' Stars and Tech Cash," Colorado Public Radio, June 17, 2018, https://www.cpr.org/2018/06/17/the-colorado-sun-to-launch-with-former-denver-post-a-team-stars-and-tech-cash/.

7. Jaclyn Peiser, "Goodbye, Denver Post. Hello, Blockchain," *New York Times*, June 17, 2018.

8. Janine S. Hiller, "The Benefit Corporation and Corporate Social Responsibility," *Journal of Business Ethics* 118 (2013): 287.

9. Hiller, "The Benefit Corporation," 299.

10. Nancy B. Kurland, "Accountability and the Public Benefit Corporation," *Business Horizons* 60, no. 4 (2017): 527.

11. Ryan Tharp, Colorado Public Benefit Corporations: Q&A. Fairfield & Woods, February 2, 2015, https://www.fwlaw.com/insights/colorado-public-benefit-corporations-qa.

12. Morgan, *Images of Organization*.

13. Morgan, *Images of Organization*.

14. Breed, "Social Control in the Newsroom."

15. For a good primer on different forms of engaged journalism, see Andrea Wenzel, *Community-Centered Journalism: Engaging People, Exploring Solutions, and Building Trust* (Champaign: University of Illinois Press, 2020).

16. Muhammad Fahad Humayun and Patrick Ferrucci, "Understanding Social Media in Journalism Practice: A Typology," *Digital Journalism* 10, no. 9 (2022): 1502–25.

17. Jacob L. Nelson, *Imagined Audiences: How Journalists Perceive and Pursue the Public* (New York: Oxford University Press, 2021).

18. Ferrucci, "It Is in the Numbers."

19. Ferrucci, "It Is in the Numbers."

Chapter 4. The *Boston Globe*

The interviews and participant observation to collect data for this chapter occurred between March and December 2022. The interviews come from several different "teams" at the *Globe* and include a mix of reporters and editors. I also conducted interviews with five employees from outside the newsroom. The participant observation took place mainly virtually, but also some in person.

1. Beth Healy, "John Henry's Purchase of the Boston Globe Completed," *Boston Globe*, October 24, 2013.

2. Dan Kennedy, *The Return of the Moguls: How Jeff Bezos and John Henry Are Remaking Newspapers for the Twenty-First Century* (Lebanon, NH: University Press of New England, 2018).

3. Dan Kennedy, "The Bezos Effect: How Amazon's Founder Is Reinventing *The Washington Post*—and What Lessons It Might Hold for the Beleaguered Newspaper Business," Shorenstein Center on Media, Politics and Public Policy, June 2016.

4. Sonja A. Sackmann, "Culture and Subcultures: An Analysis of Organizational Knowledge," *Administrative Science Quarterly* 37, no. 1 (1992): 140–61.

5. Jennifer A. Howard-Grenville, "Inside the 'Black Box': How Organizational Culture and Subcultures Inform Interpretations and Actions on Environmental Issues," *Organization & Environment* 19, no. 1 (2006): 47.

6. Martin, *Cultures in Organizations*.

7. Kennedy, *The Return of the Moguls*.

8. Patrick Ferrucci and Gregory Perreault, "The Liability of Newness: Journalism, Innovation and the Issue of Core Competencies," *Journalism Studies* 22, no. 11 (2021): 1436–49.

9. Chris Hanretty, "Media Outlets and Their Moguls: Why Concentrated Individual or Family Ownership Is Bad for Editorial Independence," *European Journal of Communication* 29, no. 3 (2014): 347.

10. Des Freedman, "Paradigms of Media Power," *Communication, Culture & Critique* 8, no. 2 (2015): 287.

11. Ken Doctor, "The Newsonomics of John Henry Buying The Boston Globe." NiemanLab, August 3, 2013, https://www.niemanlab.org/2013/08/the-newsonomics-of-john-henry-buying-the-boston-globe/.

12. For a full history of the *Boston Globe* and its purchase by John Henry, see Kennedy, *The Return of the Moguls*, ch. 2.

13. Breed, "Social Control in the Newsroom."

14. Dan Adams, "Boston Globe Moving Headquarters to Downtown Boston," *Boston Globe*, December 10, 2015.

15. For a thorough understanding of the engaged journalism movement, three books provide similar but clearly differing overviews of this phenomenon: Jake Batsell, *Engaged Journalism: Connecting with Digitally Empowered News Audiences* (New York: Columbia University Press, 2015); Nelson, *Imagined Audiences*; and Wenzel, *Community-Centered Journalism*.

16. Patrick Ferrucci and Michelle Rossi, "'Pivoting to Instability': Metajournalistic Discourse, Reflexivity and the Economics and Effects of a Shrinking Industry," *International Journal of Communication* 16 (2022): 4095–4114.

Chapter 5. The Athletic

The interviews and participant observation for this chapter occurred between May 2020 and May 2021. The journalists in this sample came from twenty-seven different geographically determined verticals (e.g., The Athletic Boston, The Athletic Denver, etc.). The participants cover all four major American professional sports and college athletics. The subjects are predominantly beat reporters for specific teams, but the participants do include nine journalists covering sports on a national level. To understand the organization and journalistic practice at The Athletic better, I also conducted in-depth interviews with six employees who work in various business positions in the company, including one founder. The participant observation included two separate days shadowing two separate journalists, primarily as a way to understand communication practices at the organization

1. For an introduction and understanding of the historical and contemporary professionalization of journalism in the United States, see Waisbord, *Reinventing Professionalism*.

2. Ben Strauss, "At the Athletic and New York Times, a Marriage with Promise and Tension," *Washington Post*, October 7, 2022.

3. Sean Leahy, "It's the First Anniversary of The Athletic Boston. Let's Celebrate," The Athletic, April 10, 2019.

4. For a more scholarly understanding of how The Athletic's paywall makes it a rather different entry into the sports journalism ecosystem, see Galen Clavio and Brian Moritz, "Here's Why I Joined: Introductory Letters from New Hires to The Athletic and the Framing of Paywall Journalism," *Communication & Sport* 9, no. 2 (2021): 198–219; or Ferrucci, "Joining the Team."

5. George Cheney, "On the Various and Changing Meanings of Organizational Membership: A Field Study of Organizational Identification," *Communications Monographs* 50, no. 4 (1983): 342.

6. Theodore L. Glasser and Marc Gunther, "The Legacy of Autonomy in American Journalism," in *Institutions of Democracy: The Press*, ed. Geneva Overholser and Kathleen Hall Jamieson (New York: Oxford University Press, 2005), 384–99.

7. Matt Carlson, *Journalistic Authority: Legitimating News in the Digital Era* (New York: Columbia University Press, 2017).

8. Ferrucci, "Money Matters?"

9. Michael McDevitt, "In Defense of Autonomy: A Critique of the Public Journalism Critique," *Journal of Communication* 53, no. 1 (2003): 162.

10. To understand the historical importance and influence of a physical newsroom, see Breed, "Social Control in the Newsroom"; or Melissa Wall, "Change the Space, Change the Practice? Re-Imagining Journalism Education with the Pop-Up Newsroom," *Journalism Practice* 9, no. 2 (2015): 123–37.

11. For a thorough understanding of how groups police themselves in terms of organizational norms, see Daniel C. Feldman, "The Development and Enforcement of Group Norms," *Academy of Management Review* 9, no. 1 (1984): 47–53; or David B. Greenberger, Marcia P. Miceli, and Debra J. Cohen, "Oppositionists and Group Norms: The Reciprocal Influence of Whistle-Blowers and Co-Workers," *Journal of Business Ethics* 6, no. 7 (1987): 527–42.

12. Jesse Fox and Bree McEwan, "Distinguishing Technologies for social Interaction: The Perceived Social Affordances of Communication Channels Scale," *Communication Monographs* 84, no. 3 (2017): 313.

13. See Susan E. McGregor, Elizabeth Anne Watkins, and Kelly Caine, "Would You Slack That? The Impact of Security and Privacy on Cooperative Newsroom Work," *Proceedings of the ACM on Human-Computer Interaction* 1 (2017): 1–22.

14. Walther, "Computer-Mediated Communication."

15. See Ferrucci, "Public Journalism No More"; and McDevitt, "In Defense of Autonomy."

16. See Arthur D. Santana, "Virtuous or Vitriolic: The Effect of Anonymity on Civility in Online Newspaper Reader Comment Boards," *Journalism Practice* 8, no. 1 (2014): 18–33; or Wolfgang, "Taming the 'Trolls.'"

17. Patrick Ferrucci and J. David Wolfgang, "Inside or Out? Perceptions of How Differing Types of Comment Moderation Impact Practice," *Journalism Studies* 22, no. 8 (2021): 1010–27.

18. See Ferrucci, "It Is in the Numbers"; or Tandoc, *Analyzing Analytics*.

19. For more on beat writing in sports, especially on how technology is changing it, see Mark Lowes and Christopher Robillard, "Social Media and Digital Breakage on the Sports Beat," *International Journal of Sport Communication* 11, no. 3 (2018): 308–18.

20. For a history of sports journalism practice, see Patrick S. Washburn and Chris Lamb, *Sports Journalism: A History of Glory, Fame, and Technology* (Lincoln: University of Nebraska Press, 2020).

21. Neil Maiden, Konstantinos Zachos, Amanda Brown, George Brock, Lars Nyre, Aleksander Nygård Tonheim, Dimitris Apsotolou, and Jeremy Evans, "Making the News: Digital Creativity Support for Journalists," *Proceedings of the 2018 CHI Conference on Human Factors in Computing Systems*, 2018, 1–11.

22. Lauren Hirsh, Kevin Draper, and Katherine Rosman, "New York Times Co. to Buy The Athletic for $550 Million in Cash," *New York Times*, January 6, 2022.

23. Laura Wagner, "Under NYT Ownership, the Athletic Lays Down 'No Politics' Rule for Staff," *Defector*, June 16, 2022.

24. Laura Wagner, "'No One Knows Anything': Staffers at the Athletic Wait in the Dark Following NYT Deal," *Defector*, January 7, 2022.

25. Jessica Toonkel, "The Athletic Burned Through $95 Million Between 2019 and 2020," *The Information*, October 4, 2021.

26. Toonkel, "The Athletic Burned Through $95 Million."

27. See McManus, *Market-Driven Journalism*; or Anthony M. Nadler, *Making the News Popular: Mobilizing US News Audiences* (Urbana: University of Illinois Press, 2016).

28. See, for an example, Ryfe, "Structure, Agency, and Change in an American Newsroom."

29. Michael A. Diamond, "Organizational Identity: A Psychoanalytic Exploration of Organizational Meaning," *Administration & Society* 20, no. 2 (1988): 166–90.

30. Clavio and Moritz, "Here's Why I Joined."

31. Geert Hofstede, "Motivation, Leadership, and Organization: Do American Theories Apply Abroad?" *Organizational Dynamics* 9, no. 1 (1980): 42–63.

Chapter 6. The *Denver Post*

The interviews and participant observation to gather data for this chapter took place between November 2021 and September 2022. I interviewed both reporters and editors from within the newsroom, but also three nonjournalists. The participant observation was mostly in person, but some was virtual.

1. Chuck Plunkett, "When the Vultures Circled the *Denver Post*, We Asked Colorado to Fight for Local News. It Did," Colorado Sun, April 2, 2023, https://coloradosun.com/2023/04/02/denver-post-colorado-opinion-plunkett/.

2. See Pompeo, "The Hedge Fund Vampire That Bleeds Newspapers Dry"; and Evan Brandt, "My Newspaper Was Gutted by Journalism's Biggest Bogeyman," as told to Noah Lanard, *Mother Jones*, May-June 2022, https://tinyurl.com/v9ba97nj.

3. For a history of the commercialization of the press, see Baldasty, *The Commercialization of News*.

4. McKay Coppins, "A Secretive Hedge Fund Is Gutting Newsrooms," *The Atlantic*, October 14, 2021.

5. Brandt, "My Newspaper Was Gutted."

6. Joshua Benton, "The Vulture Is Hungry Again: Alden Global Capital Wants to Buy a Few Hundred More Newspapers," Nieman Lab, November 22, 2021, https://tinyurl.com/4yv2843w.

7. Again, Chuck is now one of my colleagues in the Department of Journalism at the University of Colorado-Boulder.

8. Pompeo, "The Hedge Fund Vampire That Bleeds Newspapers Dry."

9. Ben H. Bagdikian, *The New Media Monopoly* (Boston: Beacon Press, 2004), 7.

10. Doug Underwood, *When MBAs Rule the Newsroom: How the Marketers and Managers Are Reshaping Today's Media* (New York: Columbia University Press, 1995).

11. Randal A. Beam, "What It Means to Be a Market-Oriented Newspaper," *Newspaper Research Journal* 19, no. 3 (1998): 2–20; McManus, *Market-Driven Journalism*, 197.

12. Morgan, *Images of Organization*.

13. Martin, "The Style and Structure of Cultures in Organizations."

14. Ferrucci and Rossi, "Pivoting to Instability."

15. For more on the emotional toll that comes with practicing journalism, see Natalee Seely, "Journalists and Mental Health: The Psychological Toll of Covering Everyday Trauma," *Newspaper Research Journal* 40, no. 2 (2019): 239–59; and Allison J. Steinke and Valerie Belair-Gagnon, "'I Know It When I See It': Constructing Emotion and Emotional Labor in Social Justice News," *Mass Communication and Society* 23, no. 5 (2020): 608–27.

Conclusion

1. Ryfe, "Broader and Deeper."

2. The ethnographies mentioned here are: Argyris, *Behind the Front Page*; Fishman, *Manufacturing the News*; Gans, *Deciding What's News*; and Tuchman, *Making News*.

3. Beam, "Professionalism as an Organizational Concept," 72.

4. Beam, "Professionalism as an Organizational Concept."

5. Terrence E. Deal and Allan A. Kennedy, *Corporate Culture: The Rites and Rituals of Corporate Life* (Reading, MA: Addison-Wesley, 1982).

6. Kunda, *Engineering Culture*, 3.

7. Schein, *Organizational Culture and Leadership*.

8. Maureen Dowd, "Requiem for the Newsroom," *New York Times*, April 29, 2023.

9. Dowd, "Requiem for the Newsroom."

10. Diamond, "Organizational Identity."

11. See both Robert W. McChesney and John Nichols, *The Death and Life of American Journalism: The Media Revolution That Will Begin the World Again* (New York: Nation Books, 2011); and Robert G. Picard, "Shifts in Newspaper Advertising Expenditures and Their Implications for the Future of Newspapers," *Journalism Studies* 9, no. 5 (2008): 704–16.

12. For a clear understanding of engagement's popularity and the difficulties in defining and quantifying it, see Jacob L. Nelson, "The Next Media Regime: The Pursuit of 'Audience Engagement' in Journalism," *Journalism* 22, no. 9 (2021): 2350–67.

13. Sue Robinson, *How Journalists Engage: A Theory of Trust Building, Identities, and Care* (New York: Oxford University Press, 2023).

14. See Penny O'Donnell, Lawrie Zion, and Merryn Sherwood, "Where Do Journalists Go after Newsroom Job Cuts?" *Journalism Practice* 10, no. 1 (2016): 35–51.

15. Stephen D. Reese, *The Crisis of the Institutional Press* (Medford, MA: Polity, 2021), 158.

16. Ben Smith, "Two Journalists Started an Argument in Boston in 1979. It's Not Over Yet," *New York Times*, October 10, 2021, https://www.nytimes.com/2021/10/10/business/journalists-objectivity.html.

17. Smith, "Two Journalists Started an Argument."

18. Singer, "Contested Autonomy," 80.

19. See Hallin and Mancini, *Comparing Media Systems*; and Henrik Örnebring, "Reassessing Journalism as a Profession," in *The Routledge Companion to News and Journalism*, ed. Stuart Allan, 568–77 (Abingdon, UK: Routledge, 2009).

20. Henrik Örnebring and Michael Karlsson, *Journalistic Autonomy: The Genealogy of a Concept* (Columbia: University of Missouri Press, 2022).

21. Bertrand, *Media Ethics and Accountability Systems*.

22. Patrick Ferrucci, "The End of Ombudsmen? 21st-Century Journalism and Reader Representatives," *Journalism & Mass Communication Quarterly* 96, no. 1 (2019): 288–307.

23. Waisbord, *Reinventing Professionalism*, 123.

24. Schudson, "The Objectivity Norm in American Journalism," 165.

25. For more on an argument about the changing nature of gatekeeping in journalism, see Axel Bruns, *Gatewatching and News Curation: Journalism, Social Media, and the Public Sphere* (New York: Peter Lang, 2018).

26. Pablo J. Boczkowski, *Digitizing the News: Innovation in Online Newspapers* (Cambridge, MA: MIT Press, 2005).

27. Caitlin Petre, *All the News That's Fit to Click: How Metrics Are Transforming the Work of Journalists* (Princeton, NJ: Princeton University Press, 2021).

28. Scott A. Eldridge II, "Journalism Coming into Being: The Timbers and Planks of a Changing Institution," in *The Institutions Changing Journalism*, ed. Patrick Ferrucci and Scott Eldridge II (New York: Routledge, 2022), 14.

29. Patrick Ferrucci, "Understanding the Institutions Affecting Journalism: Ideas for Future Work," in *The Institutions Changing Journalism*, ed. Patrick Ferrucci and Scott Eldridge II (New York: Routledge, 2022.), 190.

30. Bruce A. Williams and Michael X. Delli Carpini, *After Broadcast News: Media Regimes, Democracy, and the New Information Environment* (New York: Cambridge University Press, 2011).

31. Williams and Delli Carpini, *After Broadcast News*, 283.

32. Nelson, "The Next Media Regime."

33. Talcott Parsons, *The Social System* (New York: Free Press, 1968).

34. Adnan Almaney, "Communication and the Systems Theory of Organization," *Journal of Business Communication* 12, no. 1 (1974): 35.

35. Fremont E. Kast and James E. Rosenzweig, "General Systems Theory: Applications for Organization and Management," *Academy of Management Journal* 15, no. 4 (1972): 455.

36. Raymond Caldwell, "Systems Thinking, Organizational Change and Agency: A Practice Theory Critique of Senge's Learning Organization," *Journal of Change Management* 12, no. 2 (2012): 145–64.

37. Donde P. Ashmos and George P. Huber, "The Systems Paradigm in Organization Theory: Correcting the Record and Suggesting the Future," *Academy of Management Review* 12, no. 4 (1987): 607.

38. Breed, "Social Control in the Newsroom."

39. Marjan De Bruin, "Gender, Organizational and Professional Identities in Journalism," *Journalism* 1, no. 2 (2000): 219.

40. Ferrucci, Taylor, and Alaimo, "On the Boundaries."

41. Wilson Lowrey, "Routine News: The Power of the Organization in Visual Journalism," *Visual Communication Quarterly* 6, no 2 (1999.): 10–15.

42. Ferrucci and Kuhn, "Remodeling the Hierarchy."

43. Robert N. Stern and Stephen R. Barley, "Organizations and Social Systems: Organization Theory's Neglected Mandate," *Administrative Science Quarterly* 41, no. 1 (1996): 149.

44. See Ferrucci and Kuhn, "Remodeling the Hierarchy," for this specific model.

45. Timothy Kuhn, "Negotiating the Micro-Macro Divide: Thought Leadership from Organizational Communication for Theorizing Organization," *Management Communication Quarterly* 26, no. 4 (2012): 545.

46. Ryfe, "The Economics of News."

47. Robert King Merton, *Social Theory and Social Structure* (New Dehli: India Rawat Publications, 2017).

48. Merton, *Social Theory*, 68.

49. Amy Mitchell, Mark Jurkowitz, J. Baxter Oliphant, and Elisa Shearer, "Majorities of Americans Say News Coverage of George Floyd Protests Has Been Good, Trump's Public Message Wrong," Pew Research Center, June 12, 2020, https://tinyurl.com/4c2zzkb4.

50. Tom Cotton, "Send In the Troops," *New York Times*, June 3, 2020.

51. Elahe Izadi, Paul Farhi, and Sarah Ellison, "After Staff Uproar, *New York Times* Says Sen. Tom Cotton Op-Ed Urging Military Incursion into U.S. Cities 'Did Not Meet Our Standards,'" *Washington Post*, June 4, 2020.

52. Ezra Klein, "America Is Changing, and So Is the Media," Vox, June 10, 2020, https://tinyurl.com/4y5pwj6b.

53. Kara Swisher, "Tom Cotton's Whitewashing," *New York Times*, June 10, 2020.

54. Klein, "America Is Changing."

55. Reese, *The Crisis of the Institutional Press*.

56. Matthew Powers and Sandra Vera-Zambrano, *The Journalist's Predicament: Difficult Choices in a Declining Profession* (New York: Columbia University Press, 2023), 191.

57. Powers and Vera-Zambrano, *The Journalist's Predicament*, 194.

BIBLIOGRAPHY

Achtenhagen, Leona. 2017. "Media Entrepreneurship—Taking Stock and Moving Forward." *International Journal on Media Management* 19, no. 1: 1–10.

Adams, Dan. 2015. "*Boston Globe* Moving Headquarters to Downtown Boston." *Boston Globe*, December 10, 2015.

Almaney, Adnan. 1974. "Communication and the Systems Theory of Organization." *Journal of Business Communication* 12 (1): 35–43.

Argyris, Chris. 1974. *Behind the Front Page: Organizational Self-Renewal in Metropolition Newspapers*. San Francisco: Jossey-Bass.

Ashmos, Donde P., and George P. Huber. 1987. "The Systems Paradigm in Organization Theory: Correcting the Record and Suggesting the Future." *Academy of Management Review* 12 (4): 607–21.

Bagdikian, Ben H. 2004. *The New Media Monopoly*. Boston: Beacon Press.

Baker, C. Edwin. 1994. *Advertising and a Democratic Press*. Princeton, NJ: Princeton University Press.

Baldasty, Gerald J. 1992. *The Commercialization of News in the Nineteenth Century*. Madison, WI: University of Wisconsin Press.

Banning, Stephen A. 1999. "The Professionalization of Journalism: A Nineteenth-Century Beginning." *Journalism History* 24 (4): 157–63.

Barnouw, Erik, ed. 1997. *Conglomerates and the Media*. New York: New Press.

Batsell, Jake. 2015. *Engaged Journalism: Connecting with Digitally Empowered News Audiences*. New York: Columbia University Press.

Beam, Randal A. 1988. "Professionalism as an Organizational Concept: Journalism as a Case Study." PhD diss., University of Wisconsin-Madison.

———. 1998. "What It Means to Be a Market-Oriented Newspaper." *Newspaper Research Journal* 19 (3): 2–20.

Bélair-Gagnon, Valérie. 2022. "Web Analytics in Journalism." In *The Institutions Changing Journalism: Barbarians Inside the Gate*, edited by Patrick Ferrucci and Scott A. Eldridge II, 153–64. New York: Routledge.

Bélair-Gagnon, Valérie, and Avery E. Holton. 2018a. "Boundary Work, Interloper Media, and Analytics in Newsrooms: An Analysis of the Roles of Web Analytics Companies in News Production." *Digital Journalism* 6 (4): 492–508.

———. 2018b. "Strangers to the Game? Interlopers, Intralopers, and Shifting News Production." *Media and Communication* 6 (4): 70–78.

Benson, Rodney. 1999. "Field Theory in Comparative Context: A New Paradigm for Media Studies." *Theory and Society* 28 (3): 463–98.

Benton, Joshua. 2021. "The Vulture Is Hungry Again: Alden Global Capital Wants to Buy a Few Hundred More Newspapers." Nieman Lab, November 22, 2021, https://tinyurl.com/4yv2843w.

Bertrand, Claude-Jean. 2018. *Media Ethics and Accountability Systems*. New York: Routledge.

Boczkowski, Pablo J. 2005. *Digitizing the News: Innovation in Online Newspapers*. Cambridge, MA: MIT Press.

Brandt, Evan. "My Newspaper Was Gutted by Journalism's Biggest Bogeyman." As told to Noah Lanard. *Mother Jones*, May–June 2022, https://tinyurl.com/v9ba97nj.

Breed, Warren. 1955. "Social Control in the Newsroom: A Functional Analysis." *Social Forces* 33 (4): 326–35.

Bruns, Axel. 2018. *Gatewatching and News Curation: Journalism, Social Media, and the Public Sphere*. New York: Peter Lang.

Caldwell, Raymond. 2012. "Systems Thinking, Organizational Change and Agency: A Practice Theory Critique of Senge's Learning Organization." *Journal of Change Management* 12 (2): 145–64.

Campbell, Alexia Fernandez. 2019. "What the Mass Resignations at Deadspin Tell Us About Work in America. Vox, November 1, 2019, https://tinyurl.com/yh8vxen3.

Canham, Erwin D. 1972. *Newspaper Story: One Hundred Years of the Boston Globe*. Cambridge, MA: Harvard University Press.

Carey, James W. 2007. "A Short History of Journalism for Journalists: A Proposal and Essay." *Harvard International Journal of Press/Politics* 12 (1): 3–16.

Carlson, Matt. 2017. *Journalistic Authority: Legitimating News in the Digital Era*. New York: Columbia University Press.

Carmody, Deirdre. "*Time* Responds to Criticism over Simpson Cover." *New York Times*, June 25, 1994.

Carpenter, Serena, Jan Boehmer, and Frederick Fico. 2016. "The Measurement of Journalistic Role Enactments: A Study of Organizational Constraints and Support in For-Profit and Nonprofit Journalism." *Journalism & Mass Communication Quarterly* 93 (3): 587–608.

Casselberry, Ian. 2021. "Six Months In, Defector Looks Like a Sports Media Success Story." Awful Announcing, February 22, 2021, https://tinyurl.com/4e2j6s55.

Chadha, Monica. 2016. "What I Am versus What I Do: Work and Identity Negotiation in Hyperlocal News Startups." *Journalism Practice* 10, no. 6: 697–714.

Cheney, George. 1983. "On the Various and Changing Meanings of Organizational Membership: A Field Study of Organizational Identification." *Communications Monographs* 50 (4): 342–62.

Clavio, Galen, and Brian Moritz. 2021. "Here's Why I Joined: Introductory Letters from New Hires to The Athletic and the Framing of Paywall Journalism." *Communication & Sport* 9 (2): 198–219.

Clegg, Stewart, and David Dunkerley. 2013. *Organization, Class and Control*. New York: Routledge.

Coppins, McKay. 2021. "A Secretive Hedge Fund Is Gutting Newsrooms." *The Atlantic*, October 14, 2021.

Cottle, Simon. 2007. "Ethnography and News Production: New(s) Developments in the Field." *Sociology Compass* 1 (1): 1–16.

Cotton, Tom. 2020. "Send In the Troops." *New York Times*, June 3, 2020.

De Bruin, Marjan. 2000. "Gender, Organizational and Professional Identities in Journalism." *Journalism* 1 (2): 217–38.

Deal, Terrence E., and Allan A. Kennedy. 1982. *Corporate Culture: The Rites and Rituals of Corporate Life*. Reading, MA: Addison-Wesley.

Defector. 2022. About Us. https://defector.com/about-us.

Deuze, Mark. 2008. "The Professional Identity of Journalists in the Context of Convergence Culture." *Observatorio (Obs*)* 2 (4): 103–17.

Deuze, Mark, and Tamara Witschge. 2018. "Beyond Journalism: Theorizing the Transformation of Journalism." *Journalism* 19 (2): 165–81.

Diamond, Michael A. 1988. "Organizational Identity: A Psychoanalytic Exploration of Organizational Meaning." *Administration & Society* 20 (2): 166–90.

Doctor, Ken. 2013. "The Newsonomics of John Henry Buying The Boston Globe." NiemanLab, August 3, 2013, https://tinyurl.com/ydpfevap.

Dowd, Maureen. 2023. "Requiem for the Newsroom." *New York Times*, April 29, 2003.

Draper, Kevin. 2018. "At The Athletic, A Hiring Spree Becomes a Story in Itself." *New York Times*, August 24, 2018.

Eldridge, Scott A., II. 2017. *Online Journalism from the Periphery: Interloper Media and the Journalistic Field*. New York: Routledge.

Eldridge, Scott A. 2022. "Journalism Coming into Being: The Timbers and Planks of a Changing Institution." In *The Institutions Changing Journalism: Barbarians Inside the Gate*, edited by Patrick Ferrucci and Scott A. Eldridge II, 1–14. New York: Routledge.

Ember, Sydney. 2018. "*Denver Post* Rebels Against Its Hedge-Fund Ownership," *New York Times*, April 7, 2018.

English, Leona, and Nancy Peters. 2011. "Founders' Syndrome in Women's Nonprofit Organizations: Implications for Practice and Organizational Life." *Nonprofit Management and Leadership* 22 (2): 159–71.

Feagin, Joe R., Anthony M. Orum, and Gideon Sjoberg. 1991. *A Case for the Case Study*. Chapel Hill: University of North Carolina Press.

Feldman, Daniel C. 1984. "The Development and Enforcement of Group Norms." *Academy of Management Review* 9 (1): 47–53.

Ferrucci, Patrick. 2019a. "The End of Ombudsmen? 21st-Century Journalism and Reader Representatives." *Journalism & Mass Communication Quarterly* 96 (1): 288–307.

———. 2015. "Follow the Leader: How Leadership Can Affect the Future of Community Journalism." *Community Journalism* 4 (2): 19–35.

———. 2020. "It Is in the Numbers: How Market Orientation Impacts Journalists' Use of News Metrics." *Journalism* 21 (2): 244–61.

———. 2021. "Joining the Team: Metajournalistic Discourse, Paradigm Repair, the Athletic and Sports Journalism Practice." *Journalism Practice* 16, no. 10 (2022): 1–19.

———. 2019b. *Making Nonprofit News: Market models, Influence and Journalistic Practice*. New York: Routledge.

———. 2018. "Money Matters? Journalists' Perception of the Effects of a Weak Market Orientation." *Convergence* 24 (4): 424–38.

———. 2015. "Murder Incorporated: Market Orientation and Coverage of the Annie Le Investigation." *Electronic News* 9 (2): 108–21.

———. 2015. "Primary Differences: How Market Orientation Can Influence Content." *Journal of Media Practice* 16 (3): 195–210.

———. 2015. "Public Journalism No More: The Digitally Native News Nonprofit and Public Service Journalism." *Journalism* 16 (7): 904–19.

———. 2022. "Understanding the Institutions Affecting Journalism: Ideas for Future Work." In *The Institutions Changing Journalism*, edited by Patrick Ferrucci and Scott A. Eldridge II, 180–92. New York: Routledge.

Ferrucci, Patrick, and Kathleen I. Alaimo. 2020. "Escaping the News Desert: Nonprofit News and Open-System Journalism Organizations." *Journalism* 21 (4): 489–506.

Ferrucci, Patrick, and Scott A. Eldridge II, eds. 2022. *The Institutions Changing Journalism: Barbarians Inside the Gate*. New York: Routledge.

Ferrucci, Patrick, and Timothy Kuhn. 2022. "Remodeling the Hierarchy: An Organization-Centric Model of Influence for Media Sociology Research." *Journalism Studies* 23 (4): 525–43.

Ferrucci, Patrick, and Jacob L. Nelson. 2019. "The New Advertisers: How Foundation Funding Impacts Journalism." *Media and Communication* 7 (4): 45–55.

Ferrucci, Patrick, Chad E. Painter, and Angelika Kalika. 2019. "How Market Orientation and Ethics Affected Coverage of Marijuana Legalization." *Newspaper Research Journal* 40 (3): 391–404.

Ferrucci, Patrick, and Gregory Perreault. 2021. "The Liability of Newness: Journalism, Innovation and the Issue of Core Competencies." *Journalism Studies* 22 (11): 1436–49.

Ferrucci, Patrick, and Michelle Rossi. 2022. "Pivoting to Instability": Metajournalistic Discourse, Reflexivity and the Economics and Effects of a Shrinking Industry." *International Journal of Communication* 16 (2022): 4095–4114.

Ferrucci, Patrick, Frank Michael Russell, Heesook Choi, Margaret Duffy, and Esther Thorson. 2017. "Times Are a Changin': How a Merger Affects the Construction of News Processes." *Journalism Studies* 18 (3): 247–64.

Ferrucci, Patrick, and Edson C. Tandoc Jr. 2015. "A Tale of Two Newsrooms: How Market Orientation Affects Web Analytics Use." In *Contemporary Research Methods and Data Analytics in the News Industry*, edited by William Gibbs and Joseph McKendrick, 58–76. Philadelphia: IGI Global.

Ferrucci, Patrick, and Ross Taylor. 2019. "Blurred Boundaries: Toning Ethics in News Routines." *Journalism Studies* 20 (15): 2167–81.

Ferrucci, Patrick, Ross Taylor, and Kathleen I. Alaimo. 2020. "On the Boundaries: Professional Photojournalists Navigating Identity in an Age of Technological Democratization." *Digital Journalism* 8 (3): 367–85.

Ferrucci, Patrick, and Tim P. Vos. 2017. "Who's In, Who's Out? Constructing the Identity of Digital Journalists." *Digital Journalism* 5 (7): 868–83.

Ferrucci, Patrick, and J. David Wolfgang. 2021. "Inside or Out? Perceptions of How Differing Types of Comment Moderation Impact Practice." *Journalism Studies* 22 (8): 1010–27.

Fischer, Sara. 2021. "Scoop: New York Times in Talks to Buy The Athletic. Axios," May 25, 2021, https://www.axios.com/2021/05/25/new-york-times-nytimes-acquisition-athletic.

Fishman, Mark. 1980. *Manufacturing the News*. Austin: University of Texas Press.

Fox, Jesse, and Bree McEwan. 2017. "Distinguishing Technologies for Social Interaction: The Perceived Social Affordances of Communication Channels Scale." *Communication Monographs* 84 (3): 298–318.

Freedman, Des. 2015. "Paradigms of Media Power." *Communication, Culture & Critique* 8 (2): 273–89.

Gandy, Oscar. 1982. *Beyond Agenda-Setting: Information Subsidies and Public Policy*. Norwood, NJ: Ablex.

Gans, Herbert J. 1979. *Deciding What's News: A Study of CBS Evening News, NBC Nightly News, Newsweek, and Time*. New York: Pantheon Books.

Gaziano, Cecilie, and David C. Coulson. 1988. "Effect of Newsroom Management Styles on Journalists: A Case Study." *Journalism Quarterly* 65 (4): 869–80.

Gilsanin, Kathy. 2010. "The St. Louis Beacon: 'News That Matters' for St. Louis." *Columbia Journalism Review*, December 29, 2010, https://tinyurl.com/yck2zk5f.

Glasser, Theodore L., and Marc Gunther. 2005. "The Legacy of Autonomy in American Journalism." In *Institutions of Democracy: The Press*, edited by Geneva Overholser and Kathleen Hall Jamieson, 384–99. New York: Oxford University Press.

Gordon, Aaron. 2018. "The Sports Pages' New Clothes." Slate, September 6, 2018, https://slate.com/culture/2018/09/the-athletic-is-poaching-from-local-sports-pages-and-reading-like-them-too.html.

Green, Sue. 2018. "When the Numbers Don't Add Up: Accommodating Data Journalism in a Compact Journalism Programme." *Asia Pacific Media Educator* 28, no. 1: 78–90.

Greenberger, David B., Marcia P. Miceli, and Debra J. Cohen. 1987. "Oppositionists and Group Norms: The Reciprocal Influence of Whistle-Blowers and Co-Workers." *Journal of Business Ethics* 6: 527–42.

Grint, Keith, and Darren Nixon. 2015. *The Sociology of Work.* 4th ed. Malden, MA: Polity.

Grohmann, Rafael. 2019. "Media Workers Co-Ops: Possibilities, Contradictions and Argentinean Scenario." *Intercom: Revista Brasileira de Ciências da Comunicação* 42, no. 3: 77–90.

Groves, Jonathan, and Carrie Brown. 2020. *Transforming Newsrooms: Connecting Organizational Culture, Strategy, and Innovation.* New York: Routledge.

Hallin, Daniel C. 1992. "The Passing of the 'High Modernism' of American Journalism." *Journal of Communication* 42 (3): 14–25.

Hallin, Daniel C., and Paolo Mancini. 2011. *Comparing Media Systems Beyond the Western World.* Cambridge: Cambridge University Press.

Hamel, Jacques, Stéphane Dufour, and Dominic Fortin. 1993. *Case Study Methods.* Newbury Park, CA: Sage.

Hanitzsch, Thomas. 2007. "Deconstructing Journalism Culture: Toward a Universal Theory." *Communication Theory* 17 (4): 367–85.

Hanretty, Chris. 2014. "Media Outlets and Their Moguls: Why Concentrated Individual or Family Ownership Is Bad for Editorial Independence." *European Journal of Communication* 29 (3): 335–50.

Healy, Beth. 2013. "John Henry's Purchase of the *Boston Globe* Completed." *Boston Globe*, October 24, 2013.

Herscovitz, Heloiza G. 2004. "Brazilian Journalists' Perceptions of Media Roles, Ethics and Foreign Influences on Brazilian Journalism." *Journalism Studies* 5 (1): 71–86.

Hiller, Janine S. 2013. "The Benefit Corporation and Corporate Social Responsibility." *Journal of Business Ethics* 118: 287–301.

Hinsley, Amber. 2017. "Developing New Organizational Identity: Merger of St. Louis Public Radio and the St. Louis Beacon." *Journal of Radio & Audio Media* 24 (1): 144–60.

Hirsh, Lauren, Kevin Draper, and Katherine Rosman. 2022. "New York Times Co. to Buy The Athletic for $550 Million in Cash." *New York Times*, January 6, 2022.

Hofstede, Geert. 1980. "Motivation, Leadership, and Organization: Do American Theories Apply Abroad?" *Organizational Dynamics* 9 (1): 42–63.

Hollifield, C. Ann, Gerald M. Kosicki, and Lee B. Becker. 2001. "Organizational vs. Professional Culture in the Newsroom: Television News Directors' and Newspaper Editors' Hiring Decisions." *Journal of Broadcasting & Electronic Media* 45 (1): 92–117.

Howard-Grenville, Jennifer A. 2006. "Inside the 'Black Box': How Organizational Culture and Subcultures Inform Interpretations and Actions on Environmental Issues." *Organization & Environment* 19 (1): 46–73.

Humayun, Muhammad Fahad, and Patrick Ferrucci. 2022. "Understanding Social Media in Journalism Practice: A Typology." *Digital Journalism* 10 (9): 1502–25.

Hutchins, Corey. 2018. "The Colorado Sun Pits Civil-Backed Startup Against the *Denver Post*." *Columbia Journalism Review*, July 18, 2018, https://tinyurl.com/uf23rehc.

Izadi, Elahe, Paul Farhi, and Sarah Ellison. 2020. "After Staff Uproar, *New York Times* Says Sen. Tom Cotton Op-Ed Urging Military Incursion into U.S. Cities 'Did Not Meet Our Standards.'" *Washington Post*, June 4, 2020.

Jaakkola, Maarit, Heikki Hellman, Kari Koljonen, and Jari Väliverronen. 2015. "Liquid Modern Journalism with a Difference: The Changing Professional Ethos of Cultural Journalism." *Journalism Practice* 9 (6): 811–28.

Jian, Lian, and Nikki Usher. 2014. "Crowd-Funded Journalism." *Journal of Computer-Mediated Communication* 19 (2): 155–70.

Kast, Fremont E., and James E. Rosenzweig. 1972. "General Systems Theory: Applications for Organization and Management." *Academy of Management Journal* 15 (4): 447–65.

Kennedy, Dan. 2013. *The Wired City: Reimagining Journalism and Civic Life in the Post-Newspaper Age*. Amherst: University of Massachusetts Press.

———. 2016. "The Bezos Effect: How Amazon's Founder Is Reinventing *The Washington Post*—and What Lessons It Might Hold for the Beleaguered Newspaper Business." Shorenstein Center on Media, Politics and Public Policy, June 2016.

———. 2018. *The Return of the Moguls: How Jeff Bezos and John Henry are Remaking Newspapers for the Twenty-First Century*. Lebanon, NH: University Press of New England.

Klein, Ezra. 2020. "America Is Changing, and So Is the Media." Vox, June 10, 2020, https://tinyurl.com/4y5pwj6b

Klinenberg, Eric. 2005. "Convergence: News Production in a Digital Age." *Annals of the American Academy of Political and Social Science* 597 (1): 48–64.

Konieczna, Magda. 2014. "Do Old Norms Have a Place in New Media? A Case Study of the Nonprofit MinnPost." *Journalism Practice* 8 (1): 49–64.

———. 2018. *Journalism Without Profit: Making News When the Market Fails*. New York: Oxford University Press.

Konieczna, Magda, and Elia Powers. 2017. "What Can Nonprofit Journalists Actually Do for Democracy?" *Journalism Studies* 18 (12): 1542–58.

Koo, Ben. 2019. "The Athletic Is Worth $300 Million, But Can It Become a Billion Dollar Company? Awful Announcing," September 23, 2019, https://tinyurl.com/bdzm5cpm.

Kovach, Bill, and Tom Rosenstiel. 2007. *The Elements of Journalism: What Newspeople Should Know and the Public Should Expect*. New York: Three Rivers Press.

Kuhn, Timothy. 2008. "A Communicative Theory of the Firm: Developing an Alternative Perspective on Intra-Organizational Power and Stakeholder Relationships." *Organization Studies* 29 (8–9): 1227–54.

——. 2012. "Negotiating the Micro-Macro Divide: Thought Leadership from Organizational Communication for Theorizing Organization." *Management Communication Quarterly* 26 (4): 543–84.

Kuhn, Timothy, Karen Lee Ashcraft, and François Cooren. 2017. *The Work of Communication: Relational Perspectives on Working and Organizing in Contemporary Capitalism*. New York: Routledge.

Kuhn, Timothy, and Jared Kopczynski. 2019. "Organizational Structures, Processes, and Agency." In *Movements in Organizational Communication Research: Current Issues and Future Directions*, edited by Jamie McDonald and Rahul Mitra, 14–34. New York: Routledge.

Kunda, Gideon. 2009. *Engineering Culture: Control and Commitment in a High-Tech Corporation*. Philadelphia: Temple University Press.

Kurland, Nancy B. 2017. "Accountability and the Public Benefit Corporation." *Business Horizons* 60 (4): 519–28.

Larson, Christine. 2015. "Live Publishing: The Onstage Redeployment of Journalistic Authority." *Media, Culture & Society* 37 (3): 440–59.

Larson, Gregory S., and Phillip K. Tompkins. 2005. "Ambivalence and Resistance: A Study of Management in a Concertive Control System." *Communication Monographs* 72 (1): 1–21.

Leahy, Sean. 2019. "It's the First Anniversary of The Athletic Boston. Let's Celebrate." The Athletic, April 10, 2019.

Lee, Alfred McClung. 1990. *The Daily Newspaper in America: The Evolution of a Social Instrument*. New York: Routledge.

Levi, Lili. 2017. "The Weaponized Lawsuit Against the Media: Litigation Funding as a New Threat to Journalism." *American University Law Review* 66 (2017): 761–828.

Limor, Yehiel, and Itai Himelboim. 2006. "Journalism and Moonlighting: An International Comparison of 242 Codes of Ethics." *Journal of Mass Media Ethics* 21, no. 4: 265–85.

Linnell, Deborah. 2004. "Founders and Other Gods." *Nonprofit Quarterly* 11 (1): 8–17.

Lowes, Mark, and Christopher Robillard. 2018. "Social Media and Digital Breakage on the Sports Beat." *International Journal of Sport Communication* 11 (3): 308–18.

Lowrey, Wilson. 1999. "Routine News: The Power of the Organization in Visual Journalism." *Visual Communication Quarterly* 6 (2): 10–15.

Lowrey, Wilson, Lindsey Sherrill, and Ryan Broussard. 2019. "Field and Ecology Approaches to Journalism Innovation: The Role of Ancillary Organizations." *Journalism Studies* 20 (15): 2131–49.

Madrid-Morales, Dani, and Herman Wasserman. 2018. "Chinese Media Engagement in South Africa: What Is Its Impact on Local Journalism?" *Journalism Studies* 19 (8): 1218–35.

Maharidge, Dale. 2016. "What Happens to Journalists When No One Wants to Print Their Words Anymore?" *The Nation*, March 21, 2016.

Maiden, Neil, Konstantinos Zachos, Amanda Brown, George Brock, Lars Nyre, Aleksander Nygård Tonheim, Dimitris Apsotolou, and Jeremy Evans. 2018. "Making the News: Digital Creativity Support for Journalists." *Proceedings of the 2018 CHI Conference on Human Factors in Computing Systems*, 1–11, https://doi.org/10.1145/3173574.3174049.

Malone, Roy. 2014. "Beacon, KWMU Join Forces for the Better in St. Louis." *Gateway Journalism Review*, Winter (2014): 10.

Markus, Ben. 2018. "The Colorado Sun to Launch with Former *Denver Post* 'A-Team' Stars and Tech Cash." Colorado Public Radio, June 17, 2018, https://tinyurl.com/4wa6attv.

Martin, Joanne. 1992. *Cultures in Organizations: Three Perspectives*. Oxford: Oxford University Press.

——. 1995. "The Style and Structure of *Cultures in Organizations: Three Perspectives*." *Organization Science* 6 (2): 230–32.

McChesney, Robert W., and John Nichols. 2011. *The Death and Life of American Journalism: The Media Revolution That Will Begin the World Again*. New York: Nation Books.

McDevitt, Michael. 2003. "In Defense of Autonomy: A Critique of the Public Journalism Critique." *Journal of Communication* 53 (1): 155–64.

McGregor, Susan E., Elizabeth Anne Watkins, and Kelly Caine. 2017. "Would You Slack That? The Impact of Security and Privacy on Cooperative Newsroom Work." *Proceedings of the ACM on Human-Computer Interaction* 1: 1–22, https://doi.org/10.1145/3134710.

McManus, John H. 1994. *Market-Driven Journalism: Let the Citizen Beware?* Thousand Oaks, CA: Sage.

Merton, Robert King. 2017. *Social Theory and Social Structure*. New Dehli: India Rawat Publications.

Mitchell, Amy, Mark Jurkowitz, J. Baxter Oliphant, and Elisa Shearer. 2020. "Majorities of Americans Say News Coverage of George Floyd Protests Has Been Good, Trump's Public Message Wrong." Pew Research Center, June 12, 2020, https://tinyurl.com/4c2zzkb4.

Morgan, Gareth. 1998. *Images of Organization: The Executive Edition*. Thousand Oaks, CA: Sage.

Nadler, Anthony M. 2016. *Making the News Popular: Mobilizing US News Audiences*. Urbana: University of Illinois Press.

Nee, Rebecca Coates. 2013. "Creative Destruction: An Exploratory Study of How Digitally Native News Nonprofits Are Innovating Online Journalism Practices." *International Journal on Media Management* 15 (1): 3–22.

——. 2014. "Social Responsibility Theory and the Digital Nonprofits: Should the Government Aid Online News Startups?" *Journalism* 15 (3): 326–43.

Nelson, Jacob L. 2021a. *Imagined Audiences: How Journalists Perceive and Pursue the Public*. New York: Oxford University Press.

———. 2021b. "The Next Media Regime: The Pursuit of 'Audience Engagement' in Journalism." *Journalism* 22 (9): 2350–67.

Nicolais, Mario. 2023. "Five Years Since the Denver Post Rebellion, Colorado Journalism Has Had Its Ups and Downs." *Colorado Sun*, February 26, 2023, https://tinyurl.com/3jcbj9ve.

O'Donnell, Penny, Lawrie Zion, and Merryn Sherwood. 2016. "Where Do Journalists Go After Newsroom Job Cuts?" *Journalism Practice* 10 (1): 35–51.

Örnebring, Henrik. 2019. "Professionalization of Journalists: Historical." In *The International Encyclopedia of Journalism Studies*, edited by Tim P. Vos and Folker Hanusch. New York: Wiley.

———. 2009. "Reassessing Journalism as a Profession." In *The Routledge Companion to News and Journalism*, edited by Stuart Allan, 568–77. Abingdon, UK: Routledge.

Örnebring, Henrik, and Michael Karlsson. 2022. *Journalistic Autonomy: The Genealogy of a Concept*. Columbia: University of Missouri Press.

Parsons, Talcott. 1968. *The Social System*. New York: Free Press.

Peiser, Jaclyn. 2018. "Goodbye, *Denver Post*. Hello, Blockchain." *New York Times*, June 17, 2018.

Pershan, Caleb. 2022. "'We Have the Simplest Business in the World': A Conversation with Defector Media." *Columbia Journalism Review*, March 23, 2022, https://tinyurl.com/h4thf84b.

Peters, Jonathan. 2022. "Staying Abreast of the Law: Legal Issues Affecting Journalism." In *The Institutions Changing Journalism*, edited by Patrick Ferrucci and Scott A. Eldridge II, 46–58. New York: Routledge.

Petre, Caitlin. 2021. *All the News That's Fit to Click: How Metrics Are Transforming the Work of Journalists*. Princeton, NJ: Princeton University Press.

Picard, Robert G. 2008. "Shifts in Newspaper Advertising Expenditures and Their Implications for the Future of Newspapers." *Journalism Studies* 9 (5): 704–16.

Pirolli, Bryan. 2017. "Travel Journalists and Professional Identity: Ideology and Evolution in an Online Era." *Journalism Practice* 11 (6): 740–59.

Plunkett, Chuck. 2023. "When the Vultures Circled the *Denver Post*, We Asked Colorado to Fight for Local News. It Did." Colorado Sun, April 2, 2023, https://tinyurl.com/2wkxr8v4.

Pompeo, Joe. 2020. "The Hedge Fund Vampire That Bleeds Newspapers Dry Now Has the Chicago Tribune by the Throat." *Vanity Fair*, February 5, 2020, https://tinyurl.com/yrct3haz.

Powers, Matthew, and Sandra Vera-Zambrano. 2023. *The Journalist's Predicament: Difficult Choices in a Declining Profession*. New York: Columbia University Press.

Reese, Stephen D. 2021. *The Crisis of the Institutional Press.* Medford, MA: Polity.

Reese, Stephen D., and Jane Ballinger. 2001. "The Roots of a Sociology of News: Remembering Mr. Gates and Social Control in the Newsroom." *Journalism & Mass Communication Quarterly* 78 (4): 641–58.

Robinson, Sue. 2023. *How Journalists Engage: A Theory of Trust Building, Identities, and Care.* New York: Oxford University Press.

Ryfe, David M. 2009a. "Broader and Deeper: A Study of Newsroom Culture in a Time of Change." *Journalism* 10 (2): 197–216.

———. 2021. "The Economics of News and the Practice of News Production." *Journalism Studies* 22 (1): 60–76.

———. 2009b. "Structure, Agency, and Change in an American Newsroom." *Journalism* 10 (5): 665–83.

Sackmann, Sonja A. 1992. "Culture and Subcultures: An Analysis of Organizational Knowledge." *Administrative Science Quarterly* 37, no. 1 (1992): 140–61.

Santamaría, Sara García. 2018. "The Sovietization of Cuban Journalism: The Impact of Foreign Economy Dependency on Media Structures in a Post-Soviet Era." *Journal of Latin American Communication Research* 6 (1–2): 135–51.

Santana, Arthur D. 2014. "Virtuous or Vitriolic: The Effect of Anonymity on Civility in Online Newspaper Reader Comment Boards." *Journalism Practice* 8 (1): 18–33.

Schauster, Erin E., Patrick Ferrucci, and Marlene S. Neill. 2016. "Native Advertising Is the New Journalism: How Deception Affects Social Responsibility." *American Behavioral Scientist* 60 (12): 1408–24.

Schein, Edgar H. 2016. *Organizational Culture and Leadership.* San Francisco: Jossey-Bass.

Schneider, Nathan. 2020. "Broad-Based Stakeholder Ownership in Journalism: Co-ops, ESOPs, Blockchains." *Media Industries Journal* 7, no. 2 (2), https://doi.org/https://doi.org/10.3998/mij.15031809.0007.203.

———. 2018. "An Internet of Ownership: Democratic Design for the Online Economy." *Sociological Review* 66, no. 2: 320–40.

Schudson, Michael. 1978. *Discovering the News: A Social History of American Newspapers.* New York: Basic Books.

———. 2001. "The Objectivity Norm in American Journalism." *Journalism* 2 (2): 149–70.

———. 1992. *Watergate in American Memory: How We Remember, Forget, and Reconstruct the Past.* New York: Basic Books.

Scire, Sarah. 2022. "Defector's Most Successful Promo Email Was Too 'Creepy' to Repeat." NiemanLab, October 22, 2022, https://tinyurl.com/5n76jy2n.

Scott, Martin, Mel Bunce, and Kate Wright. 2019. "Foundation Funding and the Boundaries of Journalism." *Journalism Studies* 20 (14): 2034–52.

Seely, Natalee. 2019. "Journalists and Mental Health: The Psychological Toll of Covering Everyday Trauma." *Newspaper Research Journal* 40 (2): 239–59.

Sherman, Alex. 2020. "The Athletic Says It Hits 1 Million Subscribers after Surviving Sports Shutdown." CNBC.com, September 9, 2020, https://tinyurl.com/4appmxt7.

Shoemaker, Pamela J., and Stephen D. Reese. 2014. *Mediating the Message in the 21st Century: A Media Sociology Perspective.* 3rd ed. New York: Routledge.

Silva, Miguel Franquet Santos, and Scott A. Eldridge II. 2020. *The Ethics of Photojournalism in the Digital Age.* New York: Routledge.

Singer, Jane B. 2007. "Contested Autonomy: Professional and Popular Claims on Journalistic Norms." *Journalism Studies* 8 (1): 79–95.

——. "Journalism and Digital Technologies." In *Changing the News: The Forces Shaping Journalism in Uncertain Times*, edited by Wilson Lowrey and Peter J. Gade, 214–229. New York: Routledge, 2011.

Smith, Ben. 2021. "Two Journalists Started an Argument in Boston in 1979. It's Not Over Yet." *New York Times*, October 10, 2021.

Spencer, David Ralph, and Judith Spencer. 2007. *The Yellow Journalism: The Press and America's Emergence as a World Power.* Evanston, IL: Northwestern University Press.

Steinke, Allison J., and Valerie Belair-Gagnon. 2020. "'I Know It When I See It': Constructing Emotion and Emotional Labor in Social Justice News." *Mass Communication and Society* 23 (5): 608–27.

Stenberg, Mark. 2022. "How Defector Media Turned Its Hit Podcast into a 7% Bump in Subscribers." AdWeek, October 27, 2022, https://tinyurl.com/2p9ksyeh.

Stern, Robert N., and Stephen R. Barley. 1996. "Organizations and Social Systems: Organization Theory's Neglected Mandate." *Administrative Science Quarterly* 41 (1): 146–62.

Strauss, Ben. 2022. "At the Athletic and New York Times, a Marriage with Promise and Tension." *Washington Post*, October 7, 2022.

Sullivan, Margaret. 2021. "Defector.com's Journalistic Experiment Began with a Staff Walkout. It Might Actually Be Working." *Washington Post*, February 21, 2021.

——. 2018. "Is This Strip-Mining or Journalism? 'Sobs, Gasps, Expletives' over Latest *Denver Post* Layoffs." *Washington Post*, March 15, 2018.

Swint, Kerwin C. 2008. *Dark Genius: The Influential Career of Legendary Political Operative and Fox News Founder Roger Ailes.* New York: Union Square Press.

Swisher, Kara. 2020. "Tom Cotton's Whitewashing." *New York Times*, June 10, 2020.

Tandoc, Edson C., Jr. 2019. *Analyzing Analytics: Disrupting Journalism One Click at a Time.* New York: Routledge.

——. 2014. "Journalism Is Twerking? How Web Analytics Is Changing the Process of Gatekeeping." *New Media & Society* 16 (4): 559–75.

——. 2015. "Why Web Analytics Click: Factors Affecting the Ways Journalists Use Audience Metrics." *Journalism Studies* 16 (6): 782–99.

Tandoc, Edson C., Jr., and Joy Jenkins. 2018. "Out of Bounds? How Gawker's Outing a Married Man Fits into the Boundaries of Journalism." *New Media & Society* 20 (2): 581–98.

Taylor, Bryan C., Jamie McDonald, and James Fortney. 2013. "But Fade Away? The Current Status of 'Organizational Culture' in Organizational Communication Studies." In *Faces of Culture and Organizational Communication: Metatheoretical Perspectives*, edited by Massimo Marchiori and Sergio Bulgacov. São Caetano do Sul, Brazil: Difusão.

Tharp, Ryan. 2015. Colorado Public Benefit Corporations: Q&A. Fairfield & Woods, February 2, 2015, https://tinyurl.com/y97eu8yj.

Toonkel, Jessica. 2021. "The Athletic Burned Through $95 Million Between 2019 and 2020." The Information, October 4, 2021.

Tuchman, Gaye. 1978. *Making News: A Study in the Construction of Reality.* New York: Free Press.

Umejei, Emeka. 2018. "Hybridizing Journalism: Clash of Two 'Journalisms' in Africa." *Chinese Journal of Communication* 11 (3): 344–58.

Underwood, Doug. 1995. *When MBAs Rule the Newsroom: How the Marketers and Managers Are Reshaping Today's Media.* New York: Columbia University Press.

Vos, Tim P., and Patrick Ferrucci. 2018. "Who Am I? Perceptions of Digital Journalists' Professional Identity." In *The Routledge Handbook of Developments in Digital Journalism Studies*, edited by Scott A. Eldridge II and Bob Franklin, 40–52. New York: Routledge.

Vos, Tim P., and Frank Michael Russell. 2019. "Theorizing Journalism's Institutional Relationships: An Elaboration of Gatekeeping Theory." *Journalism Studies* 20 (16): 2331–48.

Wagner, Laura. 2022. "'No One Knows Anything': Staffers at the Athletic Wait in the Dark Following NYT Deal." Defector, January 7, 2022.

——. 2022. "Under NYT Ownership, The Athletic Lays Down 'No Politics' Rule for Staff." Defector, June 16, 2002.

Waisbord, Silvio. 2013. *Reinventing Professionalism: Journalism and News in Global Perspective.* New York: Wiley.

Wall, Melissa. 2015. "Change the Space, Change the Practice? Re-Imagining Journalism Education with the Pop-Up Newsroom." *Journalism Practice* 9 (2): 123–37.

Walther, Joseph B. 1996. "Computer-Mediated Communication: Impersonal, Interpersonal, and Hyperpersonal Interaction." *Communication Research* 23 (1): 3–43.

Ward, Ken. 2018. "America's Last Newspaper War: One Hundred and Sixteen Years of Competition between the *Denver Post* and *Rocky Mountain News*" (PhD diss., Ohio University, 2018).

Washburn, Patrick S., and Chris Lamb. 2020. *Sports Journalism: A History of Glory, Fame, and Technology.* Lincoln: University of Nebraska Press.

Weick, Karl E. 2012. *Making Sense of the Organization*, vol. 2, *The Impermanent Organization*. New York: Wiley.

Weiss, Robert Stuart. 1994. *Learning from Strangers: The Art and Method of Qualitative Interview Studies*. New York: Free Press.

Wenzel, Andrea. 2020. *Community-Centered Journalism: Engaging People, Exploring Solutions, and Building Trust*. Urbana: University of Illinois Press.

Wheeler, Thomas H., and Tim Gleason. 1995. "Photography or Photofiction: An Ethical Protocol for the Digital Age." *Visual Communication Quarterly* 2 (1): 8–12.

White, David Manning. 1950. "The 'Gate Keeper': A Case Study in the Selection of News." *Journalism Quarterly* 27 (4): 383–90.

Williams, Bruce A., and Michael X. Delli Carpini. 2011. *After Broadcast News: Media Regimes, Democracy, and the New Information Environment*. New York: Cambridge University Press.

Winfield, Betty Houchin. 2008. *Journalism 1908: Birth of a Profession*. Columbia: University of Missouri Press.

Wolfgang, J. David. 2021. "Taming the 'Trolls': How Journalists Negotiate the Boundaries of Journalism and Online Comments." *Journalism* 22 (1): 139–56.

Yiannis, Gabriel. *Organizations in Depth: The Psychoanalysis of Organizations*. Thousand Oaks, CA: Sage, 1999.

INDEX

Accrediting Council of Education in Journalism and Mass Communications, 158
advertising: Defector Media's lack of it on the website, 46; Defector Media's use of it on podcasts, 47; as a historical funding source for journalism, 2, 6–9, 11, 15; history with *Boston Globe*, 93, 107; history with *Denver Post*, 137, 139, 150; influence on the news, 176; "market for advertising" in market theory for news, 19; St. Louis' Beacon's lack of it, 28
After Broadcast News (Williams and Carpini), 174
Alden Global Capital, 22; and Colorado Sun, 67, 72, 75; and *Denver Post*, 137–147, 150, 152, 154–156, 166
alternative newsweeklies, 3
American Public Radio, 38
Amp, 60
Argyris, Chris, 11–12, 157
Athletic: approach to hiring, 112–113; as a case study, 10, 20–21, 112–135; engagement practices, 124–126; history of organization, 3, 114–116; news production processes, 126–132; organizational culture, 116–120; routines utilized, 121–124; sale to the *New York Times*, 132–133; venture capital funding, 133–135
Atlantic (magazine), 138

autonomy: at Athletic, 116, 118–120, 124–126, 132–134; at *Boston Globe*, 93, 104–105, 109; at Colorado Sun, 81, 84, 87, 91; at *Denver Post*, 140, 143, 148, 153; as influence on news production, 1, 4; role in the deprofessionalization of journalism, 171–173; at St. Louis Beacon, 29; in today's journalism ecosystem, 160–162, 165–166, 169–170

Bagdikian, Ben, 138
Baker, C. Edwin, 11
Beam, Randall, 16, 158
beat reporting, 1, 116, 126–128
Bélair-Gagnon, Valerie, 8
Bezos, Jeff, 90
Black Lives Matter, 85
Boczkowski, Pablo J., 173
Boston Globe: as case study, 10, 20, 89–111; conflict of interest covering Red Sox, 97; engagement practices, 105–106; espoused value of a "writer's paper," 91–96; history of John Henry ownership, 90–94; leadership, 96–100; mogul ownership, 96–100, 109–111; news production processes, 107–109; newsroom location, 102; organizational culture, 94–96; routines utilized, 103–105; socialization, 100–102; Spotlight team, 109; utilization of technology, 102–103

Boston Globe Media, 20, 96
Boston Red Sox, 9, 20, 90, 97–98
Brady, Tom, 106
breaking news: at Athletic, 112–114,
    133; at *Boston Globe*, 94, 106–107,
    110; at Colorado Sun, 85–86; at
    Denver Post, 136, 148, 152–152; as
    journalistic routine, 168; at St. Louis
    Beacon, 26, 37
Breed, Warren, 15, 101, 175
buddy system as a form of socializa-
    tion, 59–60, 101, 161–162

capitalism and news, 9, 177
Chartbeat, 105
Chicago Blackhawks, 119
China influence on news, 10
Cleveland, Grover, 21, 138
codes of ethics, 2, 5, 18, 55
Colacioppo, Lee Ann, 143–145
Colorado Public Radio, 85
Colorado Springs, Colorado, 80
Colorado Sun: as case study, 10,
    19–20, 67–88; engagement prac-
    tices utilized, 81–84; grant from
    Civil, 67–68, 71; history of orga-
    nization, 67–68; history with the
    Denver Post, 67–74, 86–87; lead-
    ership, 74–76; news production
    processes, 84–86; organizational
    culture, 69–74; as public benefit
    corporation, 71–73, 86–88; rou-
    tines utilized, 77–80; socialization
    within organization, 77–79; tech-
    nology utilization, 80–81
Columbia Journalism School, 170
Columbine High School massacre,
    85–86
comments (from readers) as engage-
    ment: at Athletic, 124–126; at Defec-
    tor Media, 47, 58, 60–62; impact on
    newsrooms, 9; at St. Louis Beacon,
    40
commercialization of news, 11
Cotton, Tom, 178
COVID-19 impact: at Athletic, 117, 121,
    127, 130; at *Boston Globe*, 95, 102–
    103; at Colorado Sun, 77; at *Denver
    Post*, 147

Craggs, Tommy, 57
Crisis of the Institutional Press
    (Reese), 179

Deadspin, 19, 45–47, 49–50, 57–59,
    64–65
Defector Media: Blog Cave, 63; as case
    study, 10, 19, 45–66; as coopera-
    tive organization, 48–53, 64–66;
    engagement practices, 60–62;
    ethics, 55–56; history of organiza-
    tion, 45–47; history with Deadspin,
    45–46; internal committees, 52–53;
    news production processes, 62–64;
    organizational culture, 47–53;
    socialization processes, 59–60;
    structure of leadership, 53–54;
    technology utilized, 57–58; trans-
    parency within and from organiza-
    tion, 56
Delli Carpini, Michael X., 174
Denver Broncos, 151
Denver Post: as case study, 10, 21–22,
    136–156; engagement practices,
    151–152; as hedge fund-owned orga-
    nization, 137–143, 155–156; history
    of organization, 136–137; news
    production processes, 152–155;
    organizational culture, 137–143;
    routines utilized, 147–149; socializa-
    tion processes, 145–147; structure
    of leadership, 143–145; technology
    utilized, 149–151
Denver Rebellion, 67, 139, 144
deprofessionalization, 170–179
Digital First Media, 146
digitally native news nonprofits, 6–8,
    23–44
Dorchester, Massachusetts, 102
Dowd, Maureen, 161–162

Eldridge II, Scott A., 8, 173
engagement in journalism: at Athletic,
    124–126; at *Boston Globe*, 105–106;
    at Colorado Sun, 81–84; at Defector
    Media, 60–62; at *Denver Post*, 151–
    152; in journalism today, 167–169,
    174; at St. Louis Beacon, 37–41
ESPN, 115, 131

Facebook, 8, 40, 52, 150
fantasy sports, 131
Fanueil Hall (Boston, Massachusetts), 102
Fishman, Mark, 11, 157
FiveThirtyEight, 115
Floyd, George, 85, 178
foundation funding in journalism, 7, 28, 33
Frievogel, Margaret Wolf, 26–44

Gammons, Peter, 114
Gannett, 107, 109
Gans, Herbert, 2–3, 11, 157
gatekeeping, 8, 171–173
Gawker, 9–10, 47, 65
Glazer, Jay, 113
G/O Media, 45, 47
Google, 8, 70, 80, 151
GoogleChat, 36, 43
Graham, Tim, 114
Grantland, 115
groupthink, 140, 145–146, 155–156

Hallin, Daniel, 4
Hansmann, Adam, 114–116
Henry, John, 20, 90–111, 159, 164
Henry, Linda, 96, 98, 109
hierarchy of influences, 2–10, 175–176

Insurrection Act of 1807, 178
interloping actors in journalism, 7–8, 76, 178
investigative journalism: at Athletic, 19, 21; at Boston Globe, 109; at Colorado Sun, 74, 85; at Defector Media, 8, 63

job security in journalism, 92

Kennedy, Dan, 90, 97, 107, 109
King Soopers shooting in Boulder, Colorado, 85–86
Klein, Ezra, 178
Knight Foundation, 7
Kuhn, Timothy, 176
Kunda, Gideon, 30

labor precarity: at Boston Globe, 92, 109; Colorado Sun, 68; at Denver

Post, 68, 137, 140, 147, 152–156; as driver of organizational culture, 159; in field of journalism, 11, 159, 168
leadership: at Boston Globe, 96–100; at Colorado Sun, 74–76; as concept within organizational culture, 12–15; at Defector Media, 53–54; at Denver Post, 143–145; importance in journalism studies, 160, 165–166, 169–170, 175; at St. Louis Beacon, 30–34
legacy media in American journalism: Boston Globe, 89–111; Denver Post, 136–156; organizational culture at the establishments, 159–160, 168; short understanding of history, 4–7, 9–10; St. Louis Beacon, 23–24
Ley, Tom, 53, 169

market-driven journalism, 124, 126, 133, 139
market models in journalism: as concept, 11–22; cooperative, 45–66; digitally native news nonprofit, 23–44; hedge fund-owned newsroom, 136–156; mogul-owned newsroom, 89–111; public benefit corporation, 67–88; studying in journalism studies, 159–166, 175; venture-capital-funded newsroom, 112–135
market orientation, 6, 16–17, 21
Marshall Fire, 83, 86, 136–137, 153
Martin, Joanne, 12–13
Mather, Alex, 114–116
McManus, John H., 16
media sociology: current work in, 5, 9–15; field of, 10; studying in the future, 170, 176; theories, 2
Merton, Robert, 177
middle-range theory, 177
Missouri Foundation for Health, 33
Morgan, Gareth, 74–75, 139
Morrisey Boulevard (Massachusetts), 102
Mother Jones (magazine), 137
Mr. Gates (from landmark David Manning White study), 3

National Basketball Association (NBA), 131
National Football League (NFL), 112–113, 117
National Guard, 178
National Hockey League (NHL), 119
Nelson, Jacob L., 174
news production: at Athletic, 126–132; at *Boston Globe*, 107–109; at Colorado Sun, 84–86; as concept, 5–8, 13, 16; at Defector Media, 62–64; at *Denver Post*, 152–155; importance in journalism studies, 162–163; at St. Louis Beacon, 34–41
news routines: at Athletic, 121–124; at *Boston Globe*, 103–105; at Colorado Sun, 77–80; as concept and their importance, 3–7; at *Denver Post*, 147–149; at St. Louis Beacon, 34–37; studying routines, 162–166
New York Times: Ben Smith column 170; Chris Argyris study, 11; as destination employer, 138, 142; employment of Michael Powell, 56; history with *Boston Globe*, 90–93, 97, 110, 162; Maureen Dowd column, 161; relationship with and purchase of Athletic, 18, 21, 132–133, 165; Tom Cotton editorial, 178; ways of monetization, 47
Nieman Lab, 138

objectivity, 4, 6, 28
organizational culture: at Athletic, 116–120; at *Boston Globe*, 94–96; at Colorado Sun, 69–74; as concept and theoretical framework, 11–22; at Defector Media, 47–53; at *Denver Post*, 137–143; at St. Louis Beacon, 24–34
organizational identity, 28, 124, 165

Petchesky, Barry, 45
Pew Research Center, 178
photojournalism: at *Boston Globe*, 92; at *Denver Post*, 150, 154; and ethics, 5; and National Press

Photographers Association, 5; O. J. Simpson and *Time* magazine, 5
pivot to video discourse in American journalism, 150, 156, 159, 166
Plunkett, Chuck, 67, 139
Powell, Michael, 56
Powers, Matthew, 179
Powers, Scott, 119
professionalism: culture of, 2, 5, 10; identity, 4–5, 134, 165, 168–171, 173–175; process of, 2, 5; tenets of, 170–171
psychic prison (in organizational culture), 140, 142, 145, 147, 155
Pulitzer Prize, 21, 86, 90, 138–139, 141

Reese, Stephen, 2, 170, 179
Robinson, Sue, 167
Rocky Mountain News, 82, 84
Rocky Mountain PBS, 80
Rosenthal, Ken, 114
Russia influence on news, 10
Ryckman, Larry, 74–75
Ryfe, David, 1–3, 6, 11–12, 16, 157, 165, 176

Sando, Mike, 114
Saturday Night Live, 36
Schefter, Adam, 113
Schein, Edgar H., 14, 17–18, 43, 66
Schudson, Michael, 6, 28
Shoemaker, Pamela J., 2
Simpson, O. J., 5
Slack: overall impact on newsrooms, 163; utilization at Athletic, 122–124, 126–127; utilization at *Boston Globe*, 95, 101, 103–104; utilization at Colorado Sun, 80–81; utilization at Defector Media, 57–60, 63–64, 169
Smith, Ben, 170
socialization: at *Boston Globe*, 100–102; at Colorado Sun, 77–79; as a concept, 15; at Defector Media, 59–60; at *Denver Post*, 145–147; studying in journalism studies, 161–162, 173

Society of Professional Journalism, 158
sourcing, 5–6, 80, 108, 131
South by Southwest, 36
Sports Illustrated, 115
sports reporting: at Athletic, 3, 20–21,
    112–135; at *Boston Globe*, 20, 95–98,
    103–104; at Defector Media, 3, 19,
    45–66; at *Denver Post*, 20; at St.
    Louis Beacon, 25
STEM School shooting (Highlands
    Ranch, Colorado), 85
St. Louis Beacon: Beacon and Eggs,
    38; as case study, 10, 18–19, 23–44;
    coverage, 31–34; as digitally native
    news nonprofit, 43–44; engagement
    practices, 37–41; leadership, 30–34;
    merger, 41–42; news that matters
    as a construct, 25–34, 41; organi-
    zational culture, 24–34; Public
    Insight Network, 38, 40; regular
    meetings, 35–37; routines utilized,
    34–37; strategic development, 36
St. Louis Post-Dispatch, 18–19, 24–27,
    35–38, 43
St. Louis Public Radio, 24, 31, 41–44
Strava (app), 115
subcultures in organizations: at Ath-
    letic, 118; at *Boston Globe*, 94–96,
    99–100, 103, 110–111; conceptual
    definition, 12–13; role in deprofes-
    sionalization, 163
suburban news, 110, 159, 164, 166
Swisher, Kara, 178
systems theory, 174–176

Tandoc, Jr, Edson C., 6–7
technology, use of in journalism prac-
    tice: at *Boston Globe*, 102–103; at

Colorado Sun, 80–81; as a concept,
    15–16; at Defector Media, 57–58; at
    Denver Post, 149–151; at St. Louis
    Beacon, 37–40; studying in journal-
    ism studies, 163, 175
Time magazine, 5
transparency in journalism, 54–56, 74,
    132–134, 166
Tuchman, Gaye, 2–3, 11, 157
Twitch, 60–61

University of Colorado-Boulder, 67
University of Colorado-Denver, 67
University of Missouri, 33, 42, 171
Univision Communications, 47

Vanity Fair (magazine), 137, 139
Vera-Zambrano, Sandra, 179
Voice of San Diego, 27

Washington Post, 19, 22, 47, 90, 142
Watergate, 9
web analytics/metrics: at Athletic,
    120, 124–126, 132–133; at *Boston
    Globe*, 105–106; at Colorado Sun,
    83–84, 86; at *Denver Post*, 151–152,
    156; effects on organizational
    culture, 168, 173; uses in news orga-
    nizations in general, 6–8
Weil, Richard, 27
Western Slope region of Colorado, 80
Williams, Bruce A., 174

X (Twitter), 8, 40, 112–114, 129,
    150–153

Zoom, 79–81, 104

PATRICK FERRUCCI is an associate professor and chair of the Department of Journalism at the University of Colorado Boulder. He is the author of *Making Nonprofit News: Market Models, Influence, and Journalism Practice*, coauthor of *Reviving Rural News: Transforming the Business Model of Community Journalism in the US and Beyond*, and coeditor of *The Institutions Changing Journalism: Barbarians Inside the Gate*.

The University of Illinois Press
is a founding member of the
Association of University Presses.

———————————————

Composed in 10.5/13 Mercury Text G1
with ITC Garamond Std display
by Lisa Connery
at the University of Illinois Press

University of Illinois Press
1325 South Oak Street
Champaign, IL 61820–6903
www.press.uillinois.edu